Better Homes and Gardens®

Classic International Recipes

© 1982 by Meredith Corporation, Des Moines, Iowa.
All Rights Reserved. Printed in the United States of America.
First Edition. First Printing.
Library of Congress Catalog Card Number: 80-68454
ISBN: 1-696-00715-0

On the front cover (clockwise from back right): Hazelnut Torte (Austria), Christopsomo Bread (Greece), Shrimp Larnar (Thailand), Bisschop (Holland), Churros (Mexico), Pita Bread (Middle East), Margarita (Mexico), Syllabub (British Isles), Mai Tai (South Pacific), and Fruit Trifle (England). (See index for recipe pages.)

Our seal assures you that every recipe in *Classic International Recipes* is endorsed by the Better Homes and Gardens Test Kitchen. Each recipe is tested for family appeal, practicality, and deliciousness.

Better Homes and Gardens® Books
Editor: Gerald M. Knox
Art Director: Ernest Shelton
Managing Editor: David A. Kirchner

Food and Nutrition Editor: Doris Eby
Department Head — Cook Books:
Sharyl Heiken
Senior Food Editor: Elizabeth Woolever
Senior Associate Food Editors:
Sandra Granseth,
Rosemary C. Hutchinson
Associate Food Editors:
Jill Burmeister, Julia Martinusen,
Diana McMillen, Marcia Stanley,
Diane Yanney
Recipe Development Editor:
Marion Viall
Test Kitchen Director: Sharon Stilwell
Test Kitchen Home Economists:
Jean Brekke, Kay Cargill,
Marilyn Cornelius, Maryellyn Krantz,
Marge Steenson

Associate Art Directors (Creative):
Linda Ford, Neoma Alt West
Associate Art Director (Managing):
Randall Yontz
Copy and Production Editors:
Nancy Nowiszewski, Lamont Olson,
Mary Helen Schiltz, David A. Walsh
Assistant Art Directors:
Faith Berven, Harijs Priekulis
Graphic Designers: Mike Burns,
Alisann Dixon, Mike Eagleton,
Lynda Haupert, Deb Miner,
Lyne Neymeyer, Bill Shaw,
D. Greg Thompson

Editor in Chief: Neil Kuehnl
Group Editorial Service Director:
Duane Gregg
Executive Art Director:
William J. Yates

General Manager: Fred Stines
Director of Publishing:
Robert B. Nelson
Director of Retail Marketing:
Jamie Martin
Director of Direct Marketing:
Arthur Heydendael

Classic International Recipes
Editors: Sandra Granseth,
Julia Martinusen, Diane Yanney
Copy and Production Editor:
David A. Walsh
Graphic Designer: Alisann Dixon
Consultants: Fran Paulson;
Nancy Singleton, Ph.D.

CONTENTS

8 AFRICA

18 BRITISH ISLES

30 CANADA

38 CARIBBEAN

48 CENTRAL AMERICA

56 EASTERN EUROPE

70 WESTERN EUROPE

88 FAR EAST

102 MEDITERRANEAN

120 MEXICO

130 MIDEAST

142 SCANDINAVIA

152 SOUTH AMERICA

162 SOUTHEAST ASIA

178 SOUTH PACIFIC

186 INDEX

International Cooking

Good food is a pleasure shared by people worldwide. And to share this pleasure with you, we at Better Homes and Gardens offer you this superb collection of the world's choicest dishes.

This is a cook book for those who enjoy cooking, want to know more about international cuisines, and delight thoroughly in sharing fine foods with friends. In it is a wide spectrum of world foods — classic favorites, traditional full-flavored country cooking, and distinctive or adventuresome recipes. All will satisfy the pleasure of fine food and good eating, as well as heighten your understanding of international cooking.

Our recipes are based on the cuisines of many countries and cultures, and are as authentic as possible to the originals. To make them easy to prepare, however, we selected ingredients readily available to you in supermarkets and food shops.

Also in this book are short histories about the culinary heritage of each cooking region, telling how the cuisine has evolved to the way it is today. To add to your enjoyment, the margins contain information about the origin of a specific recipe, the influences on it, or customs and folklore associated with it. And, sprinkled throughout are photographs giving a glimpse at the many wonderfully varied cultures of our world.

So, whether it is a recipe's special flavor combination, its simple but unique cooking technique, or its culinary history that delights you, use this book as a sampler of the world's delicious foods.

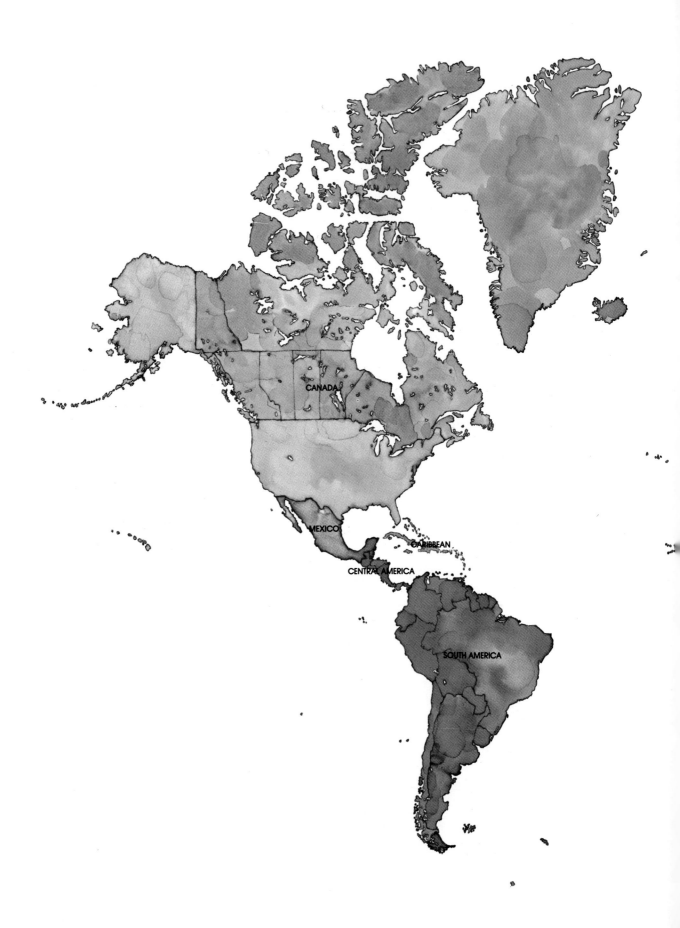

CANADA

MEXICO

CARIBBEAN

CENTRAL AMERICA

SOUTH AMERICA

The color tints indicate the 15 major culinary regions we covered in this book.

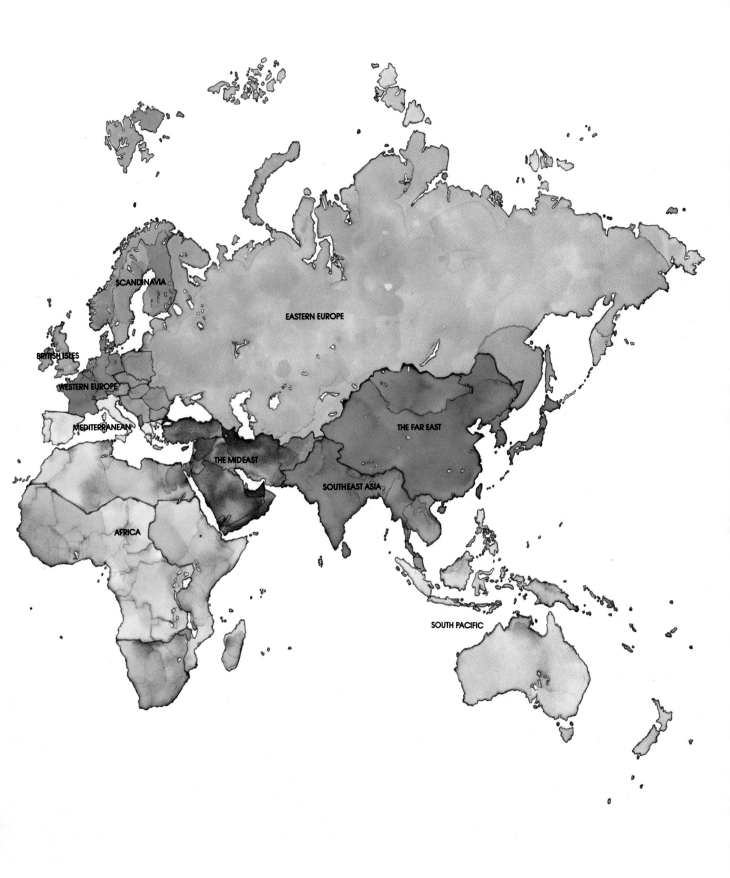

SCANDINAVIA

EASTERN EUROPE

BRITISH ISLES

WESTERN EUROPE

THE FAR EAST

MEDITERRANEAN

THE MIDEAST

SOUTHEAST ASIA

AFRICA

SOUTH PACIFIC

We grouped countries according to location or similar culinary influences, history, religion, or language.

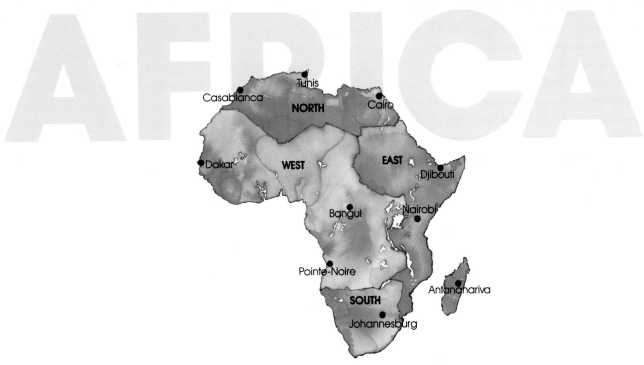

Tunis
Casablanca
NORTH
Cairo
Dakar
WEST
EAST
Djibouti
Bangui
Nairobi
Pointe-Noire
Antananarivo
SOUTH
Johannesburg

AFRICA

Africa is a continent of vast extremes, both in geography and cuisine. The coastal countries of North Africa, sandwiched between the Mediterranean Sea and the Sahara Desert, are more Middle Eastern than African. This hot, arid region is home to African Arabs who often prepare elaborate, multi-coursed banquets which they eat with their fingers, enjoying the touch and feel of their food. Available to the North African cook is a multitude of herbs and spices, compliments of the early traders from the East Indies. Dates, oranges, nuts, and olives are abundant and appear at even the simplest of meals.

Elsewhere on the continent, the African cuisine reflects its European colonists. The Portuguese imported bananas from their Brazilian colonies; the British brought their love of curry; and the French introduced their breads and croissants.

In southern Africa, a unique cuisine developed called Cape Malay. The hearty dishes of the Dutch, who settled Cape Town, were combined with curry and saffron, the favorite seasonings of the Malayan slaves who tended the Dutch farmsteads.

However, the cooking of the early colonists rarely intermingled with that of the native Africans. For most natives, the basic diet was then as it is now, a stew or soup accompanied by a starchy food. The stew is made from whatever ingredients are available. For the fortunate, meat is a welcome addition to the greens, legumes, and vegetables tossed into the pot. In equatorial central and western Africa, peanuts and red peppers are essential supplements.

Throughout Africa, the starch accompaniment varies. In North Africa, it is "couscous," a coarsely ground wheat. Elsewhere, corn, rice, yams, or bananas may round out the meal. Though the native dishes appear simple, they are exotic, flavorful contributions to African cuisine.

Pictured clockwise from top right
Groundnut Stew (see recipe, page 14), Couscous (see recipe, page 12), and Bobotie (see recipe, page 11)

AFRICA

Egyptian Eggplant Omelet

North Africa

Spices and flavorings from China, India, Spain, and tropical Africa have found their way into North African cooking. Garlic, coriander, cumin, and pepper season this open-faced *Egyptian Eggplant Omelet*. Typical Egyptian omelets are packed with vegetables and meat, making them thick, firm, and ideal for lunch or supper.

1 **medium eggplant (1 pound)**
1 **medium onion, chopped (½ cup)**
½ **pound ground beef *or* ground lamb**
2 **cloves garlic, minced**
8 **beaten eggs**
¼ **cup snipped parsley**
1 **teaspoon ground coriander**
½ **teaspoon salt**
½ **teaspoon ground cumin**
⅛ **teaspoon pepper**

Peel eggplant; halve it lengthwise. Cut crosswise into ½-inch slices. Cut slices crosswise into ½-inch strips. You should have about 4 cups eggplant. In covered saucepan cook eggplant and onion in small amount of boiling salted water about 5 minutes or just till tender; drain well.

In a 10-inch oven-going skillet cook beef or lamb and garlic till meat is brown; drain off fat. Stir in eggplant mixture; spread in bottom of skillet.

Combine eggs, parsley, coriander, salt, cumin, and pepper. Carefully pour over meat and vegetable mixture. Cook over medium heat. As eggs set, run a spatula around edge of the skillet, lifting the eggs to allow uncooked portion to flow underneath. Continue cooking and lifting till mixture is almost set. (Total cooking time is about 10 minutes.) Place under broiler, about 5 inches from heat, for 2 to 3 minutes or till set and golden. Makes 6 servings.

Beef Pilau

East Africa

Long ago, traders from India visited the eastern coast of Africa, bringing their spices with them. *Beef Pilau,* a well-loved East African specialty, combines the Indian spice coriander with several classic African ingredients — peanuts, coconut, tomatoes, and green beans.

1½ **pounds beef stew meat, cut into ¾-inch pieces**
2 **tablespoons cooking oil**
1 **medium onion, chopped**
1 **clove garlic, minced**
1 **fresh coconut**
1 **16-ounce can tomatoes, cut up**
1 **teaspoon salt**
1 **teaspoon ground coriander**
1 **9-ounce package frozen cut green beans**
1 **cup long grain rice**
1 **cup chopped unsalted peanuts**

In a large saucepan or Dutch oven brown beef, half at a time, in hot oil; remove and set aside, reserving drippings. In drippings, cook onion and garlic till tender but not brown. Return all meat to saucepan. Drain off fat.

Puncture eyes in base of coconut. Drain milk from coconut; add enough water to measure 2 cups liquid.

Stir coconut liquid, *undrained* tomatoes, salt, and coriander into meat mixture. Bring to boiling; reduce heat. Cover; simmer about 1 hour. Stir in beans, rice, and peanuts. Simmer, covered, for 25 to 30 minutes or till liquid is absorbed and meat and rice are tender. Makes 6 servings.

Jollof Rice

West Africa

It is thought that this classic one-pot dish originated in the Jollof region of Senegal, a French territory in French West Africa. The subtle flavors of *Jollof Rice* are reminiscent of New Orleans' chicken jambalaya.

1 **2½- to 3-pound broiler-fryer chicken, cut up**
2 **tablespoons peanut oil *or* cooking oil**
1 **medium onion, chopped**
1 **16-ounce can tomatoes, cut up**
1¼ **cups chicken broth**
1 **bay leaf**
½ **teaspoon salt**
½ **teaspoon ground ginger, ground cinnamon, *or* dried thyme, crushed**
¼ **teaspoon ground red pepper**
1 **cup long grain rice**

In a large skillet brown chicken pieces on both sides in hot oil about 15 minutes; remove from skillet. Set chicken aside, reserving drippings. Add the onion to drippings; cook till tender but not brown. Drain off fat. Return chicken to skillet.

Combine *undrained* tomatoes; chicken broth; bay leaf; salt; ginger, cinnamon or thyme; and ground red pepper. Pour over chicken. *Do not stir.* Bring to boiling; reduce heat. Cover; simmer for 30 minutes. Skim off fat.

Add the rice, making sure all the rice is covered with liquid. Cover; simmer for 30 minutes more or till rice is tender. Remove bay leaf. Makes 6 servings.

Ethiopian Spicy Braised Chicken
East Africa

Ethiopian cooking is known for its "berberé," a highly spiced hot red pepper sauce. "Berberé" is the characteristic flavor of many recipes, including this well-known chicken specialty called "doro wat" in Ethiopia.

1 8-ounce can tomato sauce
¼ cup paprika
¼ cup dry red wine
1 tablespoon grated gingerroot or 1 teaspoon ground ginger
1 to 2 teaspoons ground red pepper
⅛ teaspoon ground cardamom
⅛ teaspoon ground nutmeg
⅛ teaspoon ground cloves
⅛ teaspoon ground cinnamon
⅛ teaspoon ground allspice
2 medium onions, chopped
2 cloves garlic, minced
2 tablespoons cooking oil
½ teaspoon ground turmeric
1 2½- to 3-pound broiler-fryer chicken, cut up
¼ cup dry red wine
Ethiopian Flat Bread (see recipe, page 16)

For red pepper sauce, combine tomato sauce, paprika, ¼ cup red wine, grated gingerroot or ground ginger, red pepper, cardamom, nutmeg, cloves, cinnamon, and allspice. Set the red pepper sauce aside.

In a large skillet cook onion and garlic in hot oil till onion is tender but not brown. Stir in red pepper sauce, turmeric, and 1 teaspoon *salt*. Add chicken pieces to skillet. Spoon onion mixture over chicken pieces. Bring mixture to boiling; reduce heat. Cover; simmer about 30 minutes. Stir in ¼ cup dry red wine. Cook, uncovered, about 15 minutes; turn chicken pieces often. Skim off fat. Serve with Ethiopian Flat Bread. Makes 4 to 6 servings.

Pepper Chicken
West Africa

1 2½- to 3-pound broiler-fryer chicken, cut up
2 tablespoons peanut oil or cooking oil
5 medium tomatoes, finely chopped
2 medium onions, thinly sliced
1 teaspoon crushed red pepper or ½ teaspoon ground red pepper
1 teaspoon dried thyme, crushed
Hot cooked rice

In a large skillet brown chicken pieces on both sides in hot oil about 15 minutes; remove from skillet. Set aside, reserving drippings.

Add tomatoes and onion slices to pan drippings. Stir in crushed red pepper or ground red pepper, thyme, and ½ teaspoon *salt*. Bring to boiling.

Return chicken pieces to skillet. Spoon tomato mixture over chicken pieces. Return mixture to boiling; reduce heat. Cover; simmer for 35 to 40 minutes or till chicken is tender. Skim off fat. Serve with hot cooked rice. Makes 4 to 6 servings.

Bobotie *pictured on page 8*
South Africa

South African cuisine is a complex blend of many culinary heritages. The people who have had the most influence are the Dutch colonists, Asian Indians, and slaves from the Malay Peninsula.

Bobotie combines these culinary styles together. The result is this curry-seasoned ground meat dish with a delicate baked custard topping.

2 pounds ground lamb or ground beef
2 medium onions, chopped
2 tablespoons curry powder
2 cloves garlic, minced
1½ cups soft bread crumbs
½ cup milk
2 beaten eggs
½ cup raisins
½ cup chopped blanched almonds
2 tablespoons lemon juice or vinegar
2 tablespoons chutney
3 beaten eggs
⅔ cup milk

In a large skillet cook ground lamb or beef, onions, curry powder, and garlic till meat is brown; drain off fat. Stir in bread crumbs, the ½ cup milk, the 2 eggs, raisins, almonds, lemon juice or vinegar, chutney, 1 teaspoon *salt*, and ⅛ teaspoon *pepper*.

Press meat mixture into a well-greased 9x9x2-inch baking pan. In a small bowl combine the 3 eggs, the ⅔ cup milk, ⅛ teaspoon *salt*, and dash *pepper*; beat just till combined. Slowly pour over meat mixture. Bake, uncovered, in 350° oven about 45 minutes or till top is set and light brown. Let stand 5 to 10 minutes before cutting into squares. Serve with hot cooked rice and additional chutney, if desired. Serves 8.

11

AFRICA

Couscous *pictured on page 8*

pictured on page 8

North Africa

Couscous is without doubt the most famous food of North African cooking — in fact, it's the national dish of Morocco. This rich stew derives its name from the coarsely milled grain it is based upon.

Traditionally, *Couscous* is made in a special double pot called a "couscousier." The bottom part holds the meat and vegetable stew. The colander-like top section contains the couscous.

1½ **pounds boneless lamb**
2 **tablespoons cooking oil**
1 **clove garlic, minced**
3 **cups water**
2 **cups couscous**
1 **teaspoon salt**
1 **16-ounce can tomatoes, cut up**
1 **15-ounce can garbanzo beans**
1 **10½-ounce can tomato puree**
6 **cups desired vegetables***
½ **cup raisins**
2 **bay leaves**
1 **teaspoon salt**
1 **teaspoon chili powder**
¾ **teaspoon ground ginger**
¾ **teaspoon ground cumin**
¼ **cup butter *or* margarine, softened**
Homemade Harissa Sauce

Cut the lamb into 1-inch pieces. In an 8- or 10-quart Dutch oven, stockpot, or kettle brown the lamb, half at a time, in hot oil; remove lamb from pan. Cook garlic in drippings till tender but not brown. Return all lamb to pan. Add water; bring to boiling. Reduce heat; cover and simmer 30 minutes.

In a mixing bowl combine couscous and 1 teaspoon salt; add a little water. Scoop up couscous, small handfuls at a time. Rub and work couscous between fingers so each grain is separate and moistened, adding more water if necessary.

Place a colander or a steamer atop pan. (The colander or steamer must be large enough to rest on rim of the pan without touching meat mixture in bottom.) If the holes of the colander or steamer are so large the couscous falls through, line colander or steamer with a damp cheesecloth.

Slowly add *one-third* of the couscous to colander or steamer. When steam begins to rise through couscous, repeat with remaining couscous, *one-third* at a time. (Liquid in pan *cannot touch* couscous or it will become soggy.) *Do not cover* couscous during cooking. Cook 20 minutes more.

Remove colander or steamer. Stir the *undrained* tomatoes, *undrained* garbanzo beans, tomato puree, the 6 cups desired vegetables, raisins, bay leaves, 1 teaspoon salt, chili powder, ginger, and cumin into the meat. Replace colander or steamer. Cook about 20 minutes more or till vegetables and couscous are tender. Stir the softened butter or margarine into cooked couscous, stirring to coat well. Toss couscous with fork to fluff. Remove colander or steamer. Reserve ¼ cup of the hot cooking liquid from meat mixture to prepare the Homemade Harissa Sauce.

To serve, mound couscous and meat mixture on heated serving platter. Keep warm. Prepare Homemade Harissa Sauce and pass. Serves 8.

Homemade Harissa Sauce: In a blender container combine one 4-ounce jar *pimiento, undrained;* one 4-ounce can hot *green chili peppers, undrained;* the ¼ cup reserved cooking liquid; ¼ cup *tomato paste;* 1 tablespoon *lemon juice;* 1 tablespoon snipped *parsley;* 1 teaspoon ground *cumin;* and 1 teaspoon ground *coriander.* Cover; blend just till chunky. (*Or,* purchase commercial harissa at a specialty store.)

***Note:** For vegetables, choose any of the following: carrots, cut into 1-inch slices; celery, cut into 1-inch slices; zucchini, cut into ½-inch slices; green pepper, cut into 1-inch pieces; onions, cut into wedges; coarsely chopped cabbage; unpeeled, diced eggplant; or peeled, diced turnip.

Recipe note: If using packaged precooked couscous, cook meat for 50 minutes, covered. Add vegetables; cook for 10 minutes longer. Rinse and add couscous to colander or steamer as above; cook about 10 minutes more or till done.

Lamb Sosaties

South Africa

Kabobs in South Africa are known as "sosaties." Pieces of meat are marinated in a pungently spiced, slightly sweet sauce, then broiled. This Cape Malay recipe is a truly delectable eating experience.

- 2 **medium onions, finely chopped**
- 2 **cloves garlic, minced**
- 2 **tablespoons cooking oil**
- 1 **tablespoon curry powder**
- 1 **teaspoon sugar**
- ½ **teaspoon ground turmeric**
- ⅓ **cup lemon juice**
- ½ **of a 4-ounce can green chili peppers, rinsed, seeded, and finely chopped**
- 1 **bay leaf**
- 1 **pound boneless lamb, cut into 1-inch pieces**
- 1 **cup long grain rice**
- ½ **teaspoon ground turmeric**
- ⅛ **teaspoon thread saffron, crushed**

For marinade, cook onion and garlic in hot oil till onion is tender. Stir in curry powder, sugar, and ½ teaspoon turmeric. Remove from heat. Stir in lemon juice, chili peppers, bay leaf, and ½ cup *water.* Cool. Place lamb in plastic bag set in bowl. Add marinade. Chill overnight, turning bag often. Drain lamb, reserving marinade. Strain marinade; discard vegetables. Thread lamb on 8 short skewers. Combine rice, ½ teaspoon turmeric, saffron, 2 cups cold *water,* and ½ teaspoon *salt;* cover. Bring to boiling; reduce heat. Cook 14 minutes more (do not lift cover). Remove from heat; let stand, covered, 10 minutes.

Broil lamb 4 inches from heat for 10 to 12 minutes or till desired doneness, brushing with reserved marinade and giving a quarter turn every 3 minutes.

Meanwhile, bring remaining marinade to boiling; reduce heat. Simmer, uncovered, for 5 to 6 minutes. Serve lamb over rice; pass sauce. Serves 4.

Lamb Tajin

North Africa

Morocco, Algeria, and Tunisia are in the northwestern corner of Africa, and from this ancient Arabian region comes *Lamb Tajin,* a classic stew. This exotic dish is cooked to perfection in a "tajin," a shallow glazed earthenware casserole with a cone-shaped lid. A comparable substitute is a 3-quart casserole.

- 2 **medium onions, chopped**
- 2 **cloves garlic, minced**
- ½ **teaspoon ground coriander**
- ¼ **teaspoon paprika**
- ¼ **teaspoon ground cumin**
- ¼ **teaspoon ground ginger**
- ⅛ **teaspoon thread saffron, crushed**
- 1 **tablespoon cooking oil**
- 1½ **pounds boneless lamb, cut into 1-inch pieces**
- 1 **16-ounce can tomatoes, cut up**
- 1 **lemon**
- ½ **cup snipped parsley**
- ½ **cup pimiento-stuffed olives**
  Hot cooked rice

In a large skillet cook onions, garlic, coriander, paprika, cumin, ginger, saffron, and 1 teaspoon *salt* in hot cooking oil till onion is tender but not brown. Stir in lamb and *undrained* tomatoes.

Transfer mixture to a 3-quart casserole. Cover; bake in a 375° oven for 1¼ to 1½ hours or till lamb is tender. Skim off fat. Quarter lemon lengthwise and seed. Stir lemon, parsley, and olives into casserole; heat through. Serve with rice. Makes 6 servings.

- **Chicken Tajin:** Prepare Lamb Tajin as above, *except* omit lamb and use one 2½- to 3-pound broiler-fryer *chicken,* cut up. Bake in a 375° oven for 1 hour or till chicken is tender. Continue as directed. Makes 4 to 6 servings.

Lamb Bredie

South Africa

Stews play an important dietary role all over Africa, and South Africa is no exception. It was there that the slaves from Malay created *Lamb Bredie,* a thick, richly spiced meat-and-vegetable stew. This stew is served in layers with the meat and onion on the bottom and the vegetables on top.

- 2 **large onions, thinly sliced and separated into rings**
- 2 **cloves garlic, minced**
- 2 **tablespoons cooking oil**
- 1½ **pounds boneless lamb, cut into 1-inch pieces**
- 6 **cups coarsely chopped cabbage**
- 4 **medium carrots, cut into ¾-inch pieces**
- 1 **4-ounce can green chili peppers, rinsed, seeded, and chopped**
- 2 **inches stick cinnamon**
- 6 **whole cloves**

In heavy Dutch oven or large saucepan cook onion and garlic in hot oil till onion is tender but not brown. Season lamb pieces with a little salt and pepper. Add lamb to Dutch oven; brown lamb pieces in hot oil, adding more oil if necessary.

Add cabbage, carrots, green chili peppers, stick cinnamon, and whole cloves. Bring to boiling; reduce heat. Cover; simmer for 1¼ hours. *Do not stir.* Add water only if necessary.

Remove cinnamon and cloves. Skim off fat. Serve with hot cooked rice, if desired. Serves 6.

AFRICA

Palaver Sauce
West Africa

Typically, *Palaver Sauce* includes fresh beef, smoked pork or fish, and dark green leaves. In West Africa, these leaves might be "platto," "bologie," or bitter leaf, but a tasty substitute is spinach.

African natives coined "palaver" in the 19th century when European traders would parley or barter for goods.

2 **pounds beef stew meat, cut into 1-inch pieces**
3 **smoked pork hocks**
2 **pounds torn fresh spinach** *or* **two 10-ounce packages frozen chopped spinach**
2 **large onions, finely chopped**
2 **large tomatoes, peeled and chopped**
1 **tablespoon grated gingerroot** *or* **1 teaspoon ground ginger**
1 **to 2 teaspoons ground red pepper**
2 **tablespoons peanut oil** *or* **cooking oil**
2 **hard-cooked eggs, chopped**

In a large saucepan or Dutch oven combine beef, pork hocks, and 1 cup *water*. Bring to boiling; reduce heat. Cover; simmer about 50 minutes or till beef is just tender. Remove pork hocks; cool slightly. Cut meat from bones; discard bones. Return meat to saucepan.

In a large covered saucepan simmer spinach with a small amount of water for 5 minutes; drain well. (Or, cook frozen spinach according to package directions; drain well.)

In a large skillet cook onions, tomatoes, gingerroot or ground ginger, and ground red pepper in hot oil till onion is tender but not brown. Stir onion mixture, drained spinach, and chopped eggs into meat mixture. Cook, uncovered, for 30 minutes, stirring occasionally. If desired, serve over hot cooked rice in soup bowls. Makes 8 servings.

Groundnut Stew   *pictured on page 8*
West Africa

Peanuts offer a distinctive flavor to many West African dishes and provide a good source of protein.

The English colonists called peanuts groundnuts, imparting the name *Groundnut Stew* to this stew, the most celebrated peanut dish from West Africa.

1 **2½- to 3-pound broiler-fryer chicken, cut up**
3 **tablespoons cooking oil**
1 **pound beef stew meat, cut into 1-inch pieces**
2 **medium onions, chopped**
1 **medium green pepper, chopped**
1 **28-ounce can tomatoes, cut up**
1 **teaspoon salt**
1 **to 2 teaspoons ground red pepper**
¾ **cup peanut butter**
  Mashed sweet potatoes *or* **hot cooked rice (optional)**

In a large saucepan or Dutch oven brown chicken pieces in hot oil about 15 minutes; remove from pan. Set aside, reserving drippings.

Add beef, onion, and green pepper to drippings; cook till beef is brown and onion is tender. Drain off fat. Stir in *undrained* tomatoes, salt, and red pepper. Bring to boiling; reduce heat. Cover; simmer for 30 minutes. Add the chicken pieces; simmer 20 minutes more.

In small saucepan melt peanut butter over low heat. Stir into chicken mixture. Return mixture to boiling; reduce heat. Cover; simmer 20 minutes more. Skim off fat. Serve with mashed sweet potatoes or hot cooked rice, if desired. Makes 8 to 10 servings.

Fish and Eggplant Stew
West Africa

Rivers, lakes, and ocean inlets provide a variety of fish and seafood for those West African tribes living nearby. From this region comes a particularly tasty fish stew made with tomatoes, okra, and eggplant.

1 **pound fresh** *or* **frozen fish fillets**
1 **medium onion, chopped**
1 **large green pepper, chopped**
2 **tablespoons cooking oil**
1 **16-ounce can tomatoes, cut up**
1 **medium eggplant, peeled and diced**
1 **8-ounce can tomato sauce**
1 **cup water**
1½ **teaspoons salt**
¾ **teaspoon ground red pepper**
1 **10-ounce package frozen cut okra**
  Hot cooked rice

Thaw fish, if frozen. Remove any skin from fish fillets and cut fillets into 1-inch pieces; set aside.

In a Dutch oven cook onion and green pepper in hot cooking oil till onion is tender but not brown. Stir in *undrained* tomatoes, eggplant, tomato sauce, water, salt, and ground red pepper. Bring to boiling; reduce heat. Cover and simmer about 10 minutes or till eggplant is tender.

Stir in okra and fish pieces. Cover and cook 10 to 15 minutes longer or till okra is tender and fish flakes easily when tested with a fork; stir occasionally.

Ladle stew into soup bowls. Spoon some hot cooked rice atop each serving. Makes 6 servings.

Pictured from front to back
Palaver Sauce and Fish and Eggplant Stew

AFRICA

Ethiopian Flat Bread
East Africa

In Ethiopia this popular bread is known as "injera." It is similar in taste to buttermilk pancakes, but thin, like crepes.

Traditionally "injera" is formed into a large circle. Teamed with *Ethiopian Spicy Braised Chicken* (see recipe, page 11), it makes an exciting meal.

½ cup whole wheat flour
⅓ cup all-purpose flour
1 tablespoon brown sugar
½ teaspoon salt
¼ teaspoon baking powder
⅛ teaspoon baking soda
2 beaten eggs
2 cups buttermilk
1 tablespoon cooking oil

Stir together whole wheat flour, all-purpose flour, brown sugar, salt, baking powder, and baking soda.

Combine the eggs, buttermilk, and the 1 tablespoon cooking oil; add all at once to the flour mixture, stirring till smooth.

Pour *2 tablespoons* of the batter into a hot, lightly greased 6-inch heavy skillet; lift and quickly rotate pan so that batter covers bottom. Return skillet to medium heat. Cook about 1 minute or till light brown on bottom. Invert bread onto paper toweling. (If necessary, loosen with a small spatula.) Repeat with remaining batter. Roll up jelly-roll style and serve warm. Makes 24.

Fried Bread
East Africa

East Africans call this tasty bread "maandazi." The flavor and light texture is similar to a deep-fried cake doughnut. To serve *Fried Bread* as a dessert or snack, sprinkle it with powdered sugar.

2 cups all-purpose flour
2 tablespoons sugar
1 teaspoon baking powder
⅛ teaspoon salt
¼ cup shortening *or* lard
1 slightly beaten egg
⅔ cup water *or* milk
2 to 3 tablespoons all-purpose flour
   Shortening *or* cooking oil for deep-fat frying

In a medium mixing bowl combine the 2 cups flour, sugar, baking powder, and salt. Cut in shortening or lard till pieces are the size of small peas. Make a well in the center.

Stir together egg and water or milk. Add egg mixture all at once to flour mixture. Stir till mixture forms a soft dough.

Turn out onto a lightly floured surface and knead for 2 to 3 minutes, adding the 2 to 3 tablespoons flour if necessary. Shape dough into a ball. Return dough to bowl; cover with a damp towel. Let dough rest for 20 to 25 minutes.

Turn dough out onto a lightly floured surface. Divide dough in half. Roll *one* portion of the dough to a 12x6-inch rectangle. Cut rectangle into nine 4x2-inch pieces. Repeat with remaining dough. Fry pieces, a few at a time, in deep, hot fat (375°) about 1 minute per side or till crisp and golden brown. Drain on paper toweling. Serve warm. Makes 18.

Plantain Fritters
West Africa

Tempting desserts in West African cookery rely heavily on fresh fruits — coconuts, guavas, mangoes, papayas, bananas, pineapples, and plantains.

Plantain Fritters are a simple but tasty ending to a meal. Quite often West Africans just enjoy eating them as a hot snack.

1 cup all-purpose flour
2 tablespoons sugar
2 teaspoons baking powder
¼ teaspoon salt
1 very ripe medium plantain *or* 1 firm large banana (8 ounces)
½ cup milk
1 egg
1 tablespoon cooking oil
   Shortening or cooking oil for deep-fat frying
   Powdered sugar

In a mixing bowl stir together flour, sugar, baking powder, and salt; set aside. Peel plantain or banana; slice into 2-inch chunks. In a blender container combine plantain or banana, milk, egg, and 1 tablespoon cooking oil. Cover; blend till smooth. Add egg mixture to the dry ingredients, stirring just till moistened; *do not beat till smooth.*

Carefully drop *one rounded tablespoon* of the batter into deep, hot fat (375°). Fry fritters, a few at a time, for 2½ to 3 minutes or till done, turning once. Drain on paper toweling. Sprinkle fritters with powdered sugar. Serve warm. Makes about 16.

Melktert

South African cooking traditions were influenced by the Dutch settlers in the early 17th century. From that period comes this old Cape favorite, *Melktert* — which means custard tart.

This splendid dessert tastes much like a rich vanilla cream pie.

**Pastry for Single-Crust Pie
(see recipe, page 36)**
- **1 medium orange**
- **3 cups milk**
- **3 inches stick cinnamon, broken up**
- **⅔ cup sugar**
- **¼ cup cornstarch**
- **¼ teaspoon salt**
- **2 eggs**
- **3 tablespoons butter *or* margarine**
- **1½ teaspoons vanilla**
- **3 tablespoons apricot jam**
- **Ground cinnamon *or* nutmeg**

Prepare Pastry for Single-Crust Pie. Roll out pastry to circle 12 inches in diameter. Line a 9-inch pie plate. Trim pastry to ½ inch beyond edge. Flute edge; prick pastry. Bake in a 450° oven for 10 to 12 minutes or till pastry is golden. Cool thoroughly on rack.

Remove the peel from orange; scrape off excess white. Cut peel into fine strips. In a heavy medium saucepan combine orange peel strips, milk, and stick cinnamon. Cook and stir mixture over low heat for 15 minutes. Remove from heat; cool slightly. Strain milk; discard orange strips and cinnamon pieces.

For filling, in same saucepan combine sugar, cornstarch, and salt. Gradually stir in warm milk. Cook and stir till mixture is thickened and bubbly. Reduce heat; cook and stir 2 minutes more. Remove saucepan from heat.

Beat eggs slightly. Gradually stir about *1 cup* of the hot mixture into eggs. Return egg mixture to saucepan; bring just to a gentle boil. Cook and stir 2 minutes more. Remove from heat. Stir in butter or margarine and the vanilla.

In a small saucepan heat apricot jam till melted. Spoon jam onto bottom of baked pastry shell. Pour hot filling atop apricot jam. Sprinkle with cinnamon or nutmeg. Cool. Serve warm or chilled. Serves 8.

Gazelle Horns

Gazelle Horns, known as "kab el ghzal" in North Africa, are rich crescent-shaped cookies with a sweet almond filling. Traditionally they are served to guests after dinner with a cup of hot tea or rich flavored coffee.

- **1 beaten egg**
- **1 8-ounce can almond paste**
- **½ cup chopped almonds, toasted**
- **¼ cup sugar**
- **2 tablespoons butter *or* margarine, softened**
- **½ teaspoon orange extract**
- **3 cups all-purpose flour**
- **¾ teaspoon salt**
- **1½ cups butter *or* margarine**
- **½ cup cold water**
- **Powdered sugar**

For filling, in a small bowl combine egg, almond paste, chopped almonds, sugar, the 2 tablespoons softened butter or margarine, and orange extract; mix well. Cover; chill till ready for use.

In mixing bowl stir together flour and salt. Cut the 1½ cups butter or margarine into flour till mixture resembles coarse crumbs. Add cold water, one tablespoon at a time, stirring till dough is well moistened. Shape into a ball.

Divide dough into 6 parts. On lightly floured surface roll *each* part to an 8-inch square. Cut *each* square into four 4-inch squares.

For *each* of the 24 squares roll about *2 teaspoons* of the chilled filling into a 3-inch roll. For *each* crescent, position pastry square with one point toward you. Place *one* of the filling rolls horizontally across and just below center of pastry square from corner to corner. Fold bottom point of pastry over the filling; tuck point under filling. Moisten edges of pastry with water. Roll once to cover filling; continue rolling the dough up tightly. Press the pastry ends to seal tightly. Gently curve pastry into a crescent shape.

Place crescents 1 inch apart on an ungreased cookie sheet. Bake in 375° oven for 20 minutes. Remove from pan. Cool on wire rack. Sprinkle crescents with powdered sugar. Makes 24.

BRITISH ISLES

Closely linked to the history of the British Isles is its cuisine.

Norman invaders introduced the practice of eating meals in courses. And tradition has it that Mary Queen of Scots, raised in the French court, introduced the dessert course.

In Scotland a university holiday — Mealy Monday — is even food related. This holiday was initiated as a time for students to return home between terms to replenish their sacks of oatmeal, the popular grain staple of the nation.

The discovery of the New World brought the potato to Ireland's shores. And although in the late 1500s Sir Walter Raleigh planted potatoes on his estate, not until almost 300 years later did this vegetable become a staple in the peasants' diet. The potato blight in 1845 forced many Irish to leave their homeland.

Even though the traditional Anglo-Saxon staples — meat, bread, cheese, and ale — are still part of everyday fare, some newer culinary habits are interwoven with history, too. The fish-and-chips lunch, now standard noontime fare, began during the Industrial Revolution when workers needed cheap, quick nourishment.

In the latter half of the 19th century, teatime became the institution it is today. Now when the tower clock chimes at four o'clock, true Englishmen and women sit down for a cup of tea, or, as they call it, a "cuppa." Factory workers may take time for a quick cup and cookies or small cakes. But for those who want to chat and gossip, the tea table may include sandwiches and fresh vegetables along with the sweets.

In Scotland and in the English countryside, teatime becomes the evening meal with the addition of salads and hot main dishes accompanied by the required pastries. In whatever manner this tradition is observed, tea always must be served hot and must be plentiful.

Pictured clockwise from top

Black Bun (see recipe, page 27), Richmond Maids of Honor (see recipe, page 27), Treacle Tea Scones (see recipe, page 26), and Bara Brith Bread (see recipe, page 26)

BRITISH ISLES

Minced Collops Scotland

"Collops" refer to thin slices of beef, pork, or game cut across the grain. Mincing or chopping the collops tenderizes the less tender cuts of meat. *Minced Collops* are traditionally served with toast or hot mashed potatoes and sliced carrots.

1 large onion, chopped
1 tablespoon butter *or* margarine
1 pound beef round steak, thinly sliced and chopped
1 cup beef broth
¼ cup pearl barley
1 tablespoon Worcestershire sauce
1 bay leaf
¼ teaspoon ground nutmeg
¼ teaspoon pepper
4 slices bread, toasted and quartered

In a 10-inch skillet cook onion in hot butter or margarine till tender but not brown. Stir in the chopped beef, beef broth, barley, Worcestershire sauce, bay leaf, nutmeg, and pepper. Bring to boiling; reduce heat. Cover and simmer about 1¼ hours or till barley is tender. Discard bay leaf. Skim off fat. Season to taste with salt. Serve over toast quarters. Serves 4.

Melton Mowbray Pie England

England is renowned for its savory meat pies, the best known of which are shepherd's pie, steak and kidney pie, veal and ham pie, and pork pies.

The English region that stretches across the Midlands from Nottingham to the Welsh border is known as the pork pie belt. *Melton Mowbray Pie* takes its name from a market town in that region.

1 4-pound boneless pork shoulder roast
½ cup chopped apple
½ cup raisins
½ cup dried currants
¼ cup finely chopped onion
2 teaspoons salt
½ teaspoon dried marjoram, crushed
¼ teaspoon ground mace
¼ teaspoon pepper
3 cups all-purpose flour
1 teaspoon salt
¾ cup lard *or* shortening
⅔ cup milk *or* water
1 beaten egg

Trim fat from pork roast. Chop meat. (You should have about 7 cups chopped meat.)

For filling, combine chopped pork, apple, raisins, currants, onion, the 2 teaspoons salt, the marjoram, mace, and pepper.

For pastry, in large mixing bowl stir together flour and the 1 teaspoon salt. In small saucepan heat lard or shortening and milk or water till shortening is melted. Stir hot liquid into flour mixture till well combined; shape into a ball. Cover with cloth and let cool about 20 minutes. Turn out on lightly floured surface; knead dough for 3 to 4 minutes or till smooth. Set aside *one-fourth* of the pastry for the top crust. Roll remaining pastry to a circle 14 inches in diameter. Fit pastry into an 8-inch springform pan. Trim to 1 inch beyond edge of pan.

Fill with meat filling, mounding in center. Roll reserved dough to a circle 8 inches in diameter. Place atop filling. Fold edge of bottom crust over top crust to seal. Flute edges; do not seal to edge of pan. Cut a 1-inch hole in top of pie. Cut a rose and leaves from pastry trimmings. Brush pie and rose cutout with *some* of the beaten egg. Decorate crust with leaf cutouts. Brush again with egg; bake pie and rose cutout on baking sheet in 400° oven for 20 minutes. Remove rose and set aside. Reduce temperature to 300°. Continue baking pie for 2 hours, brushing with egg once or twice. With a baster, occasionally siphon off any liquid through hole. Before serving, place rose cutout over hole. Serve meat pie warm or chilled. Makes 10 to 12 servings.

Dublin Coddle

Ireland

Based on the medieval pottage or porridge, this dish builds flavor as it "coddles" or cooks slowly. The Irish have eaten *Dublin Coddle* as a Saturday evening supper dish since the late 1700s. It is usually served with *Brown Irish Soda Bread* (see recipe, page 27).

If you cannot find Irish oatmeal (which is finer than American oatmeal) in specialty stores, substitute crushed rolled oats. To crush, place the rolled oats in blender container. Cover and blend till coarsely crushed.

1 pound fully cooked ham, cubed (3 cups)
½ pound fresh pork sausage links, sliced
3 medium carrots, sliced
3 medium leeks, sliced (1 cup)
1 cup Irish oatmeal
¼ cup snipped parsley
½ teaspoon dry mustard
¼ teaspoon pepper

In large saucepan cook the ham and sausage in 4 cups boiling *water* about 5 minutes. Skim off fat. To meat mixture, add carrots, leeks, Irish oatmeal, parsley, mustard, and pepper. Turn into a 3-quart casserole. Cover and bake in 350° oven about 50 minutes or till liquid is absorbed and vegetables are tender. Stir before serving. Makes 6 servings.

Scotch Eggs

Scotland

1 pound bulk pork sausage
2 tablespoons snipped parsley
½ teaspoon ground sage
½ teaspoon dried thyme, crushed
8 hard-cooked eggs
¼ cup all-purpose flour
¼ teaspoon salt
Dash pepper
1 slightly beaten egg
½ cup fine dry bread crumbs
Cooking oil *or* shortening for deep-fat frying

In mixing bowl combine sausage, parsley, sage, and thyme. Using about ¼ *cup* mixture for each, shape into 8 patties, 4 inches in diameter. Completely wrap *one* sausage patty around *each* hard-cooked egg; cover and chill several hours. Combine flour, salt, and pepper. Roll sausage-covered eggs first in flour mixture, next in beaten egg, then in crumbs. Fry in deep hot fat (350°) for 1½ to 2 minutes or till brown. Drain on paper toweling. Serve warm or chilled. Makes 8 servings.

Michaelmas Goose

Regional

The goose is to the Irish and English what the turkey is to Americans. For centuries, roasted stuffed goose has been served for Christmas, and, more commonly, for Michaelmas on September 29 in honor of the end of harvest.

Some claim Queen Elizabeth I initiated this tradition when she decreed all her subjects should eat goose on Michaelmas to celebrate the English navy's defeat of the Spanish Armada. The reason for the proclamation? She was dining on goose when messengers brought news of the victory.

1 10-pound domestic goose *or* turkey
3 medium onions, cut into small wedges
½ cup butter *or* margarine
2 tablespoons fresh snipped sage *or* 1 teaspoon dried sage, crushed
½ teaspoon salt
⅛ teaspoon pepper
8 cups dry bread cubes (11 slices)
Salt
Cooking oil (optional)

Remove giblets from goose or turkey; reserve liver. Thoroughly rinse bird; pat dry. Set aside. For stuffing, in small saucepan place liver in enough salted water to cover; bring to boiling. Reduce heat; cover and simmer about 20 minutes. Remove and chop liver finely; reserve ¾ cup liquid.

In skillet cook onion in hot butter or margarine till tender but not brown. Stir in sage, ½ teaspoon salt, and the pepper. Combine onion mixture, bread cubes, and chopped liver; drizzle with reserved liquid. Toss to mix.

To roast bird, rub cavity with salt. If desired, spoon *some* of the stuffing into neck cavity. Skewer neck skin to back. Spoon remaining stuffing into body cavity, but *do not pack*. Tie legs to tail. Twist wing tips under back of bird.

Place bird, breast side up, on a rack in shallow roasting pan. If roasting goose, prick skin all over (for turkey, brush with cooking oil). Cover bird loosely with foil. Roast goose in a 350° oven for 3¼ to 3¾ hours, spooning off fat (for turkey, roast in a 325° oven for 4 to 4½ hours, basting occasionally).

After 2½ hours, cut string between legs. About 45 minutes before bird is done, remove foil. Bird is done when the thermometer registers 185° and legs move easily in sockets. Let stand 15 minutes before carving. Makes 8 to 10 servings.

BRITISH ISLES

Howtowdie with Drappit Eggs
Scotland

The Scots adapted the word "howtowdie" from the French term "hutaudeau," meaning pullet or chicken. "Drappit" eggs are nothing more than poached eggs dropped onto the bed of spinach. Traditionally, the eggs are poached in chicken broth that later is thickened with the grated liver. The liver sauce should never be poured atop the spinach and eggs.

    3   slices bacon
    2   small shallots, sliced
    2   cups dry bread cubes
        (3 slices)
    2   tablespoons butter or
        margarine, melted
    2   tablespoons milk
    1   tablespoon snipped parsley
    ¼   teaspoon dried marjoram,
        crushed, or dried tarragon,
        crushed
    1   2½- to 3-pound broiler-fryer
        chicken
    1½ cups water
    1   medium onion, chopped
    6   whole peppercorns
    2   whole cloves
    ½   cup whipping cream
    6   eggs
    2   pounds torn fresh spinach or
        two 10-ounce packages
        frozen leaf spinach

Cook bacon till crisp; remove, crumble, and drain on paper toweling, reserving drippings. To drippings, add shallots; cook till tender. Remove shallots; reserve drippings. Combine bacon, shallots, bread cubes, butter or margarine, milk, parsley, and marjoram or tarragon; toss to mix.

Remove giblets from chicken; reserve liver. Rinse chicken; pat dry. Rub neck and body cavities with salt; stuff loosely with bread mixture. *Do not pack.* Skewer neck skin to back. Tie legs securely to tail. Twist wing tips under back.

Place bird, breast side up, on a rack in deep roasting pan. Add water, onion, peppercorns, and cloves. Baste chicken with *some* of the reserved bacon drippings. Cover and bake chicken in 375° oven for 1 hour. Uncover and baste chicken with bacon drippings; bake 20 minutes longer. Transfer chicken to serving platter; keep warm. Skim fat off stock; reserve 1 cup stock.

For sauce, strain reserved stock into a saucepan. Add liver to stock; cook for 4 to 5 minutes or till done. Remove liver; rub through a sieve. Cook stock over medium heat till ¼ cup liquid remains. Stir in cream and liver; cook and stir till slightly thickened.

Meanwhile, poach eggs in water. Cook fresh spinach in a small amount of boiling salted water for 3 minutes. (Or, cook frozen spinach according to package directions.) Drain well. Arrange spinach around chicken; make 6 indentations with back of a tablespoon. Place *one* poached egg in *each* indentation. Garnish chicken with a strip of crisp-cooked bacon, if desired. Pass sauce. Serves 6.

Cabbie Claw
Scotland

Because Great Britain is surrounded by water, fish is a natural staple supply of food.

In England, eel, trout, and smoked salmon are considered delicacies. The national favorite is fried fish and chips, which is served with malt vinegar, salt, and catsup, and comes wrapped in newspaper.

In Scotland, *Cabbie Claw* (cod on mashed potatoes) and finnan haddie (smoked haddock) often appear on the table.

    1   pound fresh or frozen cod fillets
    4   medium potatoes (1¼ pounds),
        peeled and quartered
    ¼   cup milk
    1   tablespoon butter or
        margarine
        Paprika
    1½ cups water
    2   teaspoons grated fresh
        horseradish or prepared
        horseradish
    6   whole peppercorns
    1   bay leaf
    2   tablespoons butter or
        margarine
    2   tablespoons all-purpose flour
        Dash ground allspice
    1   hard-cooked egg, chopped
    1   tablespoon snipped parsley
        Paprika

Thaw fish, if frozen. In covered saucepan cook potatoes in boiling salted water for 20 to 25 minutes or till tender. Drain. Add milk, the 1 tablespoon butter or margarine, and ¼ teaspoon *salt.* Mash till smooth, adding more milk if necessary. Keep warm.

Meanwhile, sprinkle each fillet with salt and paprika. In skillet combine fish, water, horseradish, peppercorns, and bay leaf. Bring to boiling; reduce heat. Cover and simmer 10 to 15 minutes or till fish flakes easily when tested with a fork.

Transfer fish to serving platter. Strain cooking liquid; reserve 1¼ cups, adding water if necessary. Spoon or pipe mashed potatoes around fish. Keep warm.

For sauce, in saucepan melt the 2 tablespoons butter or margarine. Stir in flour, allspice, ½ teaspoon *salt,* and ¼ teaspoon *pepper.* Add reserved liquid all at once. Cook and stir till thickened and bubbly. Cook and stir 1 minute more. Stir in egg and parsley. Heat through. Pour sauce atop fish. Sprinkle with paprika. Pass remaining sauce. Serves 4.

Mulligatawny

Mulligatawny or "pepper water" was brought from East India by the British colonials during the 19th century. This exquisite curried chicken soup is customarily served with hot cooked rice.

1 2½- to 3-pound broiler-fryer chicken, cut up
3 cups water
3 medium carrots, sliced
2 medium onions, chopped
2 medium apples, sliced
⅓ cup flaked coconut
1 to 2 tablespoons curry powder
1 tablespoon lemon juice
2 whole cloves
1 bay leaf
2 teaspoons salt
½ teaspoon ground red pepper
1 cup light cream *or* milk
¼ cup all-purpose flour
1 3-ounce can whole mushrooms
Hot cooked rice
Snipped coriander, cilantro, *or* parsley (optional)

Rinse chicken pieces. In Dutch oven or kettle combine chicken, water, carrots, onions, apples, coconut, curry powder, lemon juice, cloves, bay leaf, salt, and red pepper. Bring to boiling; reduce heat. Cover and simmer about 50 minutes or till chicken is tender.

Remove chicken pieces from broth. Skim off fat. Remove bay leaf and cloves. When chicken is cool enough to handle, remove and discard skin and bones. Cut up chicken; return to Dutch oven.

Stir together cream or milk and flour; stir into chicken mixture. Stir in *undrained* mushrooms. Cook and stir gently till slightly thickened and bubbly. Cook and stir 1 minute more.

To serve, spoon rice into bowls. Ladle soup over rice. Sprinkle each serving with coriander, cilantro, *or* parsley, if desired. Makes 6 servings.

Pictured
Howtowdie with Drappit Eggs

BRITISH ISLES

Salmon Kedgeree

England

English colonials imported this curried salmon-and-rice dish from India. Called "kicharchi" in its native land, it originally included beans, lentils, eggs, and spices. The British added smoked or fresh salmon and now eat it for breakfast.

2 tablespoons sliced green onion
2 tablespoons butter *or* margarine
2 cups cooked rice
1 15½-ounce can salmon, drained, flaked, and skin and bones removed
1 medium tomato, chopped
2 hard-cooked eggs, sieved
½ teaspoon curry powder
¼ teaspoon ground red pepper
Snipped parsley

In skillet cook green onion in hot butter or margarine till tender but not brown. Stir in rice, salmon, tomato, *half* of the sieved egg, curry powder, and red pepper. Cook over low heat till heated through. Turn out onto serving plate. Sprinkle with remaining sieved egg and the parsley. Makes 4 to 6 servings.

Irish Stew

Ireland

Irish peasants prepared the first Irish stews with goat meat instead of the more valuable lamb or mutton. They cooked their stews in bastable ovens, large black pots that could be hung over the kitchen fire.

Irish Stew is typically a white stew, which means that the meat is never browned.

1 pound boneless lamb, cut into ¾-inch pieces
4 cups beef broth
2 medium onions, cut into wedges
1½ teaspoons salt
¼ teaspoon pepper
1 bay leaf
4 medium potatoes (1½ pounds), peeled and quartered
6 medium carrots, sliced ½ inch thick
½ teaspoon dried thyme, crushed
¼ teaspoon dried basil, crushed
½ cup cold water
¼ cup all-purpose flour
Snipped parsley

In large saucepan or Dutch oven combine lamb, beef broth, onions, salt, pepper, and bay leaf. Bring to boiling; reduce heat. Cover and simmer for 45 minutes. Skim off fat. Add potatoes, carrots, thyme, and basil. Cover and simmer for 30 to 35 minutes more or till vegetables are tender. Remove bay leaf and discard.

Combine cold water and flour. Stir into stew. Cook and stir till thickened and bubbly. Cook and stir 1 minute more. Season to taste with salt and pepper. Sprinkle each serving with parsley. Makes 6 servings.

Cock-a-Leekie Soup

Scotland

The Scots have proclaimed this chicken-and-leek soup as their national soup. Traditionally, *Cock-a-Leekie Soup* is eaten on Burn's night (January 25) to honor the great Scottish poet Robert Burns.

Some *Cock-a-Leekie Soup* recipes omit prunes, but experts say they are essential for authenticity. Leftover *Cock-a-Leekie Soup* very often is served cold.

1 2½- to 3-pound broiler-fryer chicken, cut up
4 cups water
½ cup finely chopped carrot
½ cup finely chopped celery
¼ cup finely chopped onion
2 sprigs parsley
2 teaspoons salt
¼ teaspoon white pepper
1 bay leaf
2 medium leeks, thinly sliced (1½ cups)
1 small potato, peeled and diced (½ cup)
½ cup quick-cooking barley
½ cup pitted, dried prunes, snipped
2 cups light cream *or* milk
Sliced leeks (optional)

Rinse chicken pieces. In a large saucepan or Dutch oven combine chicken pieces, water, carrot, celery, onion, parsley, salt, white pepper, and bay leaf. Bring to boiling; reduce heat. Cover and simmer about 25 minutes or till chicken is tender. Remove chicken pieces from broth. Skim off fat. Remove bay leaf and parsley. When chicken is cool enough to handle, remove and discard skin and bones. Cut up chicken. Add chicken, leeks, potato, barley, and prunes to broth. Bring to boiling; reduce heat. Cover and simmer for 15 to 20 minutes or till potato is tender. Stir in cream or milk. Heat through. Garnish each serving with additional sliced leeks, if desired. Makes 6 to 8 servings.

Colcannon

Potatoes came to the British Isles from the New World, but first were considered inedible because they looked so much like the root of the poisonous bella donna plant. By the 18th century, however, they not only had gained acceptance, but had become a dietary staple.

Potatoes are prepared in countless ways in Great Britain. Irish *Colcannon* is a mixture of mashed potatoes and cabbage. A traditional Halloween dish, the first two servings are often set on gateposts for fairies to eat.

Without the cabbage, *Colcannon* is called "champ" or "thump."

Like the Irish, the Scots also eat mashed potatoes, only they call their dish "chappit tatties." The English love "stovies," buttery potatoes boiled for a long time on the stove.

Boxty, or potato pancakes, are traditional fare for Halloween in Northern Ireland. When making *Boxty,* be sure the skillet is well seasoned so the pancakes don't stick.

4 medium potatoes (1½ pounds), peeled and quartered
2 cups finely chopped cabbage
1 medium onion, finely chopped
2 tablespoons butter *or* margarine
⅓ cup light cream *or* milk, heated
¼ cup butter *or* margarine
1 teaspoon salt
⅛ teaspoon pepper
Butter *or* margarine

Cook potatoes in boiling salted water to cover for 20 to 25 minutes or till tender. Drain. Meanwhile, cook the cabbage and onion in the 2 tablespoons butter or margarine till tender but not brown. Combine cooked potatoes, cream or milk, the ¼ cup butter or margarine, salt, and pepper. Mash till smooth, adding more cream or milk if necessary. Stir the cabbage mixture into potato mixture. Cook and stir over low heat till heated through. Transfer to serving dish and dot with additional butter or margarine. Makes 4 to 6 servings.

Boxty

4 medium potatoes (1½ pounds), peeled
½ cup all-purpose flour
½ teaspoon salt
¼ teaspoon baking powder
½ cup buttermilk
2 tablespoons butter *or* margarine
Butter *or* margarine, melted
Brown sugar

Finely shred potatoes into a bowl of cold water; set aside. In mixing bowl stir together flour, salt, and baking powder. Drain potatoes well; pat dry with paper toweling. Add potatoes and buttermilk to flour mixture; mix well.

In a 12-inch skillet heat the 2 tablespoons butter or margarine till water sprinkled on skillet sizzles. Spread about 3 *tablespoons* of the batter into small pancake in skillet, making several at a time. Cook over medium heat about 5 minutes on each side or till golden brown and crisp on the edges. Remove pancakes from skillet; cover and keep warm. Repeat with remaining batter, adding more butter or margarine to skillet, if necessary.

To serve, pour melted butter or margarine over pancakes; sprinkle with brown sugar. Makes 16 to 18 pancakes.

Leek Salad

8 medium leeks, sliced ½ inch thick (2½ cups)
2 medium tomatoes
1 hard-cooked egg, chopped
⅓ cup salad oil *or* olive oil
⅓ cup cider vinegar
1 tablespoon snipped parsley
2 teaspoons sugar
1 teaspoon Worcestershire sauce
½ teaspoon garlic salt
½ teaspoon dried tarragon, crushed
⅛ teaspoon pepper

In covered saucepan cook leeks in small amount boiling salted water for 5 minutes or till crisp-tender. Drain and cool. Cut tomatoes into thin wedges. Combine leeks, tomato wedges, and chopped hard-cooked egg.

For dressing, in screw-top jar combine salad oil or olive oil, vinegar, parsley, sugar, Worcestershire sauce, garlic salt, tarragon, and pepper. Cover and shake to mix well. Pour mixture over salad. Toss gently to coat. Cover and chill at least 1 hour, stirring occasionally. Drain the salad before serving. Makes 4 to 6 servings.

BRITISH ISLES

Bara Brith Bread *pictured on page 18* Wales

"Bara brith" in Welsh means speckled bread. Today, raisins or dried currants speckle the bread, but fresh blackberries were once just as common. Often, the bread is brushed with honey after cooling.

2¼ to 2¾ cups all-purpose flour
1 package active dry yeast
¼ teaspoon ground cinnamon
⅛ teaspoon ground nutmeg
⅛ teaspoon ground cloves
⅔ cup buttermilk
¼ cup packed brown sugar
¼ cup butter *or* margarine
½ teaspoon salt
1 egg
⅔ cup dried currants *or* raisins

Combine 1¼ cups of the flour, yeast, cinnamon, nutmeg, and cloves. In saucepan, heat buttermilk, brown sugar, butter or margarine, and salt just till warm (115° to 120°) and butter or margarine is almost melted; stir constantly. Add to flour mixture; add egg. Beat at low speed of electric mixer ½ minute. Beat 3 minutes at high speed. Stir in currants and as much of the remaining flour as you can mix in with a spoon. Turn out onto floured surface. Knead in enough remaining flour to make a moderately stiff dough that is smooth and elastic (6 to 8 minutes total). Shape into a ball. Place in greased bowl; turn once to grease surface. Cover; let rise till double (about 1¼ hours). Punch down. Shape into a loaf; place in greased 8x4x2-inch loaf pan. Cover; let rise till nearly double (about 30 minutes). Bake in 375° oven for 35 to 40 minutes; cover with foil last 20 minutes. Remove from pan; cool. Makes 1 loaf.

Treacle Tea Scones *pictured on page 18* Regional

Scones, or "sgonnes" by their Gaelic name, were first cooked on a griddle and served cut into wedges. Housewives would keep them warm before tea by wrapping them in small towels, hence the phrase tea towel. Today many cooks drop or shape scones on baking sheets to bake in the oven. Usually these famous biscuits are served with butter and jam, but for a special occasion they may be served with strawberries and cream, a combination known as cream tea.

Scones may contain dried fruit, currants or raisins, apple, cheese, syrup, or treacle. Treacle, or Scotch molasses, is sweeter and thicker than the molasses in the United States. If you cannot find Scotch treacle in specialty stores, just substitute American molasses.

2 cups all-purpose flour
1 tablespoon sugar
1 teaspoon baking soda
1 teaspoon cream of tartar
½ teaspoon ground allspice
¼ teaspoon salt
6 tablespoons butter
¾ cup milk
2 tablespoons treacle *or* molasses

Stir together flour, sugar, soda, cream of tartar, allspice, and salt. Cut in butter till mixture resembles coarse crumbs. Make a well in center; stir in milk and treacle or molasses just till moistened. Spread in lightly greased 10-inch oven-going skillet. Cook, covered, over medium-low heat for 20 to 25 minutes or till golden on bottom and set on edges. Place under broiler 4 inches from heat; broil for 4 to 5 minutes. Serves 12.

Richmond Maids of Honor   *pictured on page 18*   England

No one is sure why these almond tarts are called *Richmond Maids of Honor.* Some say King Henry VIII named them after Queen Anne Boleyn and her ladies-in-waiting. Others attribute the name to the maids of honor attending Queen Elizabeth I at the Palace of Richmond.

1   cup all-purpose flour
¼   teaspoon salt
6   tablespoons butter *or* margarine
3   to 4 tablespoons cold water
4½   teaspoons raspberry jam
½   cup sugar
3   tablespoons butter *or* margarine, softened
1   egg
⅔   cup ground almonds
¼   teaspoon almond extract

In mixing bowl stir together flour and salt. Cut in the 6 tablespoons butter till pieces are the size of small peas. Sprinkle water, one tablespoon at a time, over mixture. Toss gently with fork. Form dough into a ball. Wrap and chill 1 hour. On floured surface, roll to ⅛-inch thickness. Using a 2¾-inch cookie cutter, cut 18 circles. Fit circles into 1¾-inch muffin cups. Place ¼ *teaspoon* of jam in *each* cup.

Beat together the sugar and the 3 tablespoons butter or margarine. Beat in egg. Stir in almonds and almond extract. Spoon *1 slightly rounded tablespoon* of the almond mixture atop jam in *each* pastry shell. Bake in 375° oven for 25 to 28 minutes. Remove from pan. Cool on wire rack. Makes 18.

Black Bun   *pictured on page 18*   Scotland

The Scottish *Black Bun* is not a bun at all but a fruit cake encased in pastry. It receives added moistness and flavor when stored in an airtight container for at least a week.

Black Bun is customarily served in Scotland on Hogmanay, or as we know it, New Year's Eve.

1¼   cups raisins
1¼   cups dried currants
½   cup diced mixed candied fruits and peels
    Pastry for Double-Crust Pie
1½   cups all-purpose flour
½   cup packed brown sugar
1   teaspoon baking soda
1   teaspoon cream of tartar
1   teaspoon ground cinnamon
1   teaspoon ground ginger
1   slightly beaten egg
⅔   cup milk
½   cup Scotch whisky
2   tablespoons butter *or* margarine, melted
    Milk

In saucepan combine raisins, currants, and candied fruits and peels; cover with boiling water. Let stand 10 minutes. Drain well. Prepare Pastry for Double-Crust Pie. Using *two-thirds* of the pastry, roll out on floured surface to a circle 13 inches in diameter. Line bottom and sides of 8x1½-inch round baking pan with pastry, adjusting fullness at sides. Trim to ¾ inch beyond edge of pan. Combine flour, brown sugar, baking soda, cream of tartar, cinnamon, and ginger. Combine egg, milk, whisky, and butter; stir into flour mixture till smooth. Fold in fruit; spoon into pastry-lined pan. Roll out remaining pastry to a circle 8 inches in diameter. Place over filling. Brush edges with water. Fold bottom pastry over top; crimp to seal. Prick top crust with fork; brush with milk. Cut out decorative pieces from pastry trimmings. Place atop crust; brush with milk. Bake in 300° oven for 1¾ hours. Cool in pan; remove. Wrap; chill 1 week. Serves 12 to 16.

Pastry for Double-Crust Pie: In mixing bowl stir together 2 cups all-purpose *flour* and 1 teaspoon *salt.* Cut in ⅔ cup *shortening* till pieces are size of peas. Sprinkle 6 to 7 tablespoons cold *water* over mixture, one tablespoon at a time; toss with fork.

Brown Irish Soda Bread   Ireland

2   cups whole wheat flour
1   cup all-purpose flour
2   tablespoons brown sugar
2   teaspoons baking powder
1   teaspoon baking soda
1   teaspoon cream of tartar
½   teaspoon salt
1   cup light raisins
1¾   cups milk

In a large mixing bowl stir together the whole wheat flour, all-purpose flour, brown sugar, baking powder, baking soda, cream of tartar, and salt. Stir in the raisins. Add milk; stir till dry ingredients are moistened. Turn into a greased 9x1½-inch round baking pan. Bake in a 350° oven for 30 to 35 minutes or till brown. Cool 10 minutes in pan. Remove from pan and cool thoroughly. Wrap and store overnight. Makes 1 loaf.

BRITISH ISLES

Lemon Steamed Pudding
England

Desserts in England usually are rich in cream, eggs, butter, and fruit. They appear in the form of puddings, trifles, cakes, custards, junkets, and syllabubs.

Sweet puddings can be baked or steamed in a pudding basin. Some popular steamed puddings are the plum pudding usually served at Christmas, spotted dick (a currant-filled pudding), and the ordinary but delicious bread-and-butter pudding. They can be served hot or cold, with or without a sauce.

Fruit Trifle has evolved from a humble bread-and-butter pudding mixed with wine to a luscious layered dessert of rum-soaked sponge cake, fresh fruit, smooth custard, and mounds of whipped cream. The Scotch call it typsy laird (tipsy lord) when they pour Drambuie over the sponge cake. When made with Madeira it is often called tipsy cake.

Cream Crowdie or "cranachan" is customarily served in Scotland on Halloween night. Certain little charms can be stirred into this dessert to surprise the unwary diner. If someone finds a ring, he will be married within a year. A button is said to mean bachelorhood, and a thimble, spinsterhood. A coin indicates wealth and a horseshoe foretells good luck for the superstitious.

1 cup all-purpose flour
½ teaspoon baking powder
¼ teaspoon salt
¼ cup butter *or* margarine
¼ cup sugar
1 teaspoon vanilla
1 teaspoon finely shredded lemon peel
3 eggs
2 tablespoons lemon juice
¾ cup water
2 tablespoons sugar
1 tablespoon cornstarch
1 teaspoon finely shredded lemon peel
1 tablespoon lemon juice
1 tablespoon butter *or* margarine

For pudding, stir together flour, baking powder, and salt. In mixer bowl beat the ¼ cup butter on medium speed of electric mixer for 30 seconds. Add the ¼ cup sugar, vanilla, and 1 teaspoon lemon peel; beat till fluffy. Add eggs, one at a time, beating for 1 minute after each addition. Add flour mixture, beating till well combined. Add the 2 tablespoons lemon juice; mix well. Turn into a greased 3- or 4-cup heat-proof bowl. Cover tightly with foil. Place on rack in Dutch oven. Pour in boiling water to depth of 1 inch (just below bottom of bowl). Cover and steam for 1 to 1¼ hours; add more boiling water, if necessary. Remove from Dutch oven; remove foil. Cool for 10 minutes; invert pudding onto wire rack.

For sauce, in saucepan stir together water, the 2 tablespoons sugar, cornstarch, 1 teaspoon lemon peel, and the 1 tablespoon lemon juice. Cook and stir till thickened and bubbly. Cook and stir 2 minutes more. Stir in the 1 tablespoon butter. Serve warm over pudding. Serves 8 to 10.

Fruit Trifle   *pictured on front cover*
England

¼ cup sugar
3 tablespoons all-purpose flour
2 cups milk
3 beaten egg yolks
2 teaspoons finely shredded lemon peel
1 teaspoon vanilla
1 3-ounce package (12) ladyfingers, split
¼ cup dark rum
2 medium peaches, peeled, pitted, and chopped (1 cup)
1 cup sliced fresh strawberries
1 cup whipping cream
2 tablespoons sugar
1 teaspoon vanilla
2 cups fresh strawberries
½ cup currant jelly

For pudding, in saucepan combine the ¼ cup sugar and the flour. Stir in milk, egg yolks, and lemon peel. Cook and stir over medium heat 7 to 8 minutes or till mixture thickens and coats a spoon. Remove from heat; stir in 1 teaspoon vanilla. Cool.

In a 1½-quart soufflé dish or serving bowl arrange *half* of the split ladyfingers on bottom and sides. Sprinkle with *half* of the rum. Top with peaches. Spoon *half* of the pudding atop. Arrange remaining ladyfingers atop; sprinkle with remaining rum. Spoon sliced berries over ladyfingers. Top with remaining pudding. Chill at least 4 hours. One hour before serving, whip cream with the 2 tablespoons sugar and 1 teaspoon vanilla just to soft peaks. Spread about *half* of the whipped cream atop pudding. Use pastry tube and tip to pipe remaining whipped cream around edge. Melt jelly. Dip the 2 cups whole berries in jelly; place atop. Serves 8.

Cream Crowdie
Scotland

1½ cups fresh *or* frozen raspberries, gooseberries, *or* sliced strawberries
⅓ cup regular rolled oats
1 cup whipping cream
2 tablespoons sugar
2 tablespoons Drambuie *or* rum
1 teaspoon vanilla

Thaw berries, if frozen. To make oatmeal, place rolled oats in blender container. Cover and blend till coarsely crushed. Place oatmeal in a thin layer in a 13x9x2-inch baking pan. Bake in a 350° oven for 15 to 20 minutes, stirring the oatmeal once or twice to prevent overbrowning. Cool. Whip the cream, sugar, Drambuie or rum, and vanilla just to soft peaks. Fold in oatmeal and berries. Serve in dessert dishes. Makes 6 servings.

Burnt Cream   Scotland

Burnt Cream, a baked custard similar to a crème brûlée, evolved during the Victorian period when French cookery was popular in England.

2 **eggs**
2 **egg yolks**
2 **cups light cream**
¼ **cup sugar**
1 **teaspoon vanilla**
¼ **teaspoon ground nutmeg**
  Dash salt
2 **to 3 teaspoons sugar**

In mixing bowl lightly beat the eggs and egg yolks together. Stir in the cream, the ¼ cup sugar, vanilla, nutmeg, and salt. Place four 6-ounce custard cups in a 9x9x2-inch baking pan. Pour egg mixture into the four cups. Pour boiling water around cups in pan to a depth of 1 inch. Bake in 325° oven about 30 minutes or till knife inserted near center comes out clean. Cool on wire rack for 20 minutes. Chill. When thoroughly chilled, place custard cups in 9x9x2-inch baking pan; surround with ice water. Sprinkle the 2 to 3 teaspoons sugar evenly on surface of custards. Place under broiler; broil 3 inches from heat for 5 to 6 minutes or till sugar is melted. Makes 4 servings.

Syllabub   *pictured on front cover*   Regional

It is quite correct to let *Syllabub* stand several hours so the cream and liquor can separate.

1 **cup dry white wine**
¼ **cup sugar**
¼ **cup brandy**
1 **tablespoon lemon juice**
2 **cups whipping cream**

Combine wine, sugar, brandy, and lemon juice. Stir to dissolve sugar. Add cream; whip to soft peaks. Spoon into dessert glasses. Makes 8 servings.

Spiced Wassail   England

In its home country, *Irish Coffee* is almost as common as tea.

To make *Irish Coffee,* combine 2 tablespoons *Irish whiskey* and 1 to 2 teaspoons *brown sugar* with ¾ cup hot strong *coffee.* Pour 1 tablespoon of *whipping cream* atop.

3 **small cooking apples**
½ **cup brandy**
¼ **cup packed brown sugar**
½ **cup water**
6 **inches stick cinnamon, broken up**
½ **teaspoon whole cloves**
½ **teaspoon whole allspice, crushed**
3¼ **cups dry red wine**
1½ **cups dry sherry**

Core apples; peel strip around top of each. Place apples in 8x8x2-inch baking dish. In saucepan combine brandy and brown sugar. Bring just to boiling. Pour over apples. Cover with foil. Bake in 350° oven for 35 to 40 minutes or till tender. Drain apples, reserving ¾ cup syrup. In large saucepan or Dutch oven combine reserved syrup and water. Tie cinnamon, cloves, and allspice in cheesecloth bag; add to saucepan. Bring to boiling; reduce heat. Cover and simmer 10 minutes. Stir in wine and sherry. Heat through. Remove bag of spices. Pour into punch bowl. Float baked apples atop. Serves 12.

Marinated Salmon   England

Uncooked *Marinated Salmon* and smoked salmon are often served at high tea. Though now a luxury, salmon was so common a century ago that servants stipulated in their contracts that they would not eat salmon more than three times a week.

1 **pound fresh *or* frozen salmon, cut into 2 fillets**
1 **tablespoon sugar**
2 **teaspoons salt**
1½ **teaspoons whole black peppercorns, crushed**
1 **tablespoon snipped dill *or* 1 teaspoon dried dillweed**
  Toast *or* melba toast

Thaw salmon, if frozen. Combine sugar, salt, and peppercorns. Place *one* fish fillet on large piece of heavy-duty foil. Cover fish with dill; sprinkle with sugar mixture. Top with second fish fillet. Close foil securely, using drugstore fold; place in shallow dish or on tray. Pile several weights or 3 or 4 unopened food cans atop foil packet. Chill at least 48 hours, turning packet several times. (Be sure to keep weight on packet.) To serve, unwrap fish; scrape off seasonings. If desired, broil fish 8 inches from heat for 10 to 15 minutes. Slice thin. Serve with toast or melba toast. Makes 8 to 10 servings.

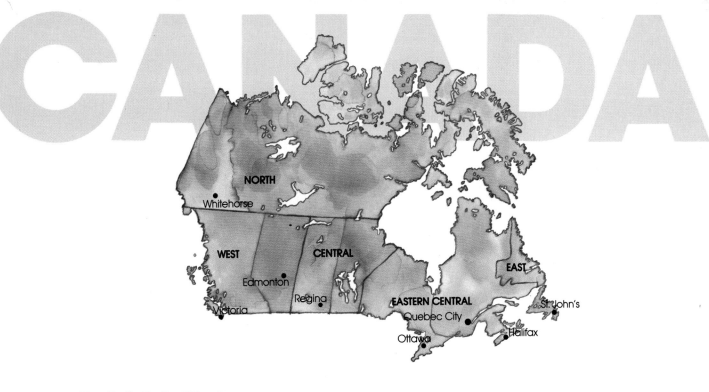

Map labels: NORTH, Whitehorse, WEST, CENTRAL, EAST, Edmonton, EASTERN CENTRAL, St. John's, Victoria, Regina, Quebec City, Halifax, Ottawa

CANADA

Canada is the second largest country in the world and home to more than 30 nationalities, but its cuisine is primarily a reflection of the cooking of the nation's early settlers — the French and the British.

The Maritime Provinces (Nova Scotia, New Brunswick, and Prince Edward Island) are famous for their seafood. Cod and the exotic New-foundland flipper (seal forepaw) are local favorites. The home-style cooking also features wild berries that flourish in the provinces.

In Canada's largest province, Quebec, the French influence on Canadian cuisine is most strongly evident. Quebec specialties include pork, apples, game, seafood; and dishes flavored with maple products.

Farther west lies Ontario, a province known for its freshwater fish, cheddar cheese, and wine.

Canada's prairie heartland — the provinces of Manitoba, Saskatchewan, and Alberta — is the provider of Canada's wheat and beef. Here, scores of European immigrants contributed their homeland favorites to the Canadian cuisine. Scots brought their shortbread, Hungarians came with their goulash, and Italians introduced lasagna.

Along the Pacific Coast, British Columbia is renowned for its excellent salmon, fruit, and vegetables.

Farther north is the rugged area of the Yukon Territory, where sourdough bread sustained prospectors during the 1898 Klondike Gold Rush. Eventually, the word sourdough became synonymous with prospector since these hardy souls kept the yeast from freezing by carrying the sourdough starter close to their bodies.

The extensive Northwest Territories stretch all the way to the Arctic Circle. In this virtually uninhabited area, the favorite foods of the Eskimos and Indians — reindeer, seal, moose, and whale meat — exemplify the diversity of the Canadian cuisine.

Pictured from bottom to top
Apple-Stuffed Salmon (see recipe, page 33), Pot-au-Feu (see recipe, page 33), Sourdough Biscuits (see recipe, page 35), and Rhubarb-Apple Pie (see recipe, page 36)

CANADA

Pot-au-Feu *pictured on page 30* East Central Canada

Pot-au-Feu is simply a fragrant stew of meat and fresh root vegetables. In old Quebec, it was always simmered for hours in a covered black cauldron. Some say that no man would marry a woman unless she possessed such a black cast-iron pot in her dowry.

1 2- to 2½-pound fresh beef brisket *or* corned beef brisket
1 bay leaf
½ teaspoon dried basil, crushed
¼ teaspoon pepper
3 medium carrots, sliced
2 medium potatoes, peeled and cubed (1¼ cups)
1 medium rutabaga, peeled and cubed (1¾ cups)
1 medium parsnip, peeled and sliced (½ cup)
1 medium onion, chopped

Cut fresh or corned beef brisket into bite-size pieces. In a large saucepan or Dutch oven combine beef, bay leaf, basil, pepper, and 4 cups *water*. Add seasoning packet from corned beef, if present. Bring to boiling; reduce heat. Cover and simmer for 1½ hours. Skim off fat.

Add carrots, potatoes, rutabaga, parsnip, and onion. Cover and simmer 30 minutes more or till vegetables are tender. Remove bay leaf and season to taste with salt and pepper. Serves 6.

Tourtière East Central Canada

Tourtière is as much of a part of the French Canadian Christmas as is "Papa Noel" (Santa Claus). This spicy pork pie is usually served cold on Christmas Eve after midnight mass.

1 pound ground pork
½ cup beef broth
1 medium onion, finely chopped
1 clove garlic, minced
1 bay leaf
½ teaspoon salt
¼ teaspoon ground ginger
¼ teaspoon pepper
⅛ teaspoon ground cloves
2 large potatoes, peeled, cooked, drained, and mashed (3 cups)
Tourtière Pastry

In Dutch oven brown pork; drain off fat. Stir in the beef broth, onion, garlic, bay leaf, salt, ginger, pepper, and cloves. Bring to boiling; reduce heat. Cover and simmer about 20 minutes or till onion is tender, stirring often. Discard bay leaf. Stir in the mashed potatoes and cool.

Prepare Tourtière Pastry. On lightly floured surface, roll out *half* of the pastry to a circle 12 inches in diameter. Line a 9-inch pie plate. Trim to ½ inch beyond edge. Fill pastry shell with meat mixture. Roll out remaining pastry to a circle 12 inches in diameter. Cut slits in top crust. Place atop filling. Seal and flute edge. Bake in a 400° oven about 25 minutes or till golden brown. Let stand 20 minutes. Serves 6.

Tourtière Pastry: In medium mixing bowl stir together 2 cups all-purpose *flour*, 2 teaspoons *baking powder*, and ½ teaspoon *salt*. Cut in ⅔ cup shortening till pieces are the size of small peas.

Stir together 1 well-beaten *egg*, ¼ cup cold *water*, 1 teaspoon *lemon juice*, and ½ teaspoon dried *thyme*, crushed. Sprinkle the egg mixture over flour mixture, 1 tablespoon at a time, gently toss with fork. Form into 2 balls.

Ranch Steak West Canada

1½ pounds beef round steak, cut ¾ inch thick
2 teaspoons dry mustard
½ teaspoon salt
¼ teaspoon ground red pepper
2 tablespoons cooking oil
1 4-ounce can mushroom stems and pieces
2 teaspoons Worcestershire sauce
1 teaspoon sugar
2 medium onions, sliced
1 8-ounce can tomatoes, cut up

Trim fat from round steak. In a bowl mix dry mustard, salt, and red pepper; pound seasonings into meat. In 12-inch skillet quickly brown steak on both sides in hot cooking oil; drain off fat.

Drain mushrooms; reserve liquid. Stir reserved liquid, Worcestershire sauce, and sugar into skillet. Add onions and *undrained* tomatoes. Bring to boiling; reduce heat. Cover and simmer for 1¼ to 1½ hours or till meat is tender. Add mushrooms; heat through. Skim off fat before serving. Serves 6.

Apple-Stuffed Salmon   *pictured on page 30*   West Canada

A favorite in both British Columbia and the Maritime Provinces, salmon best represents Canada's motto, "a mari usque ad mare" (from sea to sea).

West Coast Indian tribes depended so much upon salmon as a dietary staple that they carved it on their totem poles in a place of honor.

1   **5-pound fresh *or* frozen whole salmon**
½   **cup dry white wine**
½   **cup olive oil *or* cooking oil**
1   **tablespoon lime juice**
¼   **teaspoon dried dillweed**
¼   **teaspoon dried marjoram, crushed**
2   **medium apples, cored and diced**
3   **tablespoons butter *or* margarine**
4   **cups whole wheat bread cubes**
½   **cup shelled sunflower nuts**
1   **beaten egg**
½   **teaspoon ground sage**

Thaw salmon, if frozen. For marinade, in a bowl combine wine, oil, lime juice, dillweed, and marjoram. Place salmon in a 15x10x1-inch baking dish; brush inside and top with marinade. Pour remaining marinade over fish. Marinate salmon for 15 to 20 minutes.

For stuffing, cook apple in butter just till tender. Stir in bread, sunflower nuts, egg, sage, ½ teaspoon *salt,* and ¼ teaspoon *pepper.*

Remove salmon from marinade. Discard marinade. Stuff salmon loosely with stuffing. Return fish to baking dish. Bake stuffed fish, covered, in 350° oven for 1½ to 1¾ hours or till fish flakes easily when tested with a fork. (Stir 3 tablespoons *water* into remaining stuffing; spoon into 1-quart casserole. Bake, covered, last 30 to 40 minutes of baking time.) Garnish with apple slices and dill, if desired. Makes 8 servings.

Hugger-in-Buff   East Canada

To a "Newfie" (or Newfoundlander), fish means cod, whether fresh, dried, or salted. In the Maritime Provinces, this potato-and-salt-cod casserole may also be called Dutch mess, fish and scrunchions, or house bankin.

1   **pound salt cod**
2   **ounces salt pork *or* bacon, sliced**
2   **medium onions, chopped (1 cup)**
2   **tablespoons all-purpose flour**
¼   **teaspoon pepper**
    Dash ground nutmeg
2   **cups milk**
3   **medium potatoes (1 pound), peeled, cooked, and sliced**

Cut cod into serving-size pieces. Soak cod in enough cold water to cover for 12 hours, changing water several times. Drain.

In skillet cook salt pork or bacon till crisp. Remove, crumble, and drain. Reserve drippings. For sauce, cook onions in pan drippings till tender but not brown. Stir in flour, pepper, and nutmeg. Add milk all at once; cook and stir till thickened and bubbly.

In an 8x8x2-inch baking dish layer cod and potatoes; pour sauce atop. Sprinkle with the salt pork or bacon. Bake, covered, in a 350° oven about 40 minutes or till fish flakes easily when tested with a fork. Makes 4 to 6 servings.

Seafood Chowder   East Canada

This creamy fish soup takes its name from the container it was originally prepared in. A "chaudière" was the large cast-iron kettle brought to the New World by the French. The name was adopted in the Maritime Provinces and New England, where it was translated into chowder.

1   **pound fresh *or* frozen fish fillets**
¼   **pound salt pork *or* bacon, sliced**
1   **6½-ounce can minced clams**
3   **medium potatoes, peeled and diced**
1   **medium red onion, chopped**
1   **tablespoon butter *or* margarine, softened**
1   **tablespoon all-purpose flour**
4   **cups milk**
8   **saltine crackers, finely crushed (¼ cup)**
¾   **teaspoon dried thyme, crushed**
¼   **teaspoon ground nutmeg**
1   **tablespoon lemon juice**

Thaw fish, if frozen. Cut fish into bite-size pieces; set aside. In large saucepan or Dutch oven cook salt pork or bacon till crisp. Remove, crumble, and drain on paper toweling; reserve drippings. Drain clams; reserve liquid. Add enough water to clam liquid to measure 2 cups. To drippings in pan add reserved clam liquid, potatoes, and onion. Cover and cook about 5 minutes or till potatoes are tender. Combine softened butter or margarine and flour. Add to potato mixture along with fish, clams, milk, crackers, thyme, nutmeg, ½ teaspoon *salt,* and ¼ teaspoon *pepper.* Cook and stir till bubbly. Cook and stir 1 minute more. Stir in lemon juice. Sprinkle each serving with salt pork or bacon pieces. Makes 6 to 8 servings.

CANADA

Split Pea Soup

The *Split Pea Soup* of the Maritime Provinces contains green split peas and ham; however, pea soup of French Canada has yellow peas, salt pork, and sometimes corn.

- 1 cup dry green split peas
- 1 meaty ham bone
- ½ cup finely chopped onion
- 1 medium potato, peeled and shredded
- 1 stalk celery, finely chopped
- ½ teaspoon dried sage, crushed
  Dash ground cloves

Rinse peas. In large saucepan or Dutch oven combine peas, ham bone, onion, potato, celery, sage, cloves, 4 cups *water*, ¼ teaspoon *salt*, and ¼ teaspoon *pepper*. Bring to boiling; reduce heat. Cover and simmer for 1½ hours, stirring occasionally. Remove ham bone; cut off any meat and return to soup. Discard bone. Heat through; season to taste with salt and pepper. Makes 4 servings.

Wild Rice Bake
East Central Canada

Canada's only native grain is wild rice. And it's not really rice at all, but rather a seed that grows on tall, leafy plants found in the marshlands of Manitoba and Northern Ontario. Indians in canoes used their paddles to harvest the grain.

- 1 cup wild rice
- 2½ cups beef broth
- ¾ cup sliced fresh mushrooms
- ¾ cup sliced celery
- 2 tablespoons sliced green onion
- 1 tablespoon butter *or* margarine
- 2 teaspoons all-purpose flour
- ¼ teaspoon ground nutmeg
- ¼ teaspoon ground coriander
- ½ cup dairy sour cream
- ¼ cup milk

Run cold water over *uncooked* rice in a strainer for 1 to 2 minutes, lifting rice with fingers to rinse well. Combine rice and beef broth. Bring to boiling; reduce heat. Cover and simmer for 40 minutes.

In skillet cook mushrooms, celery, and onion in butter for 5 minutes. Stir in flour, nutmeg, and coriander. Add sour cream and milk. Cook and stir till thickened and bubbly. Cook and stir 1 minute more. Add to *undrained* rice; transfer to 1½-quart casserole. Cover and bake in a 325° oven for 20 minutes. Let stand 10 minutes. Stir before serving. Makes 6 servings.

Hodgepodge
East Canada

This creamy dish from Nova Scotia is a hodgepodge of new garden vegetables. *Hodgepodge* differs from its American cousin, succotash, in that it never contains corn.

- 8 tiny new potatoes
- 1 cup fresh *or* frozen bias-sliced green beans
- 1 cup bias-sliced carrots
- 1 cup fresh *or* frozen cauliflower flowerets
- 1 cup fresh *or* frozen peas
- ¼ pound salt pork *or* bacon, sliced
- 1 medium onion, chopped
- ½ cup light cream *or* milk
- 1 tablespoon all-purpose flour
- ¼ teaspoon salt
- ¼ teaspoon dried savory, crushed

Cook potatoes, beans, and carrots in boiling salted water to cover for 20 minutes. Add cauliflower and peas; cook 10 minutes longer. Drain, reserving ½ cup cooking liquid. Set aside.

Meanwhile, in a skillet cook salt pork or bacon till crisp. Remove, crumble, and drain; reserve drippings. To drippings in pan add onion and cook till tender but not brown. Drain off fat. Combine cream or milk, flour, salt, savory, and ¼ teaspoon *pepper*. Stir into onions along with reserved cooking liquid. Cook and stir till thickened and bubbly. Cook and stir 1 minute more. Stir cooked vegetables and salt pork into sauce. Heat through. Serves 6 to 8.

Oatcakes
East Canada

Oatcakes evolved from the unleavened oatmeal bannock introduced by Scotsmen who settled in the Canadian prairies and the Maritime Provinces.

- 1½ cups all-purpose flour
- 2 tablespoons brown sugar
- 1 tablespoon baking powder
- ½ teaspoon salt
- ¼ cup butter *or* margarine
- 1½ cups quick-cooking rolled oats
- 1 beaten egg
- ⅔ cup buttermilk
  Butter *or* margarine

In medium mixing bowl stir together flour, brown sugar, baking powder, and salt. Cut in the ¼ cup butter or margarine till pieces resemble coarse crumbs. Stir in oats. Make a well in center. Combine egg and buttermilk; add all at once to dry mixture. Stir just till dough clings together.

Spread dough evenly in greased 9x9x2-inch baking pan. Score into 16 pieces. Bake in a 400° oven for 25 minutes or till golden brown. Serve warm with butter or margarine. Makes 16 pieces.

Sourdough Biscuits   *pictured on page 30*   North Canada

Yukon gold prospectors made flapjacks (pancakes), biscuits, bread, and muffins from their precious *Sourdough Starter.*

Once *Sourdough Starter* has been made, it is easy to replenish. Stir ¾ cup all-purpose *flour,* ¾ cup warm *water,* and 1 teaspoon *sugar or honey* into remaining starter. Cover; let stand at room temperature for 1 day or till bubbly. Refrigerate for later use.

1   cup Sourdough Starter
1⅔ cups all-purpose flour
1   tablespoon sugar
2   teaspoons baking powder
½   teaspoon salt
½   teaspoon ground cinnamon
¼   teaspoon baking soda
⅓   cup shortening *or* lard
½   cup fresh *or* frozen blueberries
⅓   cup milk

Bring the Sourdough Starter to room temperature. In mixing bowl stir together the flour, sugar, baking powder, salt, cinnamon, and baking soda. Cut in shortening or lard till mixture resembles coarse crumbs. Make a well in the center. Combine Sourdough Starter, blueberries, and milk; add all at once to the dry mixture. Stir just till the dough clings together.

Drop dough by tablespoonfuls onto a lightly greased baking sheet. Bake in a 425° oven for 12 to 15 minutes or till biscuits are golden. Serve warm. Makes about 16 biscuits.

Sourdough Starter: Dissolve 1 package active dry *yeast* in ½ cup warm *water* (110° to 115°). Stir in 2 cups warm *water,* 2 cups all-purpose *flour,* and 1 tablespoon *sugar or honey.* Beat till smooth. Cover with cheesecloth. Let stand at room temperature for 5 to 10 days or till bubbly; stir 2 to 3 times each day.

To store, transfer Sourdough Starter to a jar and cover with cheesecloth; refrigerate. *Do not cover jar tightly with a metal lid.* If Starter isn't used within 10 days, stir in 1 teaspoon *sugar or honey.* Repeat every 10 days till used.

CANADA

Rhubarb-Apple Pie *pictured on page 30* Regional

Many refer to rhubarb as "wine plant" or "pie plant" since it is frequently used in making wines and pies. It also is often stewed with a little bit of sugar to make rhubarb sauce.

Pastry for Single-Crust Pie
1 **cup sugar**
1 **tablespoon cornstarch**
¼ **cup apple juice**
3 **cups sliced rhubarb**
3 **cooking apples, peeled and sliced (3 cups)**
¼ **cup all-purpose flour**
¼ **cup quick-cooking rolled oats**
¼ **cup packed brown sugar**
2 **tablespoons butter *or* margarine, melted**
½ **teaspooon ground allspice**
¼ **teaspoon salt**

Prepare Pastry for Single-Crust Pie. On lightly floured surface roll dough from center to edge forming a circle about 12 inches in diameter. Line a 9-inch pie plate. Trim to ½ inch beyond edge. Flute edge high. *Do not prick.*

For filling, in a mixing bowl combine sugar and cornstarch. Stir in apple juice, rhubarb, and apples. Pour rhubarb filling into pie shell.

For topping, stir together flour, rolled oats, brown sugar, butter or margarine, allspice, and salt. Sprinkle atop pie. To prevent overbrowning, cover edge of pie with foil. Bake in a 375° oven for 30 minutes. Remove foil; bake for 30 minutes more or till topping is golden and filling is bubbly. Cool on wire rack before serving. Makes 8 servings.

Pastry for Single-Crust Pie: Stir together 1¼ cups all-purpose *flour* and ½ teaspoon *salt.* Cut in ⅓ cup *shortening* till pieces are the size of small peas. Sprinkle 3 to 4 tablespoons of cold *water* over the mixture, one tablespoon at a time; toss gently with a fork. Form dough into a ball.

Backwoods Pie East Central Canada

At sugaring-off parties in Quebec and Ontario, hot maple syrup is poured on the snow, to be eaten as soon as it hardens.

Sap from maple trees usually starts to flow around March. It is boiled over fires, then skimmed to make maple syrup and sugar.

Pastry for Single-Crust Pie (see recipe above)
4 **eggs**
1½ **cups pure maple syrup *or* maple-flavored syrup**
¾ **cup packed brown sugar**
½ **cup light cream *or* milk**
½ **teaspoon vanilla**
½ **teaspoon ground allspice**
¼ **teaspoon salt**
Unsweetened whipped cream (optional)

Prepare Pastry for Single-Crust Pie. On lightly floured surface roll dough to a circle 12 inches in diameter. Line a 9-inch pie plate. Trim to ½ inch beyond edge. Flute edge high. *Do not prick.* Bake in a 450° oven for 5 minutes. Cool on wire rack.

In bowl beat eggs slightly with rotary beater or fork. Stir in maple syrup or maple-flavored syrup, brown sugar, light cream or milk, vanilla, allspice, and salt; beat with a rotary beater just till smooth.

Place pastry shell on oven rack; pour filling into partially baked pastry shell. To prevent overbrowning, cover edge of pie with foil. Bake in a 350° oven for 30 minutes. Remove foil; bake 30 minutes more or till knife inserted off center comes out clean. Cool on wire rack. Garnish with whipped cream, if desired. Makes 8 servings.

Cherry-Nut Roly-Poly

East Canada

The ancestor of this cherry-filled biscuit roll is the English steamed roly-poly. Other fruit fillings, such as apples and peaches, are just as delicious as cherry.

2 cups all-purpose flour
¼ cup sugar
1 tablespoon baking powder
½ teaspoon salt
⅓ cup shortening *or* lard
½ cup milk
⅓ cup packed brown sugar
3 tablespoons all-purpose flour
½ teaspoon ground cinnamon
½ cup chopped walnuts
2 tablespoons butter *or* margarine, melted
1 16-ounce can pitted tart red cherries
2 tablespoons brown sugar
2 teaspoons cornstarch

In mixing bowl stir together the 2 cups flour, the sugar, baking powder, and salt. Cut in shortening or lard till mixture resembles coarse crumbs. Make a well in center. Add the milk all at once, stirring just till dough clings together. Turn dough out onto lightly floured surface. Knead dough gently 15 to 20 strokes. On lightly floured surface, roll dough to a 12x10-inch rectangle.

Combine the ⅓ cup brown sugar, the 3 tablespoons flour, and cinnamon; stir in the nuts and melted butter or margarine. Drain cherries, reserving ¾ *cup* of the liquid. Add cherries to nut mixture. Spoon cherry mixture onto dough to within 1 inch of edges. Brush edges of dough with water. Roll up jelly-roll style, starting with long side. Seal all edges. Cut into eight 1½-inch slices. Place, cut side down, in greased 12x7½x2-inch baking dish. Bake in 350° oven for 40 to 45 minutes or till light brown.

For sauce, in saucepan combine reserved cherry juice, the 2 tablespoons brown sugar, and the cornstarch. Cook and stir till slightly thickened and bubbly. Cook and stir 2 minutes more. Serve warm; spoon sauce atop. Makes 8 servings.

Maple Divinity

East Central Canada

2 cups pure maple syrup
2 egg whites
¼ teaspoon salt
1 cup broken walnuts

In a heavy 3-quart saucepan bring maple syrup to boiling. Boil rapidly over medium-high heat till mixture reaches hard-ball stage (260° on candy thermometer), without stirring. Remove from heat. Immediately, in large mixer bowl beat egg whites and salt to stiff peaks (tips stand straight). Slowly pour hot syrup over egg whites, beating constantly at high speed with electric mixer. Continue beating 5 to 6 minutes more or till mixture forms soft peaks and begins to lose its gloss.

Quickly stir in walnuts. Drop by teaspoonfuls onto waxed paper-lined baking sheet, swirling each candy to a peak. (If mixture starts to harden, stir in a few drops water.) Makes about 40 candies.

Solomon Gundy

East Canada

2 pounds dressed salt herring
1½ cups vinegar
5 teaspoons mixed pickling spice
3 tablespoons sugar
1 tablespoon capers, drained
½ teaspoon pepper
1 medium red onion, sliced and separated into rings
  Assorted crackers
1 2-ounce jar sliced pimiento (optional)

Cut herring in 1-inch pieces. Soak herring in enough cold water to cover for 12 hours, changing water several times. Drain.

In saucepan combine vinegar, pickling spice, sugar, capers, and pepper; bring to boiling. Cool to room temperature.

Layer drained herring with onions in small glass bowl. Pour vinegar mixture over herring. Chill overnight before serving.

Serve herring on crackers. Garnish each with a pimiento strip, if desired. Store herring in refrigerator. Makes about 3 cups.

BAHAMAS

Havana

CUBA

DOMINICAN
REPUBLIC   PUERTO RICO

HAITI

VIRGIN ISLANDS

GUADELOUPE

MARTINIQUE

BARBADOS

JAMAICA

TRINIDAD

CARIBBEAN

Caribbean cuisine incorporates the flavors and cooking styles of the South American Indians, Europeans, Africans, and Asians who immigrated to these beautiful islands. Throughout the West Indies, fruits, vegetables, seafood, and fresh fish are plentiful and are often combined in hearty one-dish meals. The native dietary staples are rice and beans.

Long before Columbus discovered these islands, Carib and Arawak Indians inhabited the area. They contributed pineapple from their native South America to the island stores of cassava, sweet potatoes, arrowroot, and guava.

Oranges, limes, rice, coffee, and sugar cane were later introduced by the Spanish, Dutch, English, French, and Portuguese who settled the islands in the 1500s. The transplanted sugar cane flourished, and West African slaves provided cheap labor for the plantations. They brought along their native "akee," "callaloo," "taro," and okra — fruits and vegetables that thrived in the Caribbean — and used hot pepper to season the bland foods provided by plantation owners.

The African slaves indirectly influenced the importation of the Caribbean's second most important vegetable mainstay (after the plantain) — the breadfruit. Plantation owners needed filling foods for the slaves, and the Tahitian-grown starchy vegetable seemed perfect because it required little care or space. The infamous Captain Bligh and the HMS Bounty went to the South Seas to procure the breadfruit plants. The crew mutinied when Bligh used his men's drinking water to keep the valued breadfruit cuttings alive.

After the slaves were emancipated, indentured servants were brought from India and China to work the cane fields. Their use of curry was adopted by Caribbean cooks.

Perhaps more famous than its food is West Indies' rum — a by-product of the abundant sugar cane and the basis of many a tall, cooling refresher in this tropical paradise.

Clockwise from top right
Planter's Punch (see recipe, page 47), Plantain Circles (see recipe, page 40), Shredded Flank Steak (see recipe, page 40), Plantain Tostones (see recipe, page 43), Banana Daiquiri (see recipe, page 47), and Papaya Salad (see recipe, page 44)

CARIBBEAN

Plantain Circles   *pictured on page 38*   Puerto Rico

Long ago, migrants from India and Africa introduced the plantain, also called cooking banana, to the Caribbean Islands. From there, a Spanish-inspired spicy meat filling coupled with plantain slices evolved into this popular Puerto Rican dish known as "piononos."

½ pound ground beef *or* ground pork
½ cup finely chopped onion
1 clove garlic, minced
¼ teaspoon dried oregano, crushed
¼ teaspoon crushed red pepper
⅛ teaspoon pepper
½ of a 6-ounce can tomato paste
¼ cup raisins
¼ cup water
1 tablespoon snipped parsley
1 tablespoon capers, drained
2 teaspoons vinegar
1 hard-cooked egg, chopped
2 tablespoons chopped pimiento-stuffed olives
3 very ripe large plantains*
¼ cup butter *or* margarine
2 eggs
2 tablespoons all-purpose flour
1 tablespoon water
¼ teaspoon salt
  Cooking oil *or* shortening for deep-fat frying
  Hot cooked rice

For filling, in a skillet cook beef or pork, onion, garlic, oregano, red pepper, and pepper till meat is brown and onion is tender. Drain off fat. Stir in tomato paste, raisins, the ¼ cup water, parsley, capers, and vinegar; simmer, covered about 5 minutes. Remove from heat. Stir in the chopped hard-cooked egg and pimiento-stuffed olives.

Peel the plantains; slice *each* lengthwise into 4 slices. In a large skillet cook plantain slices, 1 or 2 at a time, in hot butter or margarine about 4 minutes on each side or till golden brown. Remove plantain slices from skillet; drain on paper toweling.

To make the meat-stuffed plantain circles, stand *each* plantain slice on edge and form into a circle, overlapping ends about ½ inch; secure with a wooden pick inserted lengthwise.

Fill *each* plantain circle with about *2 tablespoons* of the filling; pat the filling till it's firmly packed. Gently press the top till level.

In a small bowl combine beaten eggs, flour, the 1 tablespoon water, and salt. Dip the plantain circles into egg mixture, coating evenly.

Carefully place plantain circles, a few at a time, into deep, hot fat (400°) and fry about 1½ minutes; gently turn and fry about 1½ minutes more or till golden. Drain on paper toweling. Serve warm with hot cooked rice. Makes 6 servings.

*Recipe note: The skin of a very ripe plantain will be completely black.

Shredded Flank Steak   *pictured on page 38*   Cuba

This Spanish-speaking island is famous for its "ropa vieja" — shredded beef, tomatoes, chili peppers, garlic, olives, and spices that simmer together, blending flavors.

The literal translation of this delicious Cuban dish is "old clothes."

1 1-pound beef flank steak
2 medium carrots, cut up
1 medium onion, quartered
1 teaspoon salt
⅛ teaspoon pepper
1 bay leaf
1 medium onion, chopped
1 medium green pepper, chopped
1 clove garlic, minced
1 tablespoon olive oil *or* cooking oil
1 16-ounce can tomatoes, cut up
1 4-ounce can green chili peppers, rinsed, seeded, and chopped
½ teaspoon salt
⅛ teaspoon ground cinnamon
⅛ teaspoon ground cloves
⅛ teaspoon pepper
2 teaspoons capers, drained
  Plantain Tostones (see recipe, page 43) *or* hot cooked rice

Cut flank steak crosswise into thirds. In a large saucepan or Dutch oven place the flank steak. Add carrots, the quartered onion, the 1 teaspoon salt, ⅛ teaspoon pepper, bay leaf, and 3 cups *water.* Bring to boiling; reduce heat. Cover; simmer about 2 hours or till meat will shred easily. Remove meat; reserve stock. Strain stock to remove vegetables and bay leaf. Using two forks, pull meat apart into shreds; set aside.

In a medium saucepan cook the chopped onion, green pepper, and garlic in hot oil till onion is tender but not brown. Stir in *undrained* tomatoes, chili peppers, the ½ teaspoon salt, ground cinnamon, cloves, and ⅛ teaspoon pepper. Bring to boiling; reduce heat. Simmer, uncovered, for 30 minutes.

Stir in shredded meat and enough of the reserved stock to moisten (¼ to ½ cup). Stir in capers; heat through, stirring constantly. Transfer to a heated serving platter. Serve with Plantain Tostones or hot cooked rice. Makes 4 to 6 servings.

Pineapple-Rum Duckling

The French islands of Lesser Antilles are Guadeloupe, Marie Galante, Martinique, and the French half of St. Martin. These islands blend African, Asian, Indian, and French influences to provide a delightful cuisine.

Pineapple-Rum Duckling, known as "le caneton aux ananas" in Guadeloupe, combines French technique with superb tropical rum and pineapple.

1 4- to 5-pound domestic duckling, quartered
2 tablespoons butter *or* margarine
1 cup pineapple juice
½ cup rum
½ cup chopped onion
1 clove garlic, minced
½ teaspoon salt
¼ teaspoon pepper
¼ cup rum
2 tablespoons cornstarch
1 8¼-ounce can pineapple chunks

Rinse duckling; pat dry with paper toweling. Remove giblets. In covered saucepan cook in small amount of boiling salted water for 1½ hours. Remove from heat; set aside.

Meanwhile, in a Dutch oven brown duckling pieces in butter or margarine; drain off fat. Add the pineapple juice, ½ cup rum, chopped onion, garlic, salt, and pepper. Cover and simmer about 60 minutes or till duckling is tender.

Transfer duckling to platter; keep warm. Spoon fat from pan juices. Add enough giblet liquid to juices to measure 1½ cups; return to Dutch oven. Combine the ¼ cup rum and cornstarch. Stir into juice mixture. Cook and stir till thickened and bubbly. Cook and stir 2 minutes more. Stir in *undrained* pineapple chunks. Heat through; spoon over duckling. Makes 4 servings.

Fish Vinaigrette

Fish Vinaigrette is called "escoveitched" fish in Jamaica. "Escabeche" is the Spanish word for pickled, and it also describes a method of cooking fish in oil and vinegar. Jamaicans transformed the term "escabeche" into "escoveitched."

1 pound fresh *or* frozen red snapper *or* other fish fillets
2 tablespoons cooking oil
2 medium green peppers, thinly sliced into rings
1 medium onion, sliced and separated into rings
2 medium carrots, sliced
2 cloves garlic, minced
1 teaspoon grated gingerroot
2 tablespoons cooking oil
2 tablespoons dry white wine
2 tablespoons white vinegar
2 tablespoons snipped parsley

Thaw fish, if frozen. Skin fish, if desired. Sprinkle lightly with salt. In a large skillet fry fish in 2 tablespoons hot oil for 4 to 5 minutes. Turn fish and fry for 4 to 5 minutes more or till fish flakes easily when tested with a fork. Drain on paper toweling.

Meanwhile, in a saucepan cook green peppers, onion, carrots, garlic, and gingerroot in 2 tablespoons hot oil for 8 to 10 minutes or till vegetables are crisp-tender. Stir in white wine, vinegar, ½ teaspoon *salt,* and ⅛ teaspoon *pepper;* cook 1 minute more.

Transfer fish to platter. Spoon vegetable mixture over fish. Sprinkle parsley atop. Serves 4.

Red Beans and Rice

Red Beans and Rice, perhaps the most popular of Puerto Rican foods, is enjoyed for its rich and distinctive flavor.

The main contributing flavor is Sofrito — a sauce that combines tomatoes, onion, garlic, peppers, and annatto seed (sometimes called achiote). If annatto seed is unavailable, you can substitute 1½ teaspoons paprika for ¼ teaspoon annatto seed.

¼ cup Sofrito
1 pound dry red kidney beans
4 cups water
8 cups chicken broth
2 cloves garlic, minced
2 bay leaves
2½ pounds boneless pork, cut into ½-inch pieces
1 15-ounce can tomato sauce
1 pound chorizo *or* Italian sausage links, thinly sliced
2½ cups cubed winter squash
1 4-ounce can pimiento, drained and chopped
1 to 2 tablespoons vinegar
   Hot cooked rice

Prepare the Sofrito; chill. Rinse beans. In Dutch oven combine beans and water. Bring to boiling. Reduce heat; simmer 2 minutes. Remove from heat. Cover; let stand 1 hour. Drain beans and rinse.

In Dutch oven combine beans, broth, garlic, bay leaves, and 1 cup *water.* Bring to boiling; reduce heat. Cover; simmer 45 minutes. Add pork. Simmer, covered, 45 minutes. Stir in Sofrito, tomato sauce, chorizo, squash, and pimiento. Simmer, covered, 40 minutes more. Remove bay leaves. Stir in vinegar. Serve over rice. Serves 10.

Sofrito: Heat ¼ teaspoon *annatto seed* in ⅓ cup *lard* for 1 minute; strain. To lard add 3 slices *bacon,* chopped; ½ cup chopped, peeled *tomato;* ½ cup chopped *onion;* ¼ cup chopped *green pepper;* 2 cloves *garlic,* minced; and 1 teaspoon *salt.* Cook, covered, till vegetables are tender. Stir in 1 teaspoon *lime juice.*

CARIBBEAN

Callaloo

Of all Caribbean creole soups, the most celebrated is *Callaloo*. This enticing fish-and-crab chowder originated in Trinidad, but versions of it also turn up on other islands: Jamaica, Grenada, Haiti, Martinique, and Guadeloupe.

Most Caribbean versions of *Callaloo* use the young taro leaves. Since they are difficult to find, fresh spinach, Swiss chard, or mustard greens make good substitutes.

1 **pound fresh *or* frozen fish fillets**
6 **ounces frozen crab meat *or* one 6-ounce can crab meat**
2 **pounds fresh callaloo leaves, spinach, Swiss chard, *or* mustard greens**
4 **ounces salt pork with rind**
6 **cups chicken broth**
2 **medium onions, finely chopped**
2 **cloves garlic, minced**
1 **to 2 teaspoons crushed red pepper *or* ¼ to ½ teaspoon ground red pepper**
1 **teaspoon dried thyme, crushed**
2 **cups sliced okra *or* one 10-ounce package frozen cut okra**
Hot cooked rice

Partially thaw fish and crab, if frozen. Remove any skin from fish; cut into 1-inch pieces. (For canned crab, drain and flake crab; remove cartilage.) Cut up crab. Set fish and crab aside.

Discard stems of greens and any damaged portions. Tear up large leaves (should have about 12 cups greens). Chop salt pork by cutting to, but not through rind, leaving it in 1 piece. In a large kettle or Dutch oven combine greens, salt pork, chicken broth, onions, garlic, crushed red pepper or ground red pepper, and thyme. Bring to boiling; reduce heat. Cover; simmer for 1 hour. Remove and discard salt pork.

Stir in fish, crab, and okra. Return to boiling; reduce heat. Simmer, uncovered, for 5 to 7 minutes or till fish flakes easily when tested with a fork. *Do not overcook.* Season to taste with salt and pepper. Serve over rice in soup plates. Pass bottled hot pepper sauce, if desired. Serves 6 to 8.

Chicken Asopao

Two popular Puerto Rican staples are chicken and rice, which frequently are served together.

Chicken Asopao, a thick rice soup, contains chicken, ham, peas, green pepper, onions, tomatoes, olives, and capers.

The unique flavor of this dish comes from the *Adobo* — a blend of garlic, oregano, olive oil, and vinegar or fresh lime juice.

Adobo
- 1 2½- to 3-pound broiler-fryer chicken, cut up
- 1 medium onion, chopped
- 1 medium green pepper, chopped
- 2 tablespoons cooking oil
- 2 medium tomatoes, chopped
- 1 cup cubed fully cooked ham
- 1 cup water
- 1 8-ounce can tomato sauce
- 3½ cups water
- ¼ cup chopped pimiento-stuffed olives
- 1 tablespoon capers, drained
- 1 cup long grain rice
- 1 8½-ounce can peas, drained
- 1 2-ounce jar sliced pimiento, drained (optional)

Prepare the Adobo; set aside. Rinse chicken pieces; pat dry with paper toweling. Thoroughly rub *each* piece with the Adobo.

In Dutch oven brown chicken, onion, and green pepper in hot oil about 10 minutes. Drain off fat. Add chopped tomatoes, ham, the 1 cup water, and tomato sauce. Bring to boiling; reduce heat. Cover; simmer 1 hour or till chicken is tender. Remove chicken from mixture. When cool enough to handle, remove and discard skin and bones. Cut up chicken. Return chicken to mixture.

Add the 3½ cups water, olives, and capers. Bring to boiling; reduce heat. Stir in *uncooked* rice. Cover; simmer about 20 minutes or till rice is tender but still moist. Stir in peas; heat through. Serve immediately. If desired, garnish with strips of pimiento. Makes 8 to 10 servings.

Recipe note: Serve the soup as soon as it's removed from heat to prevent it from drying out.

Adobo: In a small bowl combine 2 cloves *garlic,* minced; 1½ teaspoons dried *oregano,* crushed; 1 teaspoon *salt;* and ¼ teaspoon freshly ground black *pepper.* Stir in 1 teaspoon *olive oil or cooking oil* and 1 teaspoon *vinegar or lime juice;* mix well. (Or, combine the ingredients by mixing and crushing with a mortar and pestle.)

Plantain Tostones   *pictured on page 38*

Puerto Rico

Plantains, known in the Caribbean islands as "platanos," are fried, roasted, boiled, or baked, either whole or in slices.

Fried *Plantain Tostones* have a delicious flavor and are usually served instead of bread. They taste their best when served crisp and hot.

- 2 large green plantains
- 4 cups water
- 1½ teaspoons salt
- 2 tablespoons cooking oil
  Salt

Cut off both ends of the plantains. Cut in half crosswise. With sharp knife, cut 6 lengthwise slits in the plantain's peel, cutting through to the plantain flesh. Repeat with the other half. Lift the plantain's peel away a strip at a time, pulling the peel off crosswise.

Cut plantain into 1-inch diagonal slices. In a medium mixing bowl combine water and the 1½ teaspoons salt; add plantain pieces. Let stand to soak for 60 minutes. (*Or,* in a medium saucepan combine plantain pieces, water, and the 1½ teaspoons salt. Bring to boiling; reduce heat. Cover; simmer about 15 minutes or till almost tender.)

Drain well; pat slices dry with paper toweling. In a large skillet cook plantain slices in hot oil over medium heat about 2 minutes. Turn plantain slices over and cook 2 minutes more. Drain on paper toweling. Place a large piece of clear plastic wrap or waxed paper over the plantain pieces.

Flatten each slice with palm of hand to a ½-inch thickness. Return slices to skillet; cook 2 minutes. Turn plantain slices over and cook 2 minutes more. Drain on paper toweling. Sprinkle lightly with salt. Serve immediately. Makes 4 servings.

Recipe note: The plantain slices may be set aside after flattening. Just before serving, fry plantain slices so they are crisp and hot.

CARIBBEAN

Papaya Salad   *pictured on page 38*   Bahamas

*Papaya Salad is a tasty
example of the attrac-
tive and appetizing
salads created by
Caribbeans. The
exceptional flavor of
hearts of palm, the
beautiful and tasty fruits
of the islands, and the
nutty flavor of avocado
make this salad taste
as good as it looks.*

  **1 14-ounce can hearts of palm,
     drained**
  1 pineapple
  2 medium oranges
  2 medium papayas
  1 medium avocado
  3 tablespoons lemon juice
  ⅛ teaspoon salt
  **⅛ teaspoon ground cinnamon,
     ground allspice, ground
     cloves, *or* ground coriander**
  ⅛ teaspoon paprika
  **⅛ teaspoon ground ginger
     Iceberg lettuce, *or* fresh
     spinach leaves, *or*
     watercress leaves**

Rinse hearts of palm; cut into bite-size pieces. Rinse
pineapple. Twist off crown; cut off base. Slice off
strips of rind lengthwise; cut out and discard eyes.
Slice into spears; cut off hard core. Cut pineapple
spears into chunks.

  Peel and section oranges, reserving juice. Halve
papaya lengthwise; seed, peel, and cut into 1-inch
cubes. Halve avocado lengthwise, then twist gently
and separate; seed, peel, and cut into 1-inch
cubes. Combine reserved orange juice, papaya,
avocado, and the lemon juice; toss to coat.

  In mixing bowl combine: hearts of palm;
pineapple chunks; oranges; the papaya mixture;
salt; ground cinnamon; allspice, cloves, or coriander; paprika; and ginger. Gently toss to mix.

  Serve on lettuce-, spinach-, or watercress-lined
individual salad plates or a large platter. Serves 6.

Coo-Coo   Barbados

*Traditionally Coo-Coo
is served with the Bar-
bados specialty,
steamed flying fish, but
it is also served as a
starch vegetable with
roasted pork or poultry.*

  1½ cups yellow cornmeal
  1½ cups cold water
  1½ teaspoons salt
   **2 cups sliced okra *or*
     one 10-ounce package
     frozen cut okra
     Tomato Sauce**

In mixing bowl stir together cornmeal, water, and
salt. In saucepan cook okra in boiling water for 10
minutes or till tender. (Or, cook frozen okra according to package directions.) *Do not drain.* Gradually
stir cornmeal mixture into *undrained* okra. Cook
and stir till thick. Cover and cook over very low heat
about 45 minutes; stirring often. Spread in 8x8x2-
inch pan; press firmly. Unmold onto heated serving
platter. Spoon Tomato Sauce atop. Serve immediately. Makes 6 servings.

  Tomato Sauce: In saucepan cook ⅓ cup
chopped *celery*, ¼ cup chopped *green pepper*; 1
clove *garlic*, minced, in 2 tablespoons *olive oil or
cooking oil* till onion and celery are tender. Stir in
one 16-ounce can *tomatoes*, cut up and *undrained*; ⅓ cup *tomato paste*; one 4-ounce can
green chili peppers, rinsed, seeded, and chopped;
½ teaspoon *salt*; ½ teaspoon dried *oregano*,
crushed; ¼ teaspoon *pepper*; and 1 *bay leaf*. Cook
uncovered, for 45 to 50 minutes. Remove bay leaf.

Fried Butter Biscuits   Trinidad

*Delectable Fried Butter
Biscuits, called "bakes"
in Trinidad, literally melt
in the mouth. Serve
these rich, flour-and-
butter biscuits for
breakfast with steam-
ing cups of freshly
brewed Puerto Rican or
Jamaican coffee.*

  2 cups all-purpose flour
  2 tablespoons sugar
  2 teaspoons baking powder
  ½ teaspoon salt
  **3 tablespoons butter *or*
     margarine**
  ¾ cup water
  2 tablespoons cooking oil

In mixing bowl stir together flour, sugar, baking
powder, and salt. Cut in butter or margarine till mixture resembles coarse crumbs. Make a well in center. Add water; stir to make a stiff dough. Knead
gently on lightly floured surface (10 to 12 strokes).
Divide into 10 portions. Roll or pat dough to ½-inch
thickness. Cut dough with a 2½-inch biscuit cutter.

  In a large skillet cook biscuits in hot oil, uncovered, over low heat 10 to 11 minutes on each
side or till double in volume and golden brown.
Drain on paper toweling. Makes 10.

Mango Mousse

Barbados

2 **15-ounce jars mango slices**
2 **envelopes unflavored gelatin**
½ **cup sugar**
½ **cup water**
1 **tablespoon lemon juice**
4 **egg whites**
1 **cup whipping cream**
1 **tablespoon lemon juice**
  Whipped cream (optional)
  Mango slices (optional)

Drain *one* jar mangoes, reserving syrup; chill mangoes. Place remaining jar *undrained* mangoes in a blender container. Cover and blend till nearly smooth; strain to remove seeds. Set aside. Combine gelatin and sugar; add water. Heat and stir till sugar and gelatin are dissolved. Add reserved syrup, blended mangoes, and 1 tablespoon lemon juice; gradually stir into unbeaten egg whites. Chill till the consistency of unbeaten egg whites (partially set). Beat till light. Whip whipping cream till soft peaks form; fold into gelatin. Turn mango-gelatin mixture into a 6-cup mold; chill till firm.

For sauce, in a blender container place chilled mangoes. Cover and blend till smooth; strain. Stir in the 1 tablespoon lemon juice. Unmold mousse onto a plate. Garnish with whipped cream and additional mango slices, if desired. Serve with sauce. Serves 8.

CARIBBEAN

Banana Soufflé   *pictured on page 45*   Haiti

Haiti is a French-speaking republic that shares the island of Hispaniola with the Spanish-speaking Dominican Republic.

The Haitians modified a traditional French soufflé recipe to use native foods, such as the bananas and limes in this wonderful *Banana Soufflé*.

¼ cup butter *or* margarine
¼ cup all-purpose flour
¼ teaspoon salt
¼ teaspoon ground nutmeg
½ cup milk
⅓ cup mashed banana (1 small)
1½ teaspoons finely shredded lemon peel *or* lime peel
5 egg yolks
5 egg whites
½ teaspoon vanilla
¼ cup sugar
Powdered sugar
Sweetened whipped cream (optional)

In a small saucepan melt butter or margarine. Combine flour, salt, and nutmeg; stir into butter. Combine milk, banana, and lemon or lime peel; add all at once to flour mixture. Cook and stir till thickened and bubbly. Reduce heat; cook and stir 1 minute more. Remove from heat; set aside.

Beat egg yolks about 5 minutes or till thick and lemon-colored. Slowly add banana mixture to egg yolks, stirring constantly. Wash beaters.

In a mixer bowl beat egg whites and vanilla till soft peaks form. Gradually add the sugar, beating till stiff peaks form.

Carefully fold the banana-yolk mixture into beaten egg whites. Turn into an ungreased 2-quart soufflé dish. Bake in a 325° oven for 50 to 55 minutes or till knife inserted near center comes out clean. (Do not open oven door until end of suggested baking time. Test soufflé while soufflé is still in oven.) Serve immediately. Sprinkle with powdered sugar and dollop with sweetened whipped cream, if desired. Serves 6.

Pumpkin Pudding   Puerto Rico

Like most of the Caribbeans, Puerto Ricans enjoy pudding as a light but special ending to a meal. This popular dessert, *Pumpkin Pudding* (known as "budin de calabaza") is an interesting medley of pumpkin, cinnamon, and cloves.

1 16-ounce can pumpkin
¾ cup sugar
¼ cup all-purpose flour
2 tablespoons butter *or* margarine, softened
1 teaspoon ground cinnamon
½ teaspoon salt
¼ teaspoon ground cloves
4 eggs
1¼ cups milk
½ cup whipping cream
2 teaspoons rum

In a large mixing bowl thoroughly combine the pumpkin, sugar, flour, butter, cinnamon, salt, and cloves. Add eggs; lightly beat eggs into pumpkin mixture with a fork. Add milk; mix well.

Place a 10x6x2-inch baking pan in a 13x9x2-inch baking pan on oven rack; pour in the pumpkin mixture. Pour hot water into outer pan to a depth of 1 inch. Bake in a 350° oven about 45 minutes or till knife inserted comes out clean. Cool pudding; chill.

Combine whipping cream and rum; beat till soft peaks form. Spoon pudding into 8 dessert dishes. Dollop *each* with whipped cream mixture. Makes 8 servings.

Gingerbread   Jamaica

Ginger grows wild on Jamaica. With such a plentiful supply, it seems only natural to incorporate the sweet and pungent spice into an intriguing dessert. And, this version of *Gingerbread* is a true culinary delight.

1½ cups all-purpose flour
¾ teaspoon ground allspice
½ teaspoon baking powder
½ teaspoon baking soda
½ teaspoon salt
½ cup milk
½ cup butter *or* margarine
½ cup molasses
¼ cup packed brown sugar
2 eggs
2 teaspoons grated fresh gingerroot *or* ¾ teaspoon ground ginger
1 tablespoon finely snipped candied ginger

Grease and lightly flour a 9x1½-inch round baking pan; set aside. In a mixer bowl stir together flour, allspice, baking powder, baking soda, and salt.

In a small saucepan heat together milk, butter or margarine, molasses, and brown sugar till butter is melted; stir constantly. Add to flour mixture; add eggs and gingerroot or ground ginger. Beat at low speed of electric mixer till just combined. Stir in candied ginger.

Turn into the prepared pan. Bake in a 350° oven for 30 to 35 minutes or till wooden pick inserted in center comes out clean. Cool 10 minutes on wire rack. Remove from pan; cut into wedges and serve warm. Garnish with lime twists just before serving, if desired. Makes 8 servings.

Daiquiri Regional

Truly legendary are the exotic Caribbean rum drinks. The basis for the legends is the superb liquor, a product of sugar cane, which grows profusely on the islands.

The rich volcanic land and the warm island climate are ideal for growing sugar cane. Making the golden-brown cane sugar produces a residue, black-strap molasses, which is fermented and distilled into an exceptional Caribbean rum.

Rum drinks — *Planter's Punch, Piña Colada,* or *Daiquiri* — make a delightful before- or after-dinner drink. The refreshing flavors of these drinks are sure to put you and your guests in the mood for a Caribbean dinner party.

1½ **ounces light rum**
1 **ounce lime juice**
1 **teaspoon powdered sugar**
1 **teaspoon orange liqueur**
 Cracked ice

In a cocktail shaker combine rum, lime juice, powdered sugar, orange liqueur, and cracked ice. Shake well; strain into a chilled cocktail glass. Makes 1 (4-ounce) serving.

• **Frozen Daiquiri:** In a blender container combine 3 ounces light *rum,* 2 ounces *lime juice,* 1 tablespoon *powdered sugar,* and 2 teaspoons *orange liqueur.* With blender running, add 11 or 12 *ice cubes,* one at a time, through hole in lid, to make 2½ cups slushy mixture. (Add water, if necessary.) Makes 2 (10-ounce) servings.

Pineapple Daiquiri Regional

1 **8¼-ounce can crushed pineapple**
¾ **cup light rum**
½ **cup frozen pineapple-orange juice concentrate**
20 **to 24 ice cubes**

In a blender container combine undrained pineapple, rum, and pineapple-orange juice concentrate. Cover; blend till smooth. With blender running, add ice cubes, one at a time, through hole in lid, to make 5 cups slushy mixture. (Add water, if necessary.) Makes 4 (10-ounce) servings.

Banana Daiquiri   *pictured on page 38* Regional

4 **ripe medium bananas**
¾ **cup light rum**
¼ **cup frozen limeade concentrate**
20 **to 24 ice cubes**
 Banana slices
 Mint sprigs

Peel the 4 bananas, wrap in clear plastic wrap. Freeze 1 hour. Unwrap; cut into chunks. In a blender container combine banana chunks, rum, and frozen limeade concentrate. Cover and blend till smooth. With blender running, add ice cubes, one at a time, through hole in lid, to make 5 cups slushy mixture. Garnish *each* serving with a banana slice and mint sprig. Makes 4 (10-ounce) servings.

Planter's Punch   *pictured on page 38* Regional

1 **cup sugar**
2 **cups dark rum**
1½ **cups unsweetened pineapple juice**
1½ **cups orange juice**
½ **cup lemon juice *or* lime juice**
1 **tablespoon grenadine syrup**

For syrup, combine sugar and 1 cup *boiling water;* stir till sugar dissolves. Chill.

In a pitcher stir together syrup, rum, pineapple juice, orange juice, lemon juice or lime juice, grenadine syrup, and *ice cubes.* Garnish with orange and lime slices, if desired. Makes 6 (10-ounce) servings.

Piña Colada Regional

2 **ounces chilled unsweetened pineapple juice *or* ¼ cup chilled canned crushed pineapple (juice pack)**
1½ **ounces rum**
2 **tablespoons cream of coconut**
¼ **cup cracked ice**

In a blender container combine pineapple juice or undrained crushed pineapple, rum, coconut cream, and cracked ice. Cover; blend till slushy. Pour into a chilled cocktail glass.

Garnish with a pineapple spear, if desired. Makes 1 (4-ounce) serving.

CENTRAL AMERICA

The cuisine of Central America is suggestive of its neighbors — Mexico and Colombia. In the seven countries that make up this land link between North and South America (Guatemala, Honduras, Belize, El Salvador, Panama, Costa Rica, and Nicaragua), cooking styles reflect a unique mixture of Spanish and native Indian influences.

Throughout Central America, the dietary staples are corn, beans, and rice — with beans and rice customarily served together. Also, this small area that straddles the Atlantic and Pacific oceans is rich with seafood.

Fruits and vegetables grow in profusion in Central America. Mangoes, papayas, coconuts, tangerines, pineapples, and oranges are combined in many dishes. Bananas and plantains are particularly popular when sliced and fried.

Central America is also noted for its coffee. Salvadoran, Guatemalan, and Costa Rican coffee plantations are among the most productive in the world. Their exceptional coffee beans provide not only a tasty beverage to accompany the native cuisine, but also a valuable export crop.

Some culinary exceptions do exist. In Costa Rica, the Spanish invasion resulted in the death of most of the native Indian population. Now, most Costa Ricans are of almost pure Spanish ancestry, and their cuisine reflects their heritage.

In Belize, a tiny nation south of Mexico and a British colony for almost 200 years, the British touch in local cuisine is noticeable.

Elsewhere in Central America is the Caribbean influence. In Honduras, blacks working the banana plantations provided some West Indian flavors to add to the Indian-Spanish cooking pot.

Pictured clockwise from bottom
Chicken in Wine Sauce (see recipe, page 50), Sancocho Beef Stew (see recipe, page 51), and Albondigas Tikal Soup (see recipe, page 51)

CENTRAL AMERICA

Chicken in Wine Sauce   *pictured on page 48*   El Salvador

Chicken in Wine Sauce combines many of the same flavors as the famous Latin-American chicken dish "arroz con pollo" (chicken with rice). Both include onion, green or red sweet pepper, green olives, garlic, tomato paste, and capers. Chicken in Wine Sauce may be served over rice, but in "arroz con pollo" the chicken pieces and rice are always cooked together.

- 1 2½- to 3-pound broiler-fryer chicken, cut up
- 2 tablespoons cooking oil
- 1 medium onion, chopped
- ¾ cup dry red wine
- ¼ cup cider vinegar
- 1 tablespoon Worcestershire sauce
- 1 teaspoon salt
- ¼ teaspoon garlic powder
- ¼ teaspoon ground coriander
- ⅛ teaspoon ground red pepper
- 1 large green pepper, chopped
- 12 pitted, dried prunes, halved
- 12 pimiento-stuffed olives
- ¼ cup tomato paste
- 2 tablespoons capers

Rinse chicken pieces; pat dry with paper toweling. In large skillet over medium heat, brown chicken pieces in hot oil on all sides for 15 minutes. Remove chicken and add onion to drippings; cook till tender but not brown. Drain off fat. Return chicken to skillet. Combine wine, vinegar, Worcestershire sauce, salt, garlic powder, coriander, and red pepper. Pour over chicken in skillet. Bring to boiling; reduce heat. Cover and simmer for 25 minutes.

Stir in green pepper, prunes, olives, tomato paste, and capers. Cover and simmer about 20 minutes more or till chicken is tender. Skim off fat. Transfer chicken and sauce to a heated serving platter. Makes 6 servings.

Carne en Adobo   Panama

Green and red sweet peppers, green onion, and garlic combine in this peppery dish to provide the basis of its name. Carne en Adobo, also known as "carne en jocan," refers to meat in a pickle sauce or stew. Crushed tortillas thicken the sauce, which is often served over Rice with Peas (see recipe, page 52).

- 1½ pounds beef stew meat, cut into ¾-inch pieces
- 2 tablespoons peanut oil *or* cooking oil
- ½ cup sliced green onion
- 1 clove garlic, minced
- 2 medium red *or* green sweet peppers, chopped
- 2 canned green chili peppers, rinsed, seeded, and chopped
- 1 7½-ounce can tomatoes, cut up
- 2 whole cloves
- 1 bay leaf
- ½ teaspoon dried oregano, crushed
- ½ teaspoon ground cumin
- 2 5-inch cornmeal tortillas
   Hot cooked rice

Sprinkle meat with salt and pepper. In 10-inch skillet brown beef, *half* at a time, in hot oil. Remove from skillet, reserving drippings. To drippings, add green onion and garlic; cook till onion is tender but not brown. Return all meat to skillet. Stir in red or green sweet peppers, chili peppers, *undrained* tomatoes, cloves, bay leaf, oregano, cumin, and 1 cup *water*. Bring to boiling; reduce heat. Cover and simmer 1 hour. Remove cloves and bay leaf.

Soak tortillas in cold water. Using paper toweling, press moisture out; crumble till mixture resembles coarse bread crumbs. Add to beef mixture. Cook and stir till thickened and bubbly. Serve over hot cooked rice. Makes 6 servings.

Beef with Mustard Greens   Costa Rica

- 4 slices bacon
- 1 pound ground beef
- 1 medium onion, chopped
- 1 clove garlic, minced
- 1 10-ounce package frozen mustard greens *or* turnip greens, thawed
- 1 teaspoon salt
- ¼ teaspoon pepper
- ¼ cup lemon juice
- 1 teaspoon sugar
- ¼ teaspoon paprika
- 2 hard-cooked eggs, sliced

In a 10-inch skillet cook bacon till crisp; remove, drain on paper toweling, and crumble. Reserve drippings. To drippings, add beef, onion, and garlic. Cook till meat is brown and onion is tender but not brown. Drain off fat. Stir in mustard or turnip greens, salt, and pepper. Cover and simmer mixture 10 minutes.

For sauce, stir together bacon pieces, lemon juice, sugar, and paprika.

To serve, transfer meat mixture to heated serving platter; garnish with egg slices. Pour sauce atop. Makes 4 to 6 servings.

Sancocho Beef Stew *pictured on page 48* Panama

Yams or sweet potatoes and other tropical root vegetables distinguish this flavorful beef stew from all others. Though this recipe calls for beef, boneless pork is authentic, also.

In its homeland, *Sancocho Beef Stew* is often accompanied by "casabe" (cassava cakes), yucca meal cakes, or "panecicos" (yucca meal rolls). Corn bread is a good substitute for these accompaniments.

1 **pound beef stew meat, cut into ¾-inch pieces**
2 **tablespoons cooking oil**
1 **medium onion, sliced and separated into rings**
1 **clove garlic, minced**
½ **pound chorizo *or* Italian sausage links, sliced**
1 **medium winter squash, peeled and cubed (3 cups)**
1 **medium yam *or* sweet potato, peeled and cubed (1 cup)**
1 **large plantain, peeled and sliced (1 cup)**
1 **large green pepper, sliced**
1 **9-ounce package frozen whole green beans**
1 **8¾-ounce can whole kernel corn**
1 **7½-ounce can tomatoes, cut up**
½ **teaspoon chili powder**
¼ **teaspoon ground coriander**

In a Dutch oven brown beef, *half* at a time, in hot oil; remove from pan, reserving drippings. To drippings, add onion and garlic; cook till tender but not brown. Return all meat to pan. Add 4 cups *water*. Bring to boiling; reduce heat. Cover and simmer 1 hour. Stir in chorizo or Italian sausage, squash, yam or sweet potato, plantain, green pepper, green beans, *undrained* corn, *undrained* tomatoes, chili powder, coriander, and 1 teaspoon *salt.* Cover and simmer for 15 to 20 minutes or till meat and vegetables are tender. Skim off fat. Makes 6 to 8 servings.

Albondigas Tikal Soup *pictured on page 48* Guatemala

2 **hard-cooked eggs**
½ **cup cooked brown rice**
¼ **cup soft bread crumbs**
¼ **cup chopped green onion**
¼ **cup chopped pitted ripe olives**
¼ **teaspoon dried rosemary, crushed**
  Dash ground cloves
  Dash ground cinnamon
½ **pound ground beef**
½ **pound ground pork**
  Raisins
2 **cups beef broth**
1 **10¾-ounce can condensed tomato soup**
1 **tablespoon chili powder**
½ **cup shredded Monterey Jack cheese (2 ounces)**
  Coarsely chopped pitted ripe olives (optional)
  Chopped green onion (optional)

Separate egg yolks from egg whites. Chop each separately. In a bowl combine the egg yolks, rice, bread crumbs, the ¼ cup green onion, the ¼ cup ripe olives, the rosemary, cloves, and cinnamon. Add ground beef and pork; mix well. Using 1½ *tablespoons* meat mixture for *each* meatball, wrap mixture around *two* or *three* raisins and shape into balls.

In a large saucepan combine beef broth, condensed tomato soup, chili powder, and meatballs. Bring to boiling; reduce heat. Cover and simmer for 30 minutes. Stir in chopped egg whites. To serve, ladle into soup bowls; top *each* serving with *some* of the cheese, additional olives, and chopped green onion, if desired. Makes 4 to 6 servings.

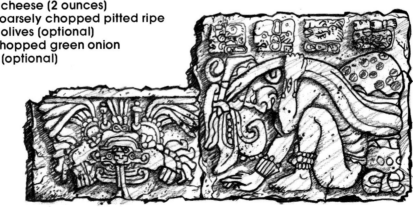

CENTRAL AMERICA

Sweet Potato Buñeulos
Regional

Certain fruits and vegetables — such as bananas, corn, potatoes, and sweet potatoes — lend themselves to mouth-watering "buñeulo" recipes. Dip *Sweet Potato Buñeulos* into syrup or honey, or sprinkle them with powdered sugar.

1 **large sweet potato (½ pound), peeled and quartered**
1 **beaten egg**
3 **tablespoons milk**
2 **tablespoons butter** *or* **margarine**
½ **cup all-purpose flour**
¼ **cup flaked coconut**
2 **teaspoons sugar**
½ **teaspoon baking powder**
¼ **teaspoon ground nutmeg**
    Shortening for deep-fat frying

Cook sweet potato in boiling water for 30 to 40 minutes or till tender. Drain and mash till smooth; cool slightly. (You should have 1 cup.) Stir in beaten egg. In small saucepan heat milk and butter to boiling; remove from heat. Stir into sweet potato mixture. Combine flour, coconut, sugar, baking powder, nutmeg, and ¼ teaspoon *salt*. Add to sweet potato mixture, stirring just to moisten. Carefully drop batter by tablespoons into deep hot fat (365°). Fry buñeulos, several at a time, for 3 to 3½ minutes or till puffy and golden, turning once. Drain on paper towel. Makes about 20.

Rice with Peas
Regional

¼ **pound salt pork, sliced**
1 **teaspoon achiote** *or* **annatto seed**
2 **medium green peppers, chopped**
1 **medium onion, chopped**
2 **cloves garlic, minced**
1 **cup long grain rice**
1 **tablespoon capers**
2 **medium tomatoes, chopped**
1 **cup fresh** *or* **frozen peas**

In skillet cook salt pork till crisp. Remove, drain, and crumble. Reserve drippings. Cook achiote or annatto seed in drippings for 5 minutes; discard achiote or annatto seed. To drippings, add green peppers, onion, and garlic; cook till tender. Stir in *uncooked* rice, capers, 2 cups *water*, and ½ teaspoon *salt*. Cover; simmer for 10 minutes. Stir in tomatoes and peas. Cover; simmer 10 minutes more or till rice is done. Stir in salt pork. Serves 6.

Red Bean Soup
El Salvador

1 **cup dry red kidney beans**
1 **medium onion, chopped**
1 **clove garlic, minced**
1 **teaspoon dried thyme, crushed**
¼ **teaspoon ground cloves**
¼ **teaspoon ground cinnamon**
1 **bay leaf**
6 **slices French bread**
2 **tablespoons cooking oil**

Rinse beans. In large saucepan combine beans and 4 cups *water*. Bring to boiling; reduce heat and simmer 2 minutes. Remove from heat. Cover; let stand 1 hour. (Or, soak beans in the water overnight in a covered pan.) Drain.

  To beans add onion, garlic, thyme, cloves, cinnamon, bay leaf, 4 cups *water*, 1 teaspoon *salt*, and ¼ teaspoon *pepper*. Bring to boiling; reduce heat. Cover and simmer for 2 to 2½ hours. Remove bay leaf. In skillet brown bread in hot oil. To serve, ladle soup atop bread in bowls. Makes 6 servings.

Mixed Vegetable Salad
Nicaragua

1 **8-ounce can red kidney beans**
1 **8-ounce can cut green beans**
4 **cups shredded cabbage**
2 **medium tomatoes, cut into wedges**
⅓ **cup salad oil**
¼ **cup cider vinegar**
½ **teaspoon sugar**
¼ **teaspoon chili powder**
1 **medium avocado**

Drain kidney beans and green beans. In a large salad bowl toss together kidney beans, green beans, cabbage, and tomato wedges.

  For dressing, in screw-top jar combine salad oil, vinegar, sugar, chili powder, and ¼ teaspoon *salt*. Cover and shake to mix well. Pour over vegetables; toss gently to coat. Cover and chill several hours or overnight. Peel, seed, and chop avocado; add to salad before serving. Makes 6 to 8 servings.

CENTRAL AMERICA

Bread and Wine Dessert Honduras

The character of this aromatic dessert depends upon the wine used in cooking. For a mellow flavor, try a dry red wine such as Burgundy or Chianti. For sweetness, add a sweet red wine such as Marsala or Madeira or use a Sangria.

2 beaten eggs
¼ cup red wine
6 slices French Bread, sliced
   ¾ inch thick
2 tablespoons butter or
   margarine
½ cup raisins
⅓ cup red wine
¼ cup honey
¼ teaspoon ground cloves
   Powdered sugar

In shallow dish combine eggs and the ¼ cup wine. Dip bread slices in egg mixture. In a 10-inch skillet cook bread in hot butter on both sides till golden brown. Remove bread and set aside.

In same skillet stir together raisins, the ⅓ cup wine, honey, and cloves. Return bread to skillet. Cover and cook over low heat 15 minutes. Invert bread slices into individual serving bowls and spoon sauce atop. Sprinkle *each* serving with powdered sugar. Makes 6 servings.

Egg Bread Rosettes Panama

These *Egg Bread Rosettes* are usually made in San Jose. This recipe calls for baking the dough, a technique uncommon in Central America where bread usually is fried. Though many people can afford ranges, they would rather cook on a kerosene stove or on a "lena," a patio oven made of stones and an open fire.

5½ to 6¼ cups all-purpose flour
2 packages active dry yeast
1 cup water
1 cup shortening or lard
¼ cup sugar
2 teaspoons salt
5 eggs

In mixer bowl combine 3 *cups* of the flour and the yeast. Heat water, shortening, sugar, and salt just till warm (115° to 120°) and shortening is almost melted; stir constantly. Add to flour mixture; add eggs. Beat at low speed of electric mixer for ½ minute, scraping bowl. Beat 3 minutes at high speed. Stir in as much of the remaining flour as you can mix in with a spoon. Turn out onto lightly floured surface. Knead in enough remaining flour to make a moderately stiff dough that is smooth and elastic (6 to 8 minutes total). Shape into a ball. Place in lightly greased bowl; turn once. Cover; let rise in warm place till double (about 1¼ hours).

Punch dough down; divide in half. Cover; let rest 10 minutes. Divide *each* half of dough into 16 pieces; roll *each* into a 12-inch rope. For *each* rosette tie rope in a loose knot, leaving 2 long ends. Tuck top end under roll; bring bottom end up and tuck into center of roll. Place 2 to 3 inches apart on greased baking sheets. Cover; let rise till nearly double (about 30 minutes). Bake in a 375° oven for 12 to 15 minutes or till golden. Makes 32 rolls.

Cake of Juices Panama

2 cups all-purpose flour
2 teaspoons baking powder
½ teaspoon salt
½ cup butter or margarine
½ cup sugar
2 teaspoons vanilla
2 eggs
1 cup orange juice or
   unsweetened pineapple
   juice
½ cup sugar
3 tablespoons water
⅛ teaspoon cream of tartar
   Dash salt
1 egg white
1½ teaspoons lemon juice

Grease and flour a 9x5x3-inch loaf pan. Stir together flour, baking powder, and the ½ teaspoon salt. Beat butter for 30 seconds. Add ½ cup sugar and vanilla; beat till fluffy. Add eggs, one at a time, beating 1 minute after each addition. Add flour mixture and juice alternately to beaten mixture, beating after each addition. Turn into pan. Bake in 325° oven for 45 to 50 minutes or till done. Cool 10 minutes. Remove from pan. Cool.

For icing, combine ½ cup sugar, water, cream of tartar, and dash salt. Cook and stir till mixture is bubbly and sugar is dissolved. In mixer bowl place egg white. Add sugar syrup to unbeaten egg white while beating constantly on high speed of electric mixer for about 7 minutes or till stiff peaks form. Beat in lemon juice. Frost cake. Serves 9.

Peach Chicha *pictured on front cover*   Panama

"Chichas," creamy fruit drinks typical of Panama, require chopped fruit as well as fruit juice.

1 16-ounce can peach slices
1½ cups cold milk
1 teaspoon vanilla
  Ice cubes
  Ground nutmeg

In blender container combine *undrained* peach slices, milk, and vanilla. Cover and blend till smooth. Pour over ice into 4 glasses. Sprinkle with nutmeg. Makes 4 servings.

Coconut Empanadas   Nicaragua

"Empanadas," or turnovers, are as common in Central America as apple pies in the United States. Depending on their size, "empanadas" can be a main dish, dessert, snack, or appetizer. Large turnovers are "empanadas" or "empadas"; the smaller ones are called "empadinhas," "empanaditas," or "empanadillas." Fillings range from sweet, as in the *Coconut Empanadas*, to savory, as in *Pork Empanaditas*. Central Americans prefer cornmeal pastry to the flour pastries used in Mexico and South America.

1⅓ cups all-purpose flour
1 teaspoon baking powder
¼ teaspoon salt
¼ cup lard *or* shortening
1 egg
¼ cup milk
¾ cup sugar
3 tablespoons butter
⅓ cup Eagle Brand sweetened condensed milk
1½ cups grated *or* flaked coconut
¼ teaspoon salt
¼ teaspoon ground nutmeg
¼ teaspoon ground cinnamon

For dough, stir together flour, baking powder, and salt. Cut in lard or shortening till pieces are size of small peas. Beat together egg and milk. Add to flour mixture, stirring till combined. Form dough into a ball; cover and chill 1 hour.

In saucepan combine sugar and ¼ cup *water*. Cook and stir till mixture is bubbly and sugar is dissolved. Reduce heat; add butter and sweetened condensed milk, stirring till butter is melted. Stir in coconut, salt, nutmeg, and cinnamon. Cool.

Divide dough into 8 portions. On lightly floured surface, roll *each* to a circle 6 inches in diameter. Place *3 tablespoons* coconut mixture, off center, on *each*. Moisten edges with water. Fold in half; seal with fork. Place on a baking sheet. Brush with more milk; sprinkle with more sugar. Bake in a 400° oven about 15 minutes or till golden. Makes 8.

Pork Empanaditas   Regional

1½ cups all-purpose flour
½ cup Masa Harina tortilla flour
½ teaspoon baking powder
¼ teaspoon salt
⅓ cup lard *or* shortening
1 egg
⅓ cup milk
¼ pound lean boneless pork, finely chopped (½ cup)
1 medium green pepper, chopped
1 medium onion, chopped (½ cup)
1 tablespoon cooking oil
⅓ cup tomato sauce
¼ teaspoon salt
¼ teaspoon chili powder
½ cup cooking oil

For pastry, stir together flour, tortilla flour, baking powder, and ¼ teaspoon salt. Cut in lard till pieces are size of peas. Beat together egg and milk. Add to flour mixture, stirring till combined. Divide into 16 balls. On lightly floured surface, roll *each* to a circle 3½ inches in diameter.

For filling, in skillet cook pork, green pepper, and onion in the 1 tablespoon hot oil till meat is brown and vegetables are tender. Remove from heat. Stir in tomato sauce, the ¼ teaspoon salt, and chili powder. Place about *1 tablespoon* filling, off center, on each pastry round. Fold in half; seal with fork. In large skillet heat ½ cup oil over medium-high heat. Fry turnovers, a few at a time, 2 to 3 minutes per side or till golden. Drain on paper toweling. Keep warm. Add more oil, if necessary. Makes 16 appetizers.

UNION OF SOVIET SOCIALIST REPUBLICS

Moscow

POLAND
CZECHOSLOVAKIA
HUNGARY
YUGOSLAVIA   ROMANIA
ALBANIA   BULGARIA

EASTERN EUROPE

In Eastern Europe, hearty dishes that satisfy hardworking people are the basis for a simple, substantial, yet interesting culinary style.

Common throughout this expansive area is the Slavic love of tart foods—most notably a fondness for sour cream and yogurt.

Carrots, cabbage, beets, turnips, and potatoes are favored Eastern European vegetables. These root crops keep well over long winters and can be pickled or preserved.

Also popular are hearty soups and stews. In Russia, the staple soup is cabbage, although beet soup—"borsch"—is liked almost as much.

The Polish prefer sauerkraut soups such as "bigos" or hunter's stew and "kapusniak." "Ciorbas" or sour soups based on the juice of unripe fruits and vegetables round out a hearty meal in Romania.

In Hungary, the national favorite is "gulyas," the herdsman's stew con-cocted by the Magyar tribesmen most Hungarians have descended from. Long ago a shepherd dish, it is now a rich stew flavored with the indispensable paprika so popular with Hungarians. Today the world recognizes this stew as the familiar goulash.

Breads and pastries are also an essential element of Eastern European cuisine. In Russia, black rye bread is the staple. In Poland, stuffed dumplings called "pierogi" are popular. And, in Czechoslovakia, sweet-filled buns, "kolache," are prized.

The Balkan countries—Albania, Bulgaria, Romania, and Yugoslavia—share the culinary styles of Eastern European neighbors with one exception. The Ottoman Empire that ruled over the Balkans for centuries left its mark. Moussakas, rice dishes, lamb entrées, and rice- or meat-stuffed vegetables serve as reminders of long-past Turkish domination.

Pictured clockwise from bottom
Tarator Yogurt Soup (see recipe, page 62), Stuffed Cabbage Rolls (see recipe, page 59), Zagreb Cake (see recipe, page 67), Hussar Roast (see recipe, page 58), and Piradzini (see recipe, page 69)

EASTERN EUROPE

Hussar Roast   *pictured on page 56*   Poland

Named after the colorful European cavalries, this pot roast absorbs the vodka or vinegar flavor as it browns. The stuffed meat slices are usually served with stewed cabbage and potatoes.

½ cup vinegar *or* vodka
1 3-pound beef eye round roast
1 cup beef broth
1 large onion, cut into wedges
1 bay leaf
¼ cup sliced green onion
1 stalk celery, chopped
2 tablespoons butter *or* margarine
1 beaten egg
⅓ cup fine dry bread crumbs
¼ cup cold water
2 tablespoons cornstarch
Parsley sprigs
Canned sliced beets, drained

In Dutch oven bring vinegar or vodka to boiling. Add meat; cook for 1 minute on each side in the boiling liquid. Discard vinegar or vodka. Add beef broth, onion wedges, and bay leaf to meat. Cover and simmer about 2 hours or till meat is tender. Remove meat and set aside; discard bay leaf.

For stuffing, in skillet cook green onion and celery in the hot butter or margarine till tender but not brown. In bowl combine egg, onion mixture, and bread crumbs.

Cut slits in meat from edge to center about ¾ inch apart to make 8 "pockets." Spoon about *2 tablespoons* stuffing into *each* pocket. Return the stuffed meat to Dutch oven. Cover and simmer over low heat 30 minutes more. Transfer meat to serving platter; keep warm. Skim fat from pan juices. Add water to juices, if necessary, to measure 2 cups; return to Dutch oven. Combine the ¼ cup water and cornstarch; stir into pan juices. Cook and stir till thickened and bubbly. Cook and stir 2 minutes more. Pass with meat. Slice meat between pockets. Garnish with parsley and beets. Serves 8 to 10.

Pork Pörkölt   Hungary

Pork Pörkölt is one of Hungary's four types of paprika stews. "Pörkölt," a thick stew, traditionally is served with "galuskas," tiny egg-and-flour dumplings. "Pörkölt" means browned or scorched, referring to the meat-browning step.

Similar to "pörkölt," only much more famous, is "gulyás," or as we know it, goulash. This stew is much thinner than the "pörkölt."

"Tokany," a third type of stew, consists of meat and vegetables, flavored with sour cream.

Like "tokany," the last stew type, "paprikas," also contains sour cream but calls for more paprika.

4 slices bacon
1½ pounds lean boneless pork, cut into ¾-inch pieces
3 medium onions, sliced and separated into rings
2 tablespoons paprika
¾ cup water
¾ teaspoon salt
1 large green pepper, thinly sliced
3 tablespoons tomato paste
Hot cooked noodles

In skillet cook bacon till crisp; remove, drain on paper toweling, and crumble. Reserve drippings. In same skillet brown meat, *half* at a time, in drippings. Remove and set aside; reserve drippings. To drippings, add onions and paprika. Cook till onion is tender but not brown. Add meat, bacon pieces, water, and salt to onion mixture. Bring to boiling; reduce heat. Cover and simmer for 20 minutes. Stir in green pepper and tomato paste; cover and simmer for 15 minutes more. Serve over hot cooked noodles. Makes 6 servings.

Veal Ragout   Latvian SSR

6 veal chops, cut ½-inch thick (1½ pounds)
2 tablespoons all-purpose flour
2 tablespoons butter *or* margarine
1 to 2 teaspoons caraway seed
½ teaspoon salt
¼ teaspoon pepper
3 medium potatoes, peeled and cubed
3 medium carrots, peeled and thinly sliced
1 cup light cream *or* milk
3 tablespoons all-purpose flour
1 tablespoon snipped parsley

Coat chops with the 2 tablespoons flour. In Dutch oven or large skillet brown meat in hot butter *or* margarine. Add caraway seed, salt, pepper, and 1 cup *water*. Bring to boiling; reduce heat. Cover and simmer for 15 minutes. Add potatoes and carrots; cover and simmer about 20 minutes or till vegetables are tender. Transfer meat and vegetables to serving platter; keep warm. Reserve cooking liquid.

For gravy, stir together cream or milk and the 3 tablespoons flour; stir into reserved cooking liquid. Cook and stir till thickened and bubbly. Cook and stir 1 minute more. Stir in parsley. Season to taste with salt and pepper. Pour gravy over meat and vegetables. Makes 6 servings.

Ghivetci Vegetables

The Balkans

Romanians say that *Ghivetci Vegetables,* their national dish, represents the melting pot of nationalities living within their homeland's borders. They think the flavors of Romania's different vegetables blend as harmoniously as her people.

In Yugoslavia, Albania, and Bulgaria, hot peppers accompany this dish.

- 1 **pound lean boneless pork, cut into ¾-inch pieces**
- ½ **pound boneless lamb *or* beef, cut into ¾-inch pieces**
- 2 **tablespoons olive oil or cooking oil**
- 3 **medium onions, chopped**
- ½ **cup long grain rice**
- 1 **small eggplant, cut into 1-inch cubes**
- 1 **cup shredded cabbage**
- 1 **medium zucchini, sliced ¼ inch thick**
- 1 **large green pepper, chopped**
- 1 **teaspoon salt**
- 1 **teaspoon paprika**
- ¼ **teaspoon pepper**
- 1 **cup cherry tomatoes, halved Paprika**

In skillet brown meat, *half* at a time, in hot oil. Remove and set aside. Reserve drippings. To drippings add onion; cook till tender but not brown. In 3-quart casserole layer meat, onion, *uncooked* rice, eggplant, cabbage, zucchini, and green pepper. Sprinkle with salt, the 1 teaspoon paprika, and the pepper. Pour 1 cup *water* over all. Cover and bake in 350° oven for 1 hour and 25 minutes. Add tomatoes; bake, uncovered, 5 minutes more. If desired, sprinkle with additional paprika. Serves 6.

Stuffed Cabbage Rolls   *pictured on page 56*

Regional

The Middle Eastern influence appears in Eastern Europe in the form of "sarma," or *Stuffed Cabbage Rolls.* A Yugoslavian national specialty, "sarma" can be made with fresh cabbage leaves or sauerkraut.

Romanians serve cabbage rolls with "mammiglia," cornmeal mush. When Hungarians make "sarma," they sour a whole head of cabbage, using leftover leaves to line the cooking pot.

- 12 **large cabbage leaves**
- ½ **cup vinegar**
- ½ **cup water**
- 1 **beaten egg**
- 1 **cup cooked rice**
- 1 **medium onion, chopped**
- ¼ **cup tomato juice**
- 1 **teaspoon salt**
- ½ **teaspoon dried savory *or* sage, crushed**
- ¼ **teaspoon pepper**
- 1¼ **pounds ground pork *or* ground veal**
- 1 **tablespoon butter *or* margarine**
- 1 **tablespoon all-purpose flour**
- ⅛ **teaspoon salt**
- 1 **cup milk**
- ¼ **cup dairy sour cream**
- 1 **hard-cooked egg, sieved Paprika**

In Dutch oven steam cabbage leaves (about 2 inches of heavy center vein may be cut out) over the boiling vinegar and water for 3 minutes or till limp; drain, reserving ¼ cup liquid.

In mixing bowl stir together egg, rice, onion, tomato juice, the 1 teaspoon salt, the savory or sage, and pepper. Stir in pork or veal; mix well. Place about ¼ *cup* of the meat mixture in center of *each* cabbage leaf; fold in edges and roll up. Fasten with wooden picks; return to Dutch oven along with reserved liquid. Bring to boiling; reduce heat. Cover and simmer for 35 minutes, adding more liquid if necessary. Drain off liquid. Remove picks.

For sauce, in saucepan melt butter or margarine. Stir in flour and the ⅛ teaspoon salt. Add milk all at once. Cook and stir till thickened and bubbly. Cook and stir 1 minute more. Stir in sour cream; heat through but *do not boil.* Pour over cabbage rolls. Top with sieved egg. Sprinkle with paprika. Makes 6 servings.

Cottage Cheese Patties

Ukrainian SSR

Ukrainians make *Cottage Cheese Patties* from "tvorog," a dry curd cheese similar to farmer's cheese or dry cottage cheese. Ukrainians often eat *Cottage Cheese Patties* for breakfast.

- 1 **beaten egg**
- 1 **cup dry cottage cheese**
- 2 **tablespoons shelled sunflower nuts**
- ¼ **teaspoon salt**
- ⅛ **teaspoon caraway seed**
- ⅓ **to ½ cup all-purpose flour**
- 2 **tablespoons butter *or* margarine**

In mixing bowl combine egg, cottage cheese, sunflower nuts, salt, and caraway seed. Stir in enough of the flour to make a stiff mixture. Shape into four ¾-inch-thick patties. Sprinkle *each* patty with some of the remaining flour. In skillet cook patties in hot butter or margarine over medium heat for 5 minutes on each side or till brown. Dollop with sour cream, if desired. Makes 4 servings.

EASTERN EUROPE

Stuffed Salmon

Fish and seafood are highly prized throughout Eastern Europe. Russians consider crawfish, salmon, and caviar from sturgeon to be great delicacies. People living inland enjoy freshwater fish such as pike, carp, perch, and trout. Fish is often prepared with a sour cream sauce.

- 1 cup chopped onion
- 1 cup chopped celery
- ½ cup chopped fresh mushrooms
- ½ cup butter or margarine
- 1 beaten egg
- 2 cups coarsely crushed rich round crackers
- 2 tablespoons snipped parsley
- 1½ teaspoons poultry seasoning
- 5 to 6 pounds fresh or frozen whole salmon
- 6 to 8 cups chicken broth
- 2 stalks celery, cut up
- 1 medium onion, quartered
- 1 medium carrot, cut up
- 2 bay leaves

For stuffing, in skillet cook the 1 cup chopped onion, 1 cup chopped celery, and mushrooms in hot butter or margarine till tender but not brown. In a mixing bowl combine egg, onion mixture, crushed crackers, parsley, poultry seasoning, 1 teaspoon salt, and dash pepper. Mix well.

Sprinkle fish cavity with salt. Spoon stuffing into cavity. Wrap fish in cheesecloth. Place on a rack in a fish poacher or large roasting pan. Add broth to depth of 1 inch. Add celery, onion, carrot, bay leaves, 2 tablespoons salt, and 1 teaspoon pepper. Place in 450° oven; poach, covered, for 1 to 1½ hours or till fish flakes easily when tested with a fork.

Remove bay leaf. Transfer fish and vegetables to heated serving platter. Makes 8 servings.

Fish with Walnut Sauce

Walnut sauces are typical to Georgia, a Soviet province on the west coast of the Caspian Sea. Chicken with walnut sauce is most common, but variations include fish, red beans, spinach, eggplant, and string beans. Fish with Walnut Sauce is customarily served cold.

To crush the walnuts, use a mortar and pestle, a rolling pin, a blender, or a food processor.

- 2 pounds fresh or frozen fish fillets
- 3 tablespoons butter or margarine, melted
- ¼ cup chopped onion
- 1 clove garlic, minced
- 2 tablespoons butter or margarine
- 1 tablespoon all-purpose flour
- 1 cup milk
- 2 tablespoons white wine vinegar
- ½ teaspoon dried basil, crushed
- ½ teaspoon ground coriander
- ¼ teaspoon salt
  Dash ground red pepper
- ½ cup chopped walnuts, crushed
- 1 tablespoon snipped parsley

Thaw fish, if frozen. Cut fillets into 8 serving size portions. Place fish in greased baking pan in single layer. Tuck under thin edges. Brush top with the 3 tablespoons melted butter or margarine. Sprinkle with salt and pepper. Bake, uncovered, in a 450° oven till fish flakes easily when tested with a fork. (Allow 5 to 6 minutes for each ½ inch of thickness.)

For sauce, in skillet cook onion and garlic in the 2 tablespoons hot butter or margarine till tender but not brown. Stir in flour. Add milk and wine vinegar all at once. Stir in basil, coriander, salt, and red pepper. Cook and stir till mixture is thickened and bubbly. Cook and stir 1 minute more. Stir in walnuts.

To serve, spoon sauce atop baked fish. Sprinkle with snipped parsley. Makes 8 servings.

Fish with Sour Cream Sauce

- 2 pounds fresh or frozen fish fillets
- ⅔ cup dry white wine
- 2 tablespoons sliced green onion
- 2 tablespoons finely chopped celery leaves
- ¼ teaspoon salt
  Dash pepper
- 1 cup dairy sour cream
- 2 beaten egg yolks
- 1 teaspoon prepared horseradish
  Snipped dill or parsley (optional)

Thaw fish, if frozen. Place in a greased 10-inch skillet. Combine wine, green onion, celery leaves, salt, and pepper; add to skillet. Bring to boiling; reduce heat. Cover and simmer for 5 to 10 minutes or till fish flakes easily when tested with a fork. Transfer fish to serving platter and keep warm; reserve ⅓ cup cooking liquid.

For sauce, combine sour cream, egg yolks, and horseradish. Slowly stir reserved liquid into yolk mixture. Return all to skillet. Cook and stir till slightly thickened; do not boil. Drain liquid from fish, if necessary. Spoon sauce over fish. Garnish with dill or parsley, if desired. Serves 8.

Kulebiaka

This classic *Kulebiaka* with a salmon-and-rice filling belongs to a family of Russian pastries called "pirogs" or "pirads."

"Pirog" supposedly was invented in times of scarcity when there wasn't enough dough or filling to make a pie. The solution was to combine fillings and encase them in pastry.

Leftover "pirog" or *Kulebiaka* is delicious served cold with a dollop of sour cream.

For a smaller version of the "pirog," known as "pirozhki," or *"Piradzini,"* see recipe, page 69.

Kulebiaka Pastry
- ¼ **cup chopped onion**
- 3 **tablespoons butter *or* margarine**
- ¼ **cup all-purpose flour**
- ½ **teaspoon salt**
- ¼ **teaspoon dried dillweed**
- 1 **cup milk**
- 1 **15½-ounce can red salmon, drained and skin and bones removed**
- 1½ **cups cooked rice**
- 1 **3-ounce can sliced mushrooms, drained**
- 2 **tablespoons snipped parsley**
- 2 **tablespoons dry white wine**
- 1 **beaten egg**
  Paprika

Prepare Kulebiaka Pastry. In saucepan cook onion in hot butter or margarine till tender. Stir in flour, salt, and dillweed; add milk all at once. Cook and stir till thickened and bubbly. Cook and stir 1 minute more. Stir in salmon, rice, mushrooms, parsley, and wine. Roll out Kulebiaka Pastry between 2 sheets of waxed paper to a 20x10-inch rectangle; trim to even edges. Remove top sheet of paper. Spoon salmon mixture down center of pastry. Fold one side of pastry over the filling; peel paper back. Repeat with the second side of pastry. Moisten the edges with water; seal.

Lifting paper, carefully transfer to large greased baking sheet, seam side down. Peel off paper. Form into horseshoe shape; brush with egg. Prick top with fork. If desired, top with decorative pastry cutouts made from pastry trimmings and sprinkle with paprika. Bake in 400° oven for 25 to 30 minutes. Makes 6 servings.

Kulebiaka Pastry: Stir together 2 cups all-purpose *flour* and ½ teaspoon *salt;* cut in ⅔ cup *shortening* till pieces are the size of small peas. Add 6 to 7 tablespoons *cold water,* 1 tablespoon at a time; toss gently with a fork.

EASTERN EUROPE

Barley and Potato Soup Poland

Served hot or cold, soups have been the mainstay of the Eastern European diet for years.

Barley and Potato Soup shares its name, "krupnik," with a potent honey mead.

Hangover Soup, otherwise known as souse's soup, was concocted to perk up tired, dizzy, and confused senses in the wee hours of the morning. It is served to after-theater crowds in Budapest coffee-houses. "Pörkölt" broth often goes in this soup to round out the sharp flavor.

The main ingredient in chilled *Tarator Yogurt Soup,* yogurt, has been dubbed "the milk of eternal life" because peasants who ate this soup daily in the fields of Bulgaria and Albania lead unexpectedly long lives. In 1908, when microbiologist Ilya Metchnikoff isolated the bacteria he thought was responsible for this longevity, he named it Lactobacillus *bulgaricus,* after the people who discovered yogurt. Today, yogurt is consumed in Southeastern Europe as frequently as sour cream is eaten in Northern Europe.

6 **cups chicken broth**
1 **cup sliced fresh mushrooms**
2 **medium carrots, peeled and sliced**
1 **medium potato, peeled and diced**
1 **cup frozen peas**
¾ **cup quick-cooking barley**
2 **tablespoons snipped parsley**
1 **tablespoon butter *or* margarine**
½ **teaspoon dried dillweed**
¼ **teaspoon pepper**
⅓ **cup dairy sour cream**
2 **hard-cooked egg yolks, sieved (optional)**

In a 3-quart saucepan combine chicken broth, mushrooms, carrots, and potato. Bring to boiling; reduce heat. Cover and simmer 10 minutes.

Stir peas, barley, parsley, butter or margarine, dill, and pepper into broth mixture. Bring to boiling; reduce heat. Cover and simmer 15 to 20 minutes or till barley is tender. Remove from heat; stir in sour cream. Garnish each serving with some sieved egg yolk, if desired. Makes 6 servings.

Hangover Soup Hungary

½ **pound Polish sausage, thinly sliced**
2 **slices bacon**
1 **medium onion, chopped**
1 **medium green pepper, chopped**
4 **cups beef broth**
1 **16-ounce can sauerkraut, rinsed, drained, and snipped**
1 **cup sliced fresh mushrooms**
2 **stalks celery, sliced**
2 **tomatoes, chopped**
2 **teaspoons paprika**
1 **teaspoon caraway seed**
½ **cup dairy sour cream**
2 **tablespoons all-purpose flour**

In Dutch oven cook sausage and bacon till sausage is brown and bacon is crisp. Remove sausage and bacon, and drain; reserve drippings. Crumble bacon. To drippings add onion and green pepper; cook till tender but not brown. Drain off fat. Stir in cooked sausage and bacon, beef broth, sauerkraut, mushrooms, celery, tomatoes, paprika, and caraway seed. Bring to boiling; reduce heat. Cover and simmer 45 minutes.

Meanwhile, combine sour cream and flour. Gradually stir about *1 cup* of the hot soup into sour cream mixture. Return all to Dutch oven. Cook and stir till thickened and bubbly. Cook and stir 1 minute more. Makes 6 servings.

Tarator Yogurt Soup *pictured on page 56* Bulgaria

2 **medium cucumbers**
2 **cups plain yogurt**
1½ **cups milk**
⅓ **cup broken walnuts**
1 **tablespoon olive oil**
1 **tablespoon snipped parsley**
1 **teaspoon salt**
½ **teaspoon dried mint, crushed**
Mint sprigs (optional)

Slice 12 thin slices from 1 cucumber; set aside. Chop remaining cucumber. In a bowl combine chopped cucumber, yogurt, milk, walnuts, olive oil, parsley, salt, and mint. Cover and chill thoroughly.

Garnish each serving with cucumber slices and sprig of mint, if desired. Makes 4 to 6 servings.

Seasoned Sauerkraut

Seasoned Sauerkraut reigns supreme as the favorite vegetable dish in Eastern Europe. In the old days, cabbage was stomped to make sauerkraut, just as grapes are for fine wines. The cabbage was spread about in a huge barrel for every family member to take turns stomping. Each stomper would toss in a few seasonings such as horseradish, peppercorns, salt, and caraway seed. When the mixture was juicy enough, or when everyone's legs tired, the barrel was sealed tightly and stored in the cellar until the kraut had "soured" enough to eat.

1 **medium onion, chopped**
2 **tablespoons butter** *or* **margarine**
1 **8-ounce can sauerkraut, drained**
1 **cup shredded cabbage**
1 **bay leaf**
2 **whole black peppercorns**
1 **teaspoon caraway seed**

In 2-quart saucepan cook onion in hot butter or margarine till tender but not brown. Add sauerkraut, cabbage, bay leaf, peppercorns, caraway seed, and ⅓ cup *water.* Bring to boiling; reduce heat. Simmer, uncovered, for 10 minutes. Remove bay leaf. Makes 4 servings.

Potato Salad

4 **medium potatoes**
¼ **cup chopped onion**
1 **tablespoon butter** *or* **margarine**
3 **small carrots, thinly sliced**
1 **medium apple, cored and diced**
1 **small cucumber, peeled, seeded, and chopped**
1 **2-ounce can sliced mushrooms, drained**
1 **hard-cooked egg, sliced**
½ **cup dairy sour cream**
½ **cup mayonnaise** *or* **salad dressing**
1 **teaspoon prepared horseradish**
½ **teaspoon paprika**

In covered saucepan cook potatoes in boiling salted water for 25 to 30 minutes or till tender; drain. Peel, halve, and slice potatoes. In small skillet cook onion in hot butter or margarine till tender.

In large bowl combine potatoes, onion, carrots, apple, cucumber, sliced mushrooms, and egg.

For dressing, combine sour cream, mayonnaise, horseradish, paprika, and ½ teaspoon *salt.* Pour over potato salad; toss lightly to coat vegetables. Chill several hours or overnight. Thin with milk, if desired. Makes 6 servings.

Lavash Bread

In its homeland by the Caspian Sea, this unleavened flat bread is baked on a "tonir," a red-hot cylindrical stove. It is eaten crisp or softened first with a few drops of water. Soft *Lavash Bread* is usually wrapped around kabobs or cheese and bean fillings. Store crisp *Lavash Bread* in an airtight container to maintain freshness.

5¾ **to 6 cups all-purpose flour**
1 **package active dry yeast**
2 **cups water**
¼ **cup butter** *or* **margarine**
1 **tablespoon sugar**
2 **teaspoons salt**
¼ **cup sesame seed, toasted**

In mixer bowl combine *2 cups* of the flour and the yeast. In saucepan heat water, butter or margarine, sugar, and salt just till warm (115° to 120°); stir constantly. Add to flour mixture. Beat at low speed with electric mixer for ½ minute, scraping bowl. Beat 3 minutes at high speed. Stir in *half* of the sesame seed and as much flour as you can mix in with a spoon. Turn out onto a lightly floured surface. Knead in enough of the remaining flour to make a moderately soft dough (3 to 4 minutes total). Shape into a ball. Place in greased bowl; turn once. Cover; let rise in warm place till double (about 2 hours). Punch down. Divide dough into 14 portions. Cover; let rest 10 minutes. On floured surface roll *each* portion to a circle 8 inches in diameter. Chill dough till ready to use. *Do not allow to rise.*

Place 2 circles on *each* of 2 greased baking sheets. Brush with cold water and sprinkle with remaining sesame seed. Prick with a fork. Bake in 350° oven for 20 to 25 minutes or till light brown and crisp. Cool on wire rack. Bake remaining dough. Makes 14.

EASTERN EUROPE

Poppy Seed Kolache

Czechoslovakia

"Kolache" is named after its shape, that of a "kolo" or circle. To Eastern Europeans, the circle symbolizes good luck, prosperity, and eternity.

Though the poppy seed filling is the most traditional, cottage cheese, apricot, prune, and other fruit fillings are also common.

3½ **to 4 cups all-purpose flour**
1 **package active dry yeast**
¾ **cup milk**
½ **cup butter** *or* **margarine**
½ **cup sugar**
1 **teaspoon finely shredded lemon peel**
2 **eggs**
¾ **cup light raisins**
½ **cup water**
¼ **cup poppy seed**
⅓ **cup honey**
1 **tablespoon butter** *or* **margarine**
⅛ **teaspoon ground allspice**
Powdered sugar

Combine 1¼ *cups* of the flour and the yeast. Heat milk, the ½ cup butter, sugar, lemon peel, and ¼ teaspoon *salt* till warm (115° to 120°); stir constantly. Add to flour mixture; add eggs. Beat at low speed of electric mixer for ½ minute, scraping bowl constantly. Beat 3 minutes at high speed. Stir in as much of the remaining flour as you can mix in with a spoon. Turn out onto lightly floured surface. Knead in enough remaining flour to make a moderately stiff dough that is smooth and elastic (8 to 10 minutes total). Place in greased bowl; turn once. Cover; let rise till double (1 to 1½ hours). Punch down; divide in half. Cover; let rest 10 minutes. Shape *each* half into 9 balls; place 3 inches apart on greased baking sheets. Flatten *each* to a circle 3½ in diameter. Cover; let rise till double (about 35 minutes). Meanwhile, for filling, in saucepan combine raisins, water, and poppy seed. Bring to boiling; remove from heat. Drain; return solids to saucepan. Stir in honey, the 1 tablespoon butter, and the allspice. Bring to boiling; reduce heat. Simmer, uncovered, for 7 to 8 minutes or till liquid is almost absorbed. Cool. Make a depression in *each* ball; fill with poppy seed filling. Bake in a 375° oven for 10 to 12 minutes. Cool on wire rack. Repeat with remaining dough. Sprinkle with powdered sugar. Makes 18.

Christmas Braid

Czechoslovakia

4¾ **to 5¼ cups all-purpose flour**
2 **packages active dry yeast**
1¼ **cups milk**
⅔ **cup packed brown sugar**
6 **tablespoons butter** *or* **margarine**
1 **teaspoon salt**
2 **eggs**
1 **egg white**
1 **teaspoon aniseed, crushed**
1 **teaspoon finely shredded lemon peel**
1½ **cups raisins**
1 **beaten egg yolk**
¼ **cup sliced almonds**

Combine 2½ *cups* of the flour and the yeast. Heat together milk, brown sugar, butter or margarine, and salt just till warm (115° to 120°) and butter is almost melted; stir constantly. Add to flour mixture; add eggs, egg white, aniseed, and lemon peel. Beat on low speed of electric mixer for ½ minute, scraping bowl. Beat 3 minutes on high speed. Stir in as much of the remaining flour as you can mix in with a spoon. Stir in raisins. On floured surface, knead in enough remaining flour to make a moderately stiff dough that is smooth and elastic (6 to 8 minutes total). Shape into a ball. Place in greased bowl; turn once. Cover; let rise till nearly double (1 to 1½ hours). Punch down; divide in half. Cover; let rest 10 minutes. Set one half of dough aside.

Divide other half of dough in half. Cut *one* piece into thirds; roll *each* third to 18-inch rope. Braid loosely. Place on greased baking sheet. Divide the other piece into quarters. Roll *three* of these quarters to 14-inch ropes. Braid loosely; place atop first braid. Cut remaining quarter into thirds. Roll *each* third to 12-inch rope; braid loosely. Place atop second braid. Tuck ends under. Repeat the directions with remaining half of dough. Cover; let rise till double (30 to 45 minutes). Brush with beaten egg yolk. Sprinkle with almonds. Bake in 350° oven for 25 to 30 minutes. Makes 2.

Eastern European homemakers demonstrate their bread-baking skills best at Christmas. They form bread into various shapes such as the Czechoslovakian *Christmas Braid* or "vanocka."

In both Czechoslovakia and the Ukraine, round unfilled "kolache" are used to make an attractive centerpiece for the Christmas dinner table. Three kolaches are stacked together to symbolize the Trinity, and a candle is inserted in the center.

Slovenians, and Serbians now living in the realm of Yugoslavia, hide coins in their Christmas braids to bring the finders good luck. Latvians twist their "klingeris" bread into a figure eight pattern for Christmas and other festive occasions.

Pictured
Christmas Braid

EASTERN EUROPE

Love Feast Buns

Czechoslovakia

The letter "M" inscribed on these golden buns stands for Moravia, the region of Czechoslovakia where this recipe originated. Moravians eat *Love Feast Buns* at religious feasts.

1 package active dry yeast
¾ cup warm water (115° to 120°)
2 well-beaten eggs
1 cup mashed potato
1 cup sugar
½ cup butter *or* margarine, melted
1 teaspoon salt
5¾ to 6¼ cups all-purpose flour
    Light cream *or* milk

Soften yeast in warm water. Combine beaten eggs, yeast mixture, mashed potato, sugar, butter or margarine, and salt; mix well. Stir in as much flour as you can mix in with a spoon. Shape into a ball. Place in greased bowl; turn once. Cover and let rise till double (about 1½ hours); punch down. Cover; let dough rest 10 minutes. Turn out onto lightly floured surface. Knead in enough of the remaining flour to make a moderately soft dough that is smooth and elastic (3 to 5 minutes total).

Divide into 12 portions. Shape into balls. Score an "M" atop each. Place on greased baking sheet; press slightly. Cover; let rise till almost double (about 45 minutes). Bake in a 375° oven for 25 to 30 minutes; brush with cream or milk after 15 minutes. Makes 12.

Piparkukas

Latvian SSR

At Christmastime, Latvian kitchens fill with the aroma of these spicy cookies as they bake. Store *Piparkukas* in an airtight container to keep them fresh.

½ cup sugar
⅓ cup butter *or* margarine
¼ cup honey
¼ cup pure maple *or* maple-flavored syrup
½ teaspoon ground ginger
¼ teaspoon ground cinnamon
¼ teaspoon ground cardamom
¼ teaspoon ground cloves
¼ teaspoon ground nutmeg
3 cups all-purpose flour
1 egg
1 beaten egg

In saucepan combine sugar, butter or margarine, honey, syrup, ginger, cinnamon, cardamom, cloves, and nutmeg. Bring to boiling. Remove from heat; stir in ½ cup of the flour and beat with a wooden spoon till smooth. Cool. Beat in 1 egg; stir in remaining flour. Cover and chill thoroughly.

Bring dough to room temperature. On lightly floured surface, roll dough to ⅛-inch thickness; cut out with 2-inch round cookie cutters. Place on greased cookie sheet; brush with the beaten egg. Bake in 375° oven for 7 to 8 minutes; cool on wire racks. Makes about 5 dozen.

Honey Cake

Ukrainian SSR

The authentic recipe for this bread-like cake calls for buckwheat honey, but you can substitute regular honey. Ukrainians serve plain or fruit-filled *Honey Cake* at Christmas, sometimes iced with sour cream. Leftover *Honey Cake* slices make delicious jam sandwiches. For less crustiness, wrap the loaf tightly and store it in the refrigerator for several days.

⅓ cup honey
1½ cups all-purpose four
1½ teaspoons baking powder
¼ teaspoon baking soda
¼ teaspoon salt
¼ teaspoon ground cinnamon
2 egg yolks
2 tablespoons butter *or* margarine
¼ cup packed brown sugar
1 tablespoon dairy sour cream
⅓ cup water
1½ teaspoons instant coffee crystals
2 egg whites
¼ teaspoon cream of tartar
1 tablespoon sugar
⅓ cup slivered almonds
    Whole almonds

Grease and lightly flour an 8x4x2-inch loaf pan; set aside. Bring honey to boiling; cool. Stir together flour, baking powder, baking soda, salt, and cinnamon. In mixer bowl beat egg yolks at high speed of electric mixer about 5 minutes or till thick and lemon colored. In small mixer bowl beat butter or margarine about 30 seconds. Add brown sugar and beat till fluffy. Add egg yolks, honey, and sour cream to sugar mixture; beat at medium speed for 1 minute. Combine water and coffee crystals. Add flour mixture and coffee liquid alternately to beaten mixture, beating on low speed after each addition till just combined.

Thoroughly wash beaters. Beat egg whites and cream of tartar till soft peaks form (tips curl over). Gradually add the sugar, beating till stiff peaks form (tips stand straight). Fold yolk mixture into egg whites. Fold in slivered almonds. Turn into loaf pan. Arrange whole almonds atop. Bake in 325° oven for 50 minutes or till done. Serves 12.

Fresh Fruit Compote

In 862, a Viking prince named Rurik was crowned first Czar of Russia. He took to Russia many of his homeland's traditions.

This Scandinavian influence on Russia surfaces in *Fresh Fruit Compote,* which is much like the Scandinavian fruit soups. *Fresh Fruit Compote* is served in the summer when pears, peaches, apples, cherries, and plums are in season. The Latvians frequently add spices, wines, liqueurs, and chopped nuts. Serve the compote with sour cream, ice cream, or whipped cream.

- ½ **cup sugar**
- ¼ **teaspoon ground cloves**
- 1 **medium apple, peeled**
- 1 **medium pear, peeled**
- 1 **medium peach, peeled**
- ½ **cup small plums, pitted and halved**
- ½ **cup pitted cherries**
- 2 **tablespoons potato flour (potato starch)** *or*
- ¼ **cup cornstarch**

In saucepan combine sugar, cloves, and 4 cups *water;* bring to boiling. Slice apple, pear, and peach. Add apple, pear, peach, plums, and cherries to saucepan. Return to boiling; reduce heat. Cover and simmer 4 minutes or till apple is tender. Stir together the potato flour and ½ cup cold *water.* Add to fruit mixture; cook and stir till thickened and bubbly. Cook and stir 1 to 2 minutes more. Remove from heat. Serve warm or chilled. Makes 10 servings.

Little Devils

- 1 **cup water**
- ½ **cup butter** *or* **margarine**
- 1 **teaspoon sugar**
- 1 **cup all-purpose flour**
- 1 **teaspoon baking powder**
- 4 **eggs**
  Cooking oil *or* **shortening for deep-fat frying**
  Powdered sugar

Combine water, butter, sugar, and ½ teaspoon *salt;* bring to boiling. Add flour and baking powder all at once, stirring vigorously till mixture leaves the sides of the pan. Remove from heat. Cool about 10 minutes. Add eggs, one at a time, beating well after each addition. Drop dough, by tablespoons, into deep hot fat (375°). Cook about 5 minutes or till puffy on both sides. Drain. Sprinkle with powdered sugar; serve warm. Makes 4 dozen.

Zagreb Cake   *pictured on page 56*

- ¾ **cup butter** *or* **margarine**
- ⅔ **cup sugar**
- 9 **egg yolks**
- 5 **squares (5 ounces) semisweet chocolate, melted**
- 2 **cups** *very finely* **ground hazelnuts (filberts)** *or* **walnuts**
- ⅓ **cup fine dry bread crumbs**
- 2 **tablespoons milk**
- 9 **stiffly beaten egg whites**
- 1 **cup sifted powdered sugar**
- 1 **tablespoon all-purpose flour**
- 4 **beaten egg yolks**
- ¼ **cup milk**
- 2 **tablespoons cherry liqueur**
- 1 **teaspoon vanilla**
- ½ **cup butter** *or* **margarine**
- 3 **squares (3 ounces) semisweet chocolate, melted and cooled**
- 1 **square (1 ounce) unsweetened chocolate**
- 1 **tablespoon butter** *or* **margarine**
- 1 **cup sifted powdered sugar**
- 1 **teaspoon vanilla**
  Whole blanched hazelnuts (filberts)

Grease and lightly flour four 8x1½-inch round cake pans. Set aside. In mixer bowl beat the ¾ cup butter or margarine on medium speed of electric mixer about 30 seconds. Add sugar and beat till fluffy. Add the 9 egg yolks, one at a time, beating for one minute after each addition. Add the 5 squares semisweet chocolate to yolk mixture. Stir in ground nuts, bread crumbs, and the 2 tablespoons milk; fold in egg whites. Turn into cake pans. Bake in a 350° oven for 15 minutes. Cool 10 minutes on wire rack; remove from pans and cool thoroughly.

For filling, combine 1 cup powdered sugar and flour; stir into the 4 egg yolks. Stir in the ¼ cup milk. Cook and stir till thickened. *Do not boil.* Remove from heat. Stir in liqueur and 1 teaspoon vanilla. Cover surface of mixture with waxed paper; cool. Beat together the ½ cup butter and the 3 squares semisweet chocolate. Stir cooked mixture into chocolate mixture. Spread the filling between the cake layers.

For glaze, melt the 1 square unsweetened chocolate and the 1 tablespoon butter over low heat, stirring constantly. Remove from heat. Stir in the 1 cup powdered sugar and the 1 teaspoon vanilla till crumbly. Stir in 1 to 2 tablespoons *boiling water* to form glaze of pouring consistency. Spread glaze over top of cake. Store in refrigerator. Garnish top of cake with whole hazelnuts (filberts). Makes 16 to 18 servings.

EASTERN EUROPE

Vargabéles Rétes
Hungary

"Rétes" is the Hungarian word for strudel. A controversy simmers between Austria and Hungary over who actually invented the paper-thin pastry.

Vargabéles Rétes originated in Transylvania, now a part of Romania. The sweet-noodle filling with nuts is typical of that region. The versatile sweetened noodles become desserts as in *Noodles with Nuts*.

Strudel Dough *or* **20 sheets frozen phyllo dough, thawed (16 ounces)**
1 **cup cream-style cottage cheese, drained**
3 **egg yolks**
½ **cup light raisins**
¼ **cup dairy sour cream**
½ **teaspoon ground nutmeg**
½ **teaspoon vanilla**
1 **cup cooked wide noodles, drained**
½ **cup slivered almonds**
3 **egg whites**
¼ **teaspoon cream of tartar**
¼ **cup sugar**
½ **to 1 cup butter** *or* **margarine, melted**

Prepare Strudel Dough. (Or use phyllo dough.)

For filling, in mixing bowl combine cottage cheese, egg yolks, raisins, sour cream, nutmeg, and vanilla. Stir in noodles and almonds. In mixer bowl beat egg whites and cream of tartar till soft peaks form (tips curl over). Gradually add sugar, beating till stiff peaks form (tips stand straight). Fold egg whites into cottage cheese mixture.

To assemble, brush ¼ *cup* of the melted butter over *half* of the strudel dough. (Using ½ cup butter for phyllo dough, brush *one* sheet with butter. Place another sheet atop and brush with butter. Repeat till you have 10 sheets of phyllo.) Spread dough with *half* of the filling. Roll strudel dough up, jelly-roll style, from short side (for phyllo, roll from long side); brush with butter. Repeat with remaining butter, dough, and filling. Place on greased baking sheet. Score slits in top. Bake in 375° oven for 25 to 30 minutes or till golden. Makes 2.

Strudel Dough: Combine 3 cups all-purpose *flour* and ½ teaspoon *salt*. Cut in ⅓ cup *butter or margarine* till pieces resemble small crumbs. Combine 2 slightly beaten *eggs,* ¾ cup warm *water,* and 2 teaspoons *lemon juice;* add to flour and stir well. On lightly floured surface, knead 3 minutes. Divide in half. Cover; let rest 30 minutes.

Cover large surface with floured cloth. On cloth roll out *half* of the dough to a square 15 inches wide. Brush with 2 tablespoons melted *butter or margarine;* let rest a few minutes. To stretch, use back of hands, working underneath dough. Start from middle; gently stretch from one corner to the next till paper thin, forming a 30x20-inch rectangle. To avoid tearing, *do not lift too high.* Trim off thick edges. Repeat with remaining dough and an additional 2 tablespoons melted *butter or margarine.*

Noodles with Nuts
Romania

4 **ounces wide noodles**
2 **tablespoons butter**
3 **tablespoons sugar**
1 **tablespoon cherry preserves**
1 **tablespoon cherry liqueur**
⅛ **teaspoon ground cloves**
¼ **cup hazelnuts (filberts), chopped**
Powdered sugar

Cook noodles according to package directions; drain. Toss noodles with butter. Stir together sugar, cherry preserves, cherry liqueur, and cloves; stir into noodles. Fold in hazelnuts (filberts). Serve warm. Sprinkle each serving with powdered sugar. Makes 6 servings.

Piradzini   *pictured on page 56*   Latvian SSR

"Zakoosky" or "Zakuski" refers to the appetizer course served in the Soviet Union and Poland. Based on the Russian word "zakooseet" (to bite), this smorgasbord-style spread shows a hint of Scandinavia. The table overflows with several hot and cold hors d'oeuvres and light and dark bread.

Some hot appetizers that may appear are buckwheat pancakes, "pirozhki," and "shashlik" (skewered meat). Cold "zakoosky" may include caviar, pickled fish, cold meats, pâtés, aspics, and cheeses.

"Zakoosky" is always served with what Russians call "little water" or, as we know it, vodka.

Piradzini, bacon-filled crescents, are the Latvian version of "pirozhki."

Mititei Sausages is Romania's answer to "shashlik." In Romania, mititei vendors are as plentiful as hot dog stands in the United States. The skinless, garlic-flavored sausages are cooked either over charcoal or under the broiler. Romanians eat *Mititei Sausages* accompanied by hot peppers.

Liptói Cheese is a cold appetizer served in Hungary. From the country of Liptó, which is now a part of Czechoslovakia, this cheese is usually made with sheep's milk. Serve *Liptói Cheese* with cherry tomatoes, green pepper slices, green onions, and radishes.

3½   cups all-purpose flour
 1   package active dry yeast
 1   cup milk
 2   tablespoons sugar
 2   tablespoons shortening
       or lard
 1   teaspoon salt
 1   egg
 ¾   pound bacon, sliced
 ¾   cup chopped onion
 ⅛   teaspoon pepper
 1   beaten egg

For dough, in mixer bowl combine *2 cups* of the flour and the yeast. In saucepan heat milk, sugar, shortening, and salt till warm (115° to 120°); stir constantly. Stir into flour mixture; add egg. Beat at low speed of electric mixer for ½ minute, scraping bowl. Beat 3 minutes at high speed.

Stir in as much of the remaining flour as you can mix in with a spoon. Turn onto lightly floured surface. Knead in enough of the remaining flour to make a moderately stiff dough that is smooth and elastic (6 to 8 minutes total). Shape into a ball. Place in lightly greased bowl; turn once. Cover; let rise till double (about 1 hour). For filling, in skillet cook bacon till crisp; remove, drain, and crumble, reserving drippings. To drippings, add onion. Cook till tender but not brown; drain. Add onion to bacon; sprinkle with pepper. Cover and chill till dough has risen.

Punch dough down; divide into thirds. Cover; let rest 10 minutes. Divide *each* third into 12 balls; pat *each* ball to a circle 3 inches in diameter Cover; let rise till nearly double (about 30 minutes). Place *1½ teaspoons* filling in center of *each* round. Roll up; place, seam side down, on greased baking sheet. Pinch edges to seal. Bend to a crescent shape. Prick top; brush with beaten egg. Bake in 375° oven for 15 to 20 minutes or till crust is golden brown. Makes 36 crescents.

Mititei Sausages   Romania

 1   beaten egg
 ¼   cup beef broth
 1   clove garlic, minced
 ½   teaspoon salt
 ½   teaspoon dried thyme, crushed
 ¼   teaspoon ground allspice
 ¼   teaspoon pepper
 1   pound ground beef

In bowl stir together egg, beef broth, garlic, salt, thyme, allspice, and pepper. Add meat; mix well. Using about *one rounded teaspoon* per sausage, shape the meat mixture into 2½x½-inch sausage links. Place on rack of unheated broiler pan. Broil 3 to 4 inches from heat about 15 minutes or to desired doneness, turning once. (Or grill over *hot* coals about 15 minutes or to desired doneness, turning once.) Makes 40 sausages.

Liptói Cheese   Hungary

 1   8-ounce package cream cheese
 ½   cup cream-style cottage cheese
 6   tablespoons butter *or* margarine, softened
 2   tablespoons finely chopped green onion
 1   tablespoon paprika
 1   tablespoon anchovy paste
 1   teaspoon dry mustard
 ½   teaspoon caraway seed
     Assorted vegetables

Soften cream cheese at room temperature. Sieve cottage cheese into small mixer bowl. Add cream cheese, softened butter or margarine, chopped green onion, paprika, anchovy paste, mustard, and caraway seed; beat well. Turn into serving bowl; cover and chill. Serve as an appetizer with assorted vegetables. Makes 1¾ cups.

EUROPE

WESTERN EUROPE

From substantial stews to elegant entrées, Western Europe cuisine encompasses a broad range of foods and cooking styles that overlaps geographic boundaries.

In Switzerland, three regions— each having its own language and culture—reflect the influences of neighboring France, Germany, and Italy. In Belgium, cooking in the north is similar to adjoining Holland, and food preferences in the south tend to be more like neighboring France.

But each nation has its own specialties. Most famous of all cuisines is the French—home of classic and nouvelle cuisines, and provincial cooking. The highly structured classic cuisine is based on five sauces and the elegant, meticulous preparation of each dish; nouvelle cuisine is a lighter version of its centuries-old predecessor. Provincial cooking depends on fresh, local ingredients and simple recipes to produce delectable dishes.

In Germany, sausages, breads, and cheeses—long the backbone of the national diet—are complemented extremely well by excellent domestic beer. Potatoes, though only introduced to Germany in the mid-1700s, now are virtually the national vegetable.

In neighboring Austria, Viennese pastries are world famous. Yeast cakes, tortes, and coffee cakes are actually of Czechoslovakian and Hungarian origin since the Viennese kitchens of the Austro-Hungarian Empire were ruled by Bohemia's cooks.

Unique to the Netherlands is the "rijsttafel" or rice table. In it are as many as 25 dishes of seafood, vegetables, eggs, and meat prepared in a variety of sauces to accompany a plentiful amount of rice. Holland adopted this culinary tradition from its Indonesian colonies. And now it is more common to find the rice table served in Holland than in Indonesia!

Pictured clockwise from top right
Goose with Apple Stuffing (see recipe, page 75), Stamppot (see recipe, page 74), and Artichoke-Shallot Soufflé (see recipe, page 78)

WESTERN EUROPE

Veal with Cream Sauce Switzerland

One of the glories of Swiss cooking is juicy, tender veal sautéed in butter and served with a rich white wine and cream sauce. "Emince de veau," the Swiss name for *Veal with Cream Sauce,* is served traditionally with "rösti" (*Fried Potato Cakes* — see recipe, page 81).

1 pound veal leg round steak, cut ¼ inch thick
1 tablespoon lemon juice *or* brandy
¼ teaspoon salt
  Dash freshly ground black pepper
2 tablespoons butter *or* margarine
⅓ cup finely sliced shallots *or* green onions
1 tablespoon butter *or* margarine
¼ cup dry white wine
⅓ cup whipping cream
  Fried Potato Cakes (see recipe, page 81) *or* mashed potatoes

Partially freeze veal; slice very thinly across the grain into bite-size strips. In mixing bowl combine lemon juice or brandy, salt, and pepper; add veal strips and toss to coat evenly. Let stand 10 minutes.

In a large skillet cook the veal, *half* at a time, in 2 tablespoons hot butter or margarine for 2 minutes. Transfer to a heated serving platter; keep warm.

For sauce, in same skillet cook shallots or green onions in the 1 tablespoon hot butter or margarine till tender but not brown. Add wine and bring to boiling, stirring constantly; cook for 3 minutes or till reduced to ¼ cup mixture. Gradually add whipping cream, stirring constantly. Stir in veal strips; heat through but *do not boil.* Serve immediately with Fried Potato Cakes or mashed potatoes. Makes 4 servings.

Wine-Braised Beef pictured on page 77 France

In France this splendid *Wine-Braised Beef* is known as "boeuf en daube à la proven-çale." The French cuisine has emerged with several imaginative and savory country dishes — "cassoulet," "beef bourguignonne," "choucroute garni," "ragout," and bouilla-baisse" — to name only a few of these simmered specialties. Traditionally, braised French stews are cooked in a heavy cast-iron pot called a "daubière," also known as a "doufeu."

2 cups burgundy
4 medium carrots, sliced into ½-inch pieces
2 medium onions, thinly sliced and separated into rings
2 tablespoons red wine vinegar
2 tablespoons olive oil *or* cooking oil
2 cloves garlic, halved
2 bay leaves
6 whole black peppercorns
4 whole cloves
3 juniper berries
1 teaspoon dried thyme
1 teaspoon dried marjoram
½ teaspoon fennel seed
2 pounds beef stew meat, cut into 1-inch pieces
4 slices bacon
1 16-ounce can tomatoes, cut up
1 cup beef broth
2 teaspoons finely shredded orange peel
¼ cup sliced, pitted ripe olives
3 tablespoons all-purpose flour
3 tablespoons butter *or* margarine, softened
1½ teaspoons salt
¼ teaspoon pepper

For marinade, in a mixing bowl combine burgundy, carrots, onions, red wine vinegar, and olive oil or cooking oil. For a *bouquet garni,* cut a small square from several thicknesses of cheesecloth; place garlic, bay leaves, peppercorns, cloves, juniper berries, thyme, marjoram, and fennel seed in center. Bring edges together; tie with string. Place beef in plastic bag set in shallow dish. Pour marinade over meat; add *bouquet garni.* Close bag. Marinate the meat in the refrigerator for 10 hours or overnight, turning bag occasionally.

Drain beef; reserve the marinade, vegetables, and *bouquet garni.* Pat beef dry with paper toweling. In a heavy oven-going Dutch oven cook bacon till crisp; remove, drain, and crumble. Reserve drippings. Add beef to Dutch oven; brown over high heat. Remove the beef; set aside.

Cook the reserved onions and carrots in drippings till onion is tender but not brown, adding more cooking oil if necessary. Drain off fat. Add beef, reserved marinade, *bouquet garni,* and the bacon.

Add *undrained* tomatoes, beef broth, and orange peel. Bring to boiling. Remove from heat. Cover with a tight-fitting lid; bake in a 350° oven for 1 to 1½ hours. Stir in black olives; heat through. Remove meat and vegetables from wine mixture; arrange in serving dish. Keep warm. Discard the *bouquet garni.*

Stir the flour, softened butter or margarine, salt, and pepper into a smooth paste. Stir paste into hot mixture in Dutch oven. Cook and stir till thickened and bubbly. Cook and stir 1 minute more. To serve, pour the wine mixture over meat and vegetables. Makes 8 servings.

Beef and Vegetable Platter

Austria

Around the mid-1800s Austria's ruler, Emperor Franz Josef, preferred the flavor of boiled beef over all the dishes his palace chefs prepared. The influence of his preference remains even today as the Austrian cuisine ranks boiled beef, "gekochter tafelspitz," as one of the most beloved Viennese dishes.

Boiled beef is a choice cut of beef that simmers delectably with vegetables and herbs. The beef is thinly sliced and garnished with *Parslied Carrots* and *Creamed Spinach* (see recipes, pages 80 and 81).

1 **3- to 4-pound beef round tip roast *or* beef chuck pot roast**
8 **cups water**
2 **medium onions, quartered**
2 **stalks celery with leaves, cut up**
2 **medium carrots, cut up**
1 **medium turnip *or* parsnip, cut up**
6 **sprigs parsley**
6 **whole black peppercorns**
3 **bay leaves**
1 **tablespoon salt**
   Parslied Carrots (see recipe, page 80)
   Creamed Spinach (see recipe, page 81)
   Dill Sauce

In a Dutch oven place beef roast. Add the water, onions, celery, carrots, turnip or parsnip, parsley, peppercorns, bay leaves, and salt.

Bring mixture to boiling; reduce heat. Cover; simmer for 1½ to 1¾ hours or till meat is tender. Remove meat. Reserve 1½ *cups* beef broth for Dill Sauce or Chive Sauce. (Reserve the remaining broth for Beef Broth with Strudel Dumplings, see recipe, page 76.)

Thinly slice meat diagonally across the grain. Arrange slices down the center of a heated serving platter. Place Parslied Carrots on one side of meat slices and Creamed Spinach on the other side. Serve with Dill Sauce. Serves 12 to 14.

Dill Sauce: Cook ¼ cup chopped *onion* in 2 tablespoons hot *butter* till tender but not brown. Stir in 2 tablespoons all-purpose *flour*. Add reserved 1½ cups *beef broth* all at once. Cook and stir over medium heat till thickened and bubbly. Cook and stir 1 minute more. Combine ½ cup dairy *sour cream,* 1 tablespoon snipped *parsley,* 1 tablespoon all-purpose *flour,* and ½ teaspoon dried *dillweed;* gradually stir some of the hot broth mixture into sour cream mixture. Return to saucepan. Cook and stir the sauce till thickened and bubbly. Cook and stir 1 minute more.

WESTERN EUROPE

Chicken with Cider and Cream
France

Northern France is famous for its wonderful apples, cider, and Calvados—a dark-brown apple brandy. A classic dish from Normandy is "poulet vallée d'auge," *Chicken with Cider and Cream.*

This savory chicken recipe is reminiscent of "coq au vin."

Crème Fraiche
1 2½- to 3-pound broiler-fryer chicken, cut up
¼ cup butter *or* margarine
2 cups apple cider *or* apple juice
2 cups fresh mushrooms
12 small boiling onions
½ cup chopped celery
2 tablespoons Calvados, applejack, *or* brandy
Almond-Baked Apples

Prepare Crème Fraiche. Let mixture stand, covered, at room temperature overnight, stirring once.

Brown chicken pieces on all sides in hot butter or margarine about 15 minutes; remove from skillet. To skillet add cider or apple juice, mushrooms, onions, and celery. Bring to boiling; return chicken to skillet. Reduce heat. Cover; simmer 35 minutes or till chicken is tender. Remove chicken and vegetables to a platter; keep warm.

For sauce, skim fat from pan juices; return juices to boiling. Boil 5 minutes or till reduced to 1 cup liquid. Remove from heat. Stir in Crème Fraiche and Calvados, applejack, or brandy. Pour sauce over chicken and vegetables. Serve with Almond-Baked Apples. Makes 6 servings.

Crème Fraiche: In a blender container combine ¾ cup *whipping cream* and 3 tablespoons dairy *sour cream.* Cover; blend 15 to 20 seconds at low speed or till smooth and slightly thickened. Turn mixture into a small bowl.

Almond-Baked Apples: Core 6 large cooking *apples;* peel a strip from the top of each. Place apples in a 12x7x2-inch baking dish. Place 1 teaspoon toasted sliced *almonds* in the center of *each* apple; dot with *butter or margarine.* Bake in a 350° oven for 30 minutes. Meanwhile, in a small saucepan combine ½ cup *apple cider or juice* and ½ cup *sugar.* Bring to boiling; boil hard for 10 minutes. Immediately pour syrup over apples to form a glaze. Return to oven. Bake 10 minutes more or till apples are just tender. Garnish with additional toasted sliced *almonds.*

Stamppot
pictured on page 70
Holland

½ pound kale *or* one 10-ounce package frozen chopped kale
6 medium potatoes (2 pounds), peeled and quartered
1 medium onion, chopped (½ cup)
¼ cup butter *or* margarine
½ teaspoon salt
⅛ teaspoon pepper
⅛ teaspoon ground nutmeg
¼ to ½ cup light cream *or* milk
1 pound knackwurst *or* frankfurters
2 tablespoons butter *or* margarine
Shredded carrot

Cut roots off fresh kale and remove any damaged portions. Cut stems and leaves into small pieces. In a covered saucepan cook fresh kale in large amount of boiling salted water 60 to 75 minutes. Drain well; squeeze out excess liquid. (Or, cook frozen chopped kale according to package directions; drain well, squeeze out excess liquid.)

In a covered saucepan cook potatoes and onion in boiling salted water for 20 to 25 minutes or till potatoes are tender; drain well.

In a mixer bowl beat hot kale, hot potatoes, and onion on low speed of electric mixer till smooth. Beat in the ¼ cup butter or margarine, salt, pepper, and nutmeg. Add as much light cream or milk as necessary to make fluffy.

Meanwhile, cook knackwurst or frankfurters in the 2 tablespoons hot butter or margarine for 5 to 10 minutes or till heated through. Arrange meat atop vegetable mixture. Garnish with shredded carrot. Serves 4.

Goose with Apple Stuffing *pictured on page 70*   Germany

German home cooking is simple and substantial. The robust flavor of roasted goose with a seasoned bread stuffing is a dish that typifies the German cook's attitude about food — good, plain cooking.

Goose with Apple Stuffing is a favorite holiday entrée throughout Germany, especially for Christmas dinner.

1 **10-pound domestic goose**
2 **cups water**
1 **cup pitted, dried prunes (6 ounces), quartered *or* raisins**
1 **medium onion, chopped**
2 **tablespoons butter *or* margarine**
½ **teaspoon salt**
5 **cups dry rye bread cubes**
2 **medium apples, peeled, cored, and finely chopped**
⅓ **cup chopped blanched almonds**
½ **cup snipped parsley**
¼ **cup brandy**
1 **teaspoon dried marjoram, crushed**
⅛ **teaspoon pepper**

Remove giblets. Rinse goose in cold running water; pat dry with paper toweling. For broth, in a medium saucepan cook the giblets in water; salt lightly. Bring to boiling; reduce heat. Cover; simmer for 1½ hours. Remove from heat. Strain giblet liquid; discard giblets and reserve broth.

In same saucepan combine ⅔ cup reserved broth, the prunes or raisins, onion, butter or margarine, and salt. Bring to boiling; reduce heat. Cover; simmer 5 minutes or till onion is tender.

In a large mixing bowl combine bread cubes, chopped apple, almonds, parsley, brandy, marjoram, and pepper. Pour broth mixture over bread mixture; toss lightly to moisten. Add enough of the remaining reserved giblet broth to make desired moistness.

Season the body cavity with salt, if desired. To stuff the goose, spoon some stuffing loosely into the neck cavity; pull the neck skin over the stuffing and fasten securely to the back of the bird with a small skewer. Lightly spoon the remaining stuffing into the body cavity. If the goose has a band of skin across the tail, tuck the drumsticks under the band; otherwise, tie the legs securely to the tail. Twist the tips of the wings under the back. Prick skin well all over to allow fat to escape.

Place goose, breast side up, on a rack in a shallow roasting pan. Insert meat thermometer in center of inside thigh muscle, making sure bulb does not touch bone. Roast in uncovered pan in a 350° oven for 2 to 2½ hours; skim off fat during roasting. Cut band of skin or string between legs so thighs will cook evenly. Continue roasting 1 to 1¼ hours more or till meat thermometer registers 185° and drumstick moves easily in socket. Remove from oven; cover loosely with foil to keep warm. Let stand 15 minutes before carving. Garnish the platter with additional apple and prunes, if desired. Serves 8 to 10.

Duck with Apple Stuffing: Prepare Goose with Apple Stuffing as above, *except* omit goose and use two 5-pound whole domestic *ducklings*. Continue as directed. Roast in a 350° oven for 1½ to 2¼ hours or till meat thermometer registers 185° and drumstick moves easily in socket.

WESTERN EUROPE

Swiss Cheese Soup
Switzerland

Switzerland is known throughout the world for its excellent cheeses. Emmentaler (a type of natural Swiss cheese) and Gruyère are the two best-known cheeses.

Emmentaler cheese is named after the Emmental Valley, a pastoral mountain region northeast of Berne. Gruyère cheese gets its name from the Gruyère Valley in the canton of Fribourg.

1½ cups finely chopped onion *or* shallots
2 cloves garlic, minced
2 tablespoons butter *or* margarine
1½ cups chicken broth
½ teaspoon caraway seed
⅛ teaspoon salt
⅛ teaspoon pepper
⅛ teaspoon ground nutmeg
1½ cups light cream *or* milk
3 tablespoons all-purpose flour
1½ cups shredded Emmentaler *or* Swiss cheese (6 ounces)

In a large saucepan cook onion or shallots and garlic in hot butter or margarine till onion is tender but not brown. Stir in chicken broth, caraway seed, salt, pepper, and ground nutmeg. Bring to boiling; reduce heat. Cover; simmer 15 minutes.

Combine light cream or milk and flour; add to mixture in saucepan. Cook and stir till thickened and bubbly. Cook and stir 1 minute more. Reduce heat. Add cheese; cook and stir till cheese is partially melted. Serve immediately with crusty white bread, if desired. Makes 6 to 8 servings.

● **Swiss Cheese-Cabbage Soup:** Prepare Swiss Cheese Soup as above, *except* increase milk to *2 cups* and stir in 2 cups coarsely chopped *cabbage* and ½ cup cooked *rice* with milk and cook till cabbage is tender. Continue as directed. Makes 6 to 8 servings.

Beef Broth with Strudel Dumplings
Austria

In the traditional Viennese home, a dinner always starts with soup. Since soups play an important part in the Viennese cuisine, the Viennese cooks are masters of rich, steaming soup dishes.

"Lungenstrudellsuppe" is the Austrian name for *Beef Broth with Strudel Dumplings.* Dumpling dough is rolled out, and a savory beef filling is spread atop. Then, the mixture is rolled up, creating several layers similar to strudel. This light and fragrant bread dumpling, served with hot beef broth, is typically Viennese in flavor and splendor.

2 cups all-purpose flour
½ teaspoon salt
2 beaten eggs
⅓ cup water
1 teaspoon cooking oil
⅓ cup all-purpose flour
1 medium onion, chopped
1 tablespoon butter *or* margarine
2 cups finely chopped cooked beef
2 tablespoons snipped parsley
1 teaspoon dried marjoram, crushed
½ teaspoon salt
⅛ teaspoon pepper
2 beaten eggs
8 cups water
6 cups beef broth

For dumplings, in a mixing bowl stir together the 2 cups flour and ½ teaspoon salt. Make a well in center. Combine 2 beaten eggs, the ⅓ cup water, and cooking oil; add to flour mixture. Mix well.

Sprinkle kneading surface with the ⅓ cup flour. Turn dough out onto the floured surface. Knead till dough is smooth and elastic (8 to 10 minutes total). Cover and let rest 10 minutes. On a floured surface roll dough to an 18x16-inch rectangle. (If dough becomes too elastic during rolling, cover and let rest 5 minutes.)

For filling, in a skillet cook onion in hot butter or margarine till tender but not brown. Stir in beef, parsley, marjoram, ½ teaspoon salt, and pepper. Heat through. Remove from heat; stir in 2 beaten eggs. Cool slightly.

Spoon the beef filling over rectangle of dough. Roll up jelly-roll style, beginning from long end. Moisten edges of dough with water and pinch together to seal firmly.

Slice the roll crosswise into eighteen 1-inch pieces. On 1 side of *each* dumpling bring edges of dough up around filling, stretching a little till edges just meet; moisten and pinch to seal.

In a Dutch oven or large saucepan bring the 8 cups water to boiling. Drop dumplings, one at a time, filling side up, into boiling water. Simmer, uncovered, about 5 minutes. Remove from heat; drain. Place 3 of the dumplings in each individual soup plate. Meanwhile, in another saucepan bring beef broth to boiling. Ladle beef broth atop the dumplings. Serve immediately. Serves 6.

Pictured clockwise from back
Swiss Cheese Soup, Wine-Braised Beef (see recipe, page 72), and Beef Broth with Strudel Dumplings

WESTERN EUROPE

Asparagus Cream Soup Germany

The most cherished of all the vegetables in Germany is asparagus. Although the green variety is enjoyed in many dishes, the most prized is white asparagus.

Either variety works well in this *Asparagus Cream Soup.*

2 15-ounce cans asparagus spears *or* two 10-ounce packages frozen asparagus spears, thawed
3 cups milk *or* light cream
¼ cup finely chopped shallots *or* onion
2 tablespoons butter *or* margarine
2 teaspoons all-purpose flour
½ teaspoon salt
⅛ teaspoon white pepper
⅛ teaspoon ground nutmeg
2 slightly beaten egg yolks

Drain canned asparagus; cut tips off canned or frozen asparagus spears and set aside. In a blender container combine asparagus stalks and milk; cover and blend till smooth.

In a saucepan cook shallots or onion in hot butter or margarine till tender but not brown. Stir in flour, salt, pepper, and nutmeg. Add asparagus mixture all at once. Cook and stir till thickened and bubbly. Cook and stir 1 minute more.

Slowly stir about *half* of the hot mixture into egg yolks. Return all to pan. Stir in reserved asparagus tips. Cook and stir over low heat for 2 to 3 minutes. Sprinkle snipped parsley atop, if desired. Makes 6 to 8 side-dish servings.

Artichoke-Shallot Soufflé *pictured on page 70* France

Artichoke-Shallot Soufflé is a pleasure to the palate and a delight to the eye.

This is what French cooking is all about. Taking the freshest of ingredients, the French create exquisite dishes that taste delicious and look dazzling.

⅓ cup finely chopped shallots *or* onion
6 tablespoons butter *or* margarine
⅓ cup all-purpose flour
¼ teaspoon salt
1½ cups milk
½ cup grated Parmesan cheese
6 egg yolks
1 14-ounce can artichoke hearts, drained and chopped
6 egg whites

In a saucepan cook shallots or onion in hot butter or margarine till tender but not brown. Stir in flour and salt. Add milk all at once. Cook and stir till mixture is thickened and bubbly. Remove from heat. Stir in Parmesan cheese.

Beat egg yolks about 6 minutes or till very thick and light colored. Slowly stir cheese mixture into yolks. Stir in artichokes. Cool slightly. Thoroughly wash beaters. Beat egg whites till stiff peaks form (tips stand straight); fold yolk mixture into whites. Turn into *ungreased* 2-quart soufflé dish. Bake in a 350° oven for 55 to 60 minutes. Serves 6 to 8.

Cheese and Onion Tart Switzerland

Basic Rich Pastry (see recipe, page 83)
Dry beans (optional)
½ cup finely chopped shallots *or* onion
2 tablespoons butter *or* margarine
3 beaten eggs
¾ cup light cream
¾ cup milk
½ teaspoon salt
⅛ teaspoon ground nutmeg *or* paprika
¾ cup shredded Gruyère cheese (3 ounces)
¾ cup shredded Emmentaler *or* Swiss cheese (3 ounces)
1 tablespoon all-purpose flour

Prepare Basic Rich Pastry. For flan or quiche pastry shell, on a lightly floured surface roll dough to a circle 12 inches in diameter. Line a 10- or 11-inch flan pan or quiche dish with dough. Turn overlapping dough edges to inside and press against sides of pan or dish. Prick sides with fork. (If dough is quite soft, freeze dough in flan pan or quiche dish for 30 minutes.) Line the bottom and sides of pan or dish with heavy-duty foil; fill with dry beans. Bake in a 400° oven for 20 minutes. Remove foil and beans. Bake for 10 to 15 minutes more or till golden. Set aside. Reduce the oven temperature to 325°.

Cook shallots or onion in hot butter or margarine till tender. Stir together onion mixture, eggs, light cream, milk, salt, and nutmeg or paprika. Combine the Gruyère and Emmentaler or Swiss cheese with the flour; add to egg mixture. If using flan pan, place on a baking sheet. Pour cheese mixture into hot pastry shell. Bake in a 325° oven 30 to 35 minutes or till knife inserted near center comes out clean. Let stand 10 minutes before serving. If using flan pan, remove side of pan. Serves 6.

Flemish Fish Waterzooi

Belgium

The Flemish are very fond of "waterzooi," an elegant and distinctive fish stew full of fresh vegetables and simmered in wine and herbs.

Flemish Fish Waterzooi originated in Ghent, a historical city in northern Belgium.

1 **pound fresh** *or* **frozen perch fillets** *or* **other fish fillets**
2 **medium carrots, cut into julienne strips**
1 **stalk celery, cut into julienne strips**
1 **stalk celery, cut into julienne strips**
2 **medium leeks, thinly sliced (about ⅔ cup)** *or* **1 medium onion, coarsely chopped**
2 **tablespoons butter** *or* **margarine**
¼ **cup dry white wine**
1 **tablespoon lemon juice**
¾ **teaspoon dried thyme, crushed**
¼ **teaspoon salt**
⅛ **teaspoon ground cloves, nutmeg,** *or* **mace**
1 **bay leaf**
2 **tablespoons snipped parsley**
 Lemon wedges (optional)

Thaw fish, if frozen. Remove skin, if present. In a large skillet cook carrots, celery, and leeks or onion in hot butter or margarine about 5 minutes or just till tender. Place fish fillets on top of vegetables in skillet. Combine: wine; lemon juice; thyme; salt; ground cloves, nutmeg, or mace; the bay leaf, and ¼ cup *water.* Pour over fish.

Cover and simmer for 5 to 10 minutes or till fish flakes easily when tested with a fork. Remove fish to a heated serving platter; keep warm.

Boil vegetable mixture gently, uncovered, for 3 minutes or till liquid is reduced by half. Remove bay leaf. Spoon vegetable mixture over fish fillets. Sprinkle with snipped parsley. If desired, serve with lemon wedges. Makes 4 servings.

Flemish Eel Waterzooi: Prepare Flemish Fish Waterzooi as above, *except* substitute ½ pound cleaned *eel* for ½ pound of the fish fillets. Cut eel, crosswise, into 2-inch pieces. In a saucepan bring 2 cups *chicken broth* to boiling. Add eel; return to boiling. Reduce heat and simmer for 15 minutes or till eel is tender. Drain. Add eel to fish fillets atop vegetables in skillet. Continue as directed.

Fish with White Butter Sauce

France

4 **cups water**
1½ **cups dry white wine**
1 **medium onion, cut into wedges**
1 **medium carrot, cut up**
1 **stalk celery with leaves, cut up**
4 **whole cloves**
4 **whole black peppercorns**
2 **sprigs parsley**
1 **clove garlic, halved**
1 **bay leaf**
1 **teaspoon dried thyme, crushed**
1 **teaspoon salt**
1 **2- to 2½-pound fresh** *or* **frozen dressed haddock, red snapper, turbot,** *or* **whiting (head and tail removed)**
¼ **cup white wine vinegar**
¼ **cup dry white wine**
3 **shallots, finely chopped**
10 **tablespoons butter** *or* **margarine, softened**
¼ **teaspoon salt**
⅛ **teaspoon white pepper**
 Parsley sprigs

For *court-bouillon,* in a large saucepan combine water, the 1½ cups wine, onion, carrot, celery, cloves, peppercorns, parsley, garlic, bay leaf, thyme, and the 1 teaspoon salt. Bring to boiling; reduce heat. Cover; simmer for 30 minutes. Remove from heat. Strain; discard solids. Cool to room temperature.

Thaw fish, if frozen. Place on a large piece of cheesecloth; fold cloth over fish. Place on rack in poaching pan. Add the *court-bouillon.* Cover and simmer about 20 minutes or till fish flakes easily when tested with a fork. Remove from pan; cover with foil and keep warm. (The *court-bouillon* can be stored in the refrigerator or frozen and used as fish stock.)

Meanwhile, for butter sauce, in a medium saucepan combine vinegar, the ¼ cup wine, and shallots. Bring to boiling; boil, uncovered, for 4 to 5 minutes or till reduced to 2 tablespoons mixture. Remove from heat. Cool for 1 minute.

Add softened butter or margarine, 1 tablespoon at a time, to the shallot mixture, heating and beating constantly with a wire whisk till the butter is completely absorbed into the shallot mixture. (The butter should cream without turning oily.) Stir in the ¼ teaspoon salt and white pepper. Transfer to a small, warm serving dish and serve immediately.

Pull foil and cheesecloth away from fish; remove and discard skin. Transfer fish to a heated serving platter using 2 spatulas; garnish platter with parsley. Pass the butter sauce. Serves 8.

WESTERN EUROPE

Fried Potato Cake
Switzerland

Fried Potato Cakes, called "rösti" in Switzerland, are considered to be the national potato dish. Traditionally, the potatoes are cooked in their skins, then chilled and peeled before they're shredded.

The Swiss shred the potatoes with a special shredder, which is standard kitchen equipment to them. Rightly so; "rösti" is eaten daily.

3 medium potatoes (1 pound)
¼ cup finely chopped onion
½ teaspoon salt
   Dash pepper
2 tablespoons butter *or* margarine
½ cup shredded Gruyère, Emmentaler, *or* Swiss cheese

Thoroughly scrub potatoes. In a large covered saucepan cook whole potatoes in enough boiling salted water to cover for 20 to 25 minutes or till almost tender; drain. Chill several hours or overnight.

Peel potatoes; shred to make 3 cups. Combine shredded potatoes, onion, salt, and pepper. In a 10-inch skillet melt the butter or margarine. Using a spatula, pat potato mixture into skillet, leaving ½-inch space around the edge. Cook potato mixture, uncovered, over low heat about 20 minutes or till underside is crisp and golden brown.

Use a spatula to loosen the potatoes from skillet. Place plate or baking sheet atop skillet. Invert skillet to remove potatoes. If necessary, add more butter or margarine to the skillet. Slide potato cake into skillet, browned side up; cook unbrowned side 5 minutes. Sprinkle the shredded cheese atop; cover and cook 5 minutes more or till potatoes are golden brown and cheese is melted. Cut potato cake into 4 wedges. Makes 4 servings.

Brussels Sprouts Puree
Belgium

Delicately flavored brussels sprouts are a culinary treasure from Belgium. They are named for Brussels, the capital of the tiny country, where they were first grown during the 14th century.

A popular method for preparing brussels sprouts is this recipe, *Brussels Sprouts Puree.* It's also known as "purée des choux de bruxelles."

1 pint brussels sprouts *or* one 10-ounce package frozen brussels sprouts
2 medium potatoes, peeled and quartered
½ cup dairy sour cream
¼ cup finely chopped onion
1 tablespoon butter *or* margarine
1 tablespoon all-purpose flour
¼ teaspoon salt
   Dash pepper
½ cup milk
1 slightly beaten egg yolk

In a large covered saucepan cook fresh or frozen brussels sprouts and potatoes in boiling salted water for 20 to 25 minutes or till vegetables are tender; drain well. In saucepan shake vegetables over low heat to dry. Remove pan from heat.

In a mixer bowl beat brussels sprouts and potatoes on low speed of electric mixer till nearly smooth. Beat in sour cream.

In the same saucepan cook onion in hot butter or margarine till tender but not brown. Stir in flour, salt, and pepper. Add milk all at once. Cook and stir till thickened and bubbly. Cook and stir 1 minute more. Gradually stir the hot mixture into egg yolk, stirring constantly. Stir into brussels sprouts mixture. Return to saucepan. Cook and stir the mixture over low heat for 2 to 3 minutes or till heated through. Serves 4.

Parslied Carrots
Austria

8 carrots, cut into julienne strips
½ cup water
3 tablespoons butter *or* margarine
2 tablespoons lemon juice
1 tablespoons sugar
¼ teaspoon salt
⅛ teaspoon pepper
2 tablespoons snipped parsley

In a medium saucepan combine carrots, water, butter or margarine, lemon juice, sugar, salt, and pepper. Bring to boiling; reduce heat. Cover; cook over low heat for 20 minutes or till carrots are tender.

Uncover; continue to cook 10 minutes more or till liquid has evaporated, carefully stirring occasionally to prevent carrots from sticking. To serve, sprinkle with snipped parsley. Makes 6 servings.

Creamed Spinach

Austrian cooks transform plain, simple vegetables into elegant, delicious dishes. *Creamed Spinach,* known as "spinat," is a favorite with Austrians — and can be found on the menus of many fine restaurants. Flavored with lemon juice and butter, and enriched with the addition of beef broth and sour cream, this truly is a worthwhile cooking venture.

 1 **pound fresh spinach (12 cups) or one 10-ounce package frozen chopped spinach**
 2 **tablespoons lemon juice**
⅓ **cup finely chopped onion**
 3 **tablespoons butter *or* margarine**
 2 **tablespoons all-purpose flour**
¼ **teaspoon salt**
⅛ **teaspoon ground nutmeg Dash pepper**
¾ **cup beef broth *or* milk**
½ **cup dairy sour cream**
 2 **tablespoons snipped parsley**

Thoroughly wash fresh spinach. Cut fresh spinach stems into 1-inch pieces; tear leaves into bite-size pieces. In a large covered saucepan cook spinach in lemon juice for 3 to 4 minutes; drain well. (*Or,* cook frozen spinach according to package directions, *except* use lemon juice instead of water; drain well.)

In a saucepan cook the finely chopped onion in hot butter or margarine till tender but not brown. Stir in flour, salt, nutmeg, and pepper. Add the beef broth or milk all at once. Cook and stir over medium heat till mixture is thickened and bubbly. Cook and stir 1 minute more. Stir in the drained spinach, sour cream, and parsley; heat through but *do not boil.* Makes 4 servings.

• **Creamed Dilled Spinach:** Prepare Creamed Spinach as above, *except* omit chopped onion and use 1 clove *garlic,* minced, and omit snipped parsley and use 1 teaspoon dried *dillweed.* Continue as directed.

WESTERN EUROPE

Hazelnut Torte *pictured on the front cover*   Austria

Viennese cakes and pastries are some of the world's most remarkable culinary creations. And "haselnusstorte" is one of these great Viennese specialties.

This *Hazelnut Torte* is everything a dessert should be. It has three nutty meringue-like cake layers filled with a rich butter cream filling. The torte is lavishly decorated with chocolate frosting and nuts.

This torte, like other traditional Austrian tortes, uses ground nuts instead of flour. For excellent results in making this cake, the consistency of the nuts is critical. Grind the nuts very finely in a blender or in a food processor. They should be the consistency of coarse cornmeal.

For a perfect accompaniment to the torte, treat yourself to coffee Viennese style — rich and strong, and served with milk and cream.

6   egg yolks
2   teaspoons finely shredded
      lemon peel
¾   teaspoon ground cinnamon
½   cup sugar
6   egg whites
1   teaspoon cream of tartar
½   cup sugar
3   cups *very finely* ground
      hazelnuts (filberts) *or* walnuts
½   cup fine dry bread crumbs
      Coffee-Butter Cream Filling
      Chocolate Butter Frosting
      Whole hazelnuts (filberts)
½   cup finely ground hazelnuts
      (filberts) *or* walnuts

Grease bottom of a 9-inch springform pan. Line bottom with waxed paper; grease paper.

In a small mixer bowl beat the egg yolks, lemon peel, and cinnamon at high speed of electric mixer about 6 minutes or till very thick and light colored. Gradually add ½ cup sugar, 1 tablespoon at a time, beating till sugar dissolves. Set aside.

Wash beaters. In a large mixer bowl beat egg whites and cream of tartar at high speed of electric mixer till soft peaks form. Gradually add ½ cup sugar, 1 tablespoon at a time. Continue beating till stiff peaks form.

Fold egg yolk mixture into the beaten egg whites. Stir together the 3 cups very finely ground nuts and the bread crumbs. Sprinkle about ⅓ cup of the nut mixture over eggs; fold in gently. Repeat with remaining nut mixture, ⅓ cup at a time, folding in gently. Turn into the prepared pan. Bake in a 325° oven for 55 to 60 minutes or till cake tests done. (Cake will have a slight dip.) Remove from oven; cool in pan for 15 minutes. If necessary, loosen sides of cake from pan with spatula. Remove sides of pan. Invert onto wire rack; remove bottom of pan. Cool cake completely. Wrap cake tightly; chill overnight.

Slice cake horizontally into 3 equal layers. To assemble, spread one layer with ⅓ of the Coffee-Butter Cream Filling. Repeat with 1 more cake layer and another ⅓ of the filling. Top with remaining cake layer. Frost top and sides with Chocolate Butter Frosting. Using a decorating bag fitted with a tip, pipe remaining cream filling around edge of the top layer. Garnish top with whole hazelnuts (filberts). Press the ½ cup finely ground nuts onto sides. Chill overnight. Serves 14 to 16.

Coffee-Butter Cream Filling: In small mixer bowl cream ½ cup softened *butter* till fluffy; remove from bowl and set aside. Wash bowl and beaters; in same bowl beat 2 *egg yolks* till thick and lemon colored. Set aside. Combine 1 cup sifted *powdered sugar,* 1 tablespoon instant *coffee crystals,* and ½ cup *orange juice or water;* bring to boiling, stirring till sugar and coffee are dissolved. Cook over low heat without stirring to soft ball stage (236°). Quickly pour the hot syrup in steady stream into egg yolks, beating constantly at high speed of electric mixer. Continue beating till thick and smooth; cool about 15 minutes. Beat in the creamed butter, a tablespoon at a time. Cover bowl and chill about 30 minutes.

Chocolate Butter Frosting: In a small mixer bowl beat ⅓ cup *butter* till light and fluffly. Gradually add 1¼ cups sifted *powdered sugar,* beating well. Beat in: 1 square (1 ounce) *unsweetened chocolate,* melted and cooled; 1 tablespoon *milk;* 1 tablespoon *cognac or brandy;* and ¾ teaspoon *vanilla.* Gradually beat in ½ cup sifted *powdered sugar;* beat in additional milk or powdered sugar, if necessary, to make the frosting of spreading consistency.

Fruit Tarte

During the Renaissance, French cooks created many noble and impressive desserts.

The cooks developed and refined recipes for delicious cakes, elegant pastries, and impressive fruit specialties — pies, compotes, and tarts.

Today, fruit orchards are everywhere in Southern France, yielding delectable apples, apricots, pears, and peaches. Serving an elaborate fruit dessert, such as this *Fruit Tarte*, is typical after a satisfying French dinner.

Basic Rich Pastry
Dry beans
5 **very ripe medium cooking apples, peeled, cored, and chopped (5 cups)**
⅔ **cup sugar**
⅓ **cup dry white wine**
¼ **cup butter** *or* **margarine**
⅛ **teaspoon ground cinnamon**
1 **tablespoon quick-cooking farina**
¼ **cup Kirsch** *or* **cherry liqueur**
½ **teaspoon vanilla**
¼ **cup dry white wine**
¼ **cup apricot preserves**
1 **teaspoon sugar**
⅛ **teaspoon ground cinnamon**
2 **medium cooking apples, cored and sliced**
1 **medium pear, peeled, cored, and sliced**
1 **tablespoon cognac** *or* **brandy**

Prepare Basic Rich Pastry. For flan pastry shell, on a lightly floured surface roll dough to a circle 12 inches in diameter. Fit dough into a 10- or 11-inch flan pan, pressing bottom and sides gently to remove any air bubbles. Turn overlapping dough edges to inside and press against sides of pan. Prick sides with fork. (If dough is quite soft, freeze dough in flan pan for 30 minutes.) Line the bottom and sides of pan with heavy-duty foil; fill with dry beans. Bake in a 400° oven for 20 minutes. Remove foil and beans. Bake 10 to 15 minutes more or till golden. Set aside.

For apple filling, in a medium saucepan combine the 5 cups chopped apples, the ⅔ cup sugar, the ⅓ cup wine, butter or margarine, and ⅛ teaspoon cinnamon. Cook, covered, about 10 minutes or till apples are tender and mixture is bubbly. Slowly sprinkle farina over apples, stirring constantly. Bring to boiling; reduce heat and simmer 5 minutes or till mixture is thickened, stirring frequently. Remove from heat; stir in Kirsch or cherry liqueur and vanilla. Cool slightly. Spread in bottom of baked flan shell.

In medium saucepan combine the ¼ cup dry white wine, apricot preserves, the 1 teaspoon sugar, and ⅛ teaspoon cinnamon. Bring to boiling; add the 2 sliced apples and the pear slices; cook about 7 minutes or till apples are translucent. Drain fruit, reserving liquid. Arrange apple slices in a ring around outside edge of shell. Arrange ring of pear slices, overlapping ring of apples. Cook reserved liquid till reduced to 2 tablespoons; stir in cognac or brandy. Spoon over fruit to glaze. Serves 8 to 10.

Basic Rich Pastry

1 **cup all-purpose flour**
¼ **teaspoon salt**
¼ **cup cold butter**
1 **tablespoon shortening**
1 **egg yolk**
2 **tablespoons cold water**

In a mixing bowl combine the flour and salt. Cut in butter and shortening with a fork (or pastry cutter) till mixture resembles coarse crumbs. Make a well in the center. Beat together egg yolk and water. Add to flour mixture. Using fork, stir just till dough forms a ball. Turn onto floured surface and knead 3 or 4 times. Wrap in clear plastic wrap and chill 20 minutes in freezer or 1½ hours in refrigerator before rolling to desired shape. Makes one 10-inch shell.

WESTERN EUROPE

Kirsch Torte

Germany

From the Black Forest region in Southern Germany comes Kirschwasser (Kirsch), an exquisite cherry brandy.

Kirsch Torte has a baked nutty meringue layer topped with a kirsch-flavored sponge cake, followed by a thick layer of butter filling and another meringue layer.

Decorated with even more butter filling and chopped nuts, this dessert becomes a German culinary masterpiece.

1 cup sifted powdered sugar
1 tablespoon cornstarch
5 egg whites
½ cup *very finely* ground hazelnuts (filberts) *or* toasted almonds
½ cup all-purpose flour
½ cup cornstarch
½ teaspoon baking powder
3 egg yolks
2 tablespoons hot water
½ cup sifted powdered sugar
3 egg whites
¼ cup sifted powdered sugar
1 cup butter *or* margarine
2 cups sifted powdered sugar
2 egg yolks
½ cup currant jelly
¼ cup Kirsch *or* cherry brandy
¼ cup water
2 tablespoons sugar
½ cup chopped hazelnuts (filberts)*or* toasted almonds
Powdered sugar

Line two 9x1½-inch round cake pans with waxed paper. Grease and flour an 8x1½-inch round cake pan.

For meringue layer, combine the 1 cup powdered sugar and the 1 tablespoon cornstarch. In a large mixer bowl beat the 5 egg whites till soft peaks form (tips curl over). Gradually add powdered sugar mixture, beating till stiff peaks form (tips stand straight). Fold in ground nuts. Spread *half* of the meringue into *each* prepared 9x1½-inch round cake pan. Bake in a 300° oven 18 to 20 minutes. *Cool in pans only 5 minutes.* Without removing waxed paper, remove meringues from cake pans using a wide metal spatula. Place, waxed paper side down, on wire rack. Cool. Increase oven temperature to 375°.

Stir together the flour, the ½ cup cornstarch, and baking powder; set aside. Wash large mixer bowl thoroughly; set aside.

For sponge cake, in a small mixer bowl beat the 3 egg yolks; gradually add the 2 tablespoons hot water, beating well. Gradually add the ½ cup powdered sugar, beating for 6 minutes or till very thick and light colored. Wash small bowl and beaters thoroughly.

In a large mixer bowl beat the 3 egg whites till soft peaks form (tips curl over). Gradually add the ¼ cup powdered sugar, beating till stiff peaks form (tips stand straight). By hand, gently fold egg yolk mixture into the beaten whites. Sprinkle about ⅓ of the flour mixture over eggs; fold in gently. Repeat with the remaining flour mixture, ⅓ at a time; fold in gently.

Pour batter into prepared 8x1½-inch round cake pan. Bake in a 375° oven 20 minutes. Cool in pan 10 minutes; remove from pan. Cool on wire rack.

For butter filling, in a small mixer bowl beat butter or margarine on medium speed of electric mixer for 30 seconds. Gradually add the 2 cups powdered sugar and beat till well combined. Add the 2 egg yolks, one at a time, beating on medium speed for 1 minute after each addition. Beat in currant jelly; set aside.

Combine Kirsch or cherry brandy, the ¼ cup water, and sugar. Pierce surface of cake layer with a fork. Place the cake layer on a rack over a tray and drizzle Kirsch mixture over.

Place one meringue layer on cake plate; carefully peel off waxed paper. Spread with ¼ *cup* of the butter filling. Top with the sponge cake layer. Spread with ½ *cup* of the butter filling. Top with second meringue layer; peel off paper. Frost top and sides of torte with the remaining butter filling. Press the ½ cup chopped nuts onto sides of cake. Sprinkle with additional powdered sugar. Mark a crisscross pattern with a knife over top of torte. Chill at least 3 hours. To serve, cut into wedges. Makes 12 to 16 servings.

Malakoff Torte

Germany

4 **egg yolks**
½ **cup milk**
½ **cup butter** *or* **margarine**
¾ **cup sugar**
1 **teaspoon vanilla**
1½ **cups** *very finely* **ground toasted almonds**
18 **to 24 ladyfingers, split**
1 **cup whipping cream**
Strawberries

Bring egg yolks, milk, and butter or margarine to room temperature. In a large mixer bowl beat butter or margarine on medium speed of electric mixer for 30 seconds. Add sugar and vanilla and beat till fluffy. Add egg yolks, one at a time, beating after each addition. Continue beating while gradually adding milk. Stir in almonds.

Arrange *half* of the split ladyfingers on bottom and sides of a 6-cup bowl, breaking ladyfingers to fit. Pour ⅓ of the almond mixture over to cover. Top with the *half* of the remaining ladyfingers; pour another ⅓ of almond mixture over to cover. Top with remaining ladyfingers and cover with remaining almond mixture. Cover; chill for several hours or overnight.

To serve, loosen from bowl; invert onto plate. Whip the whipping cream to soft peaks; frost torte. Garnish with strawberries. Pass additional strawberries, if desired. Makes 12 servings.

Pictured from left to right
Malakoff Torte and Kirsch Torte

WESTERN EUROPE

Cherry Bread Pudding
Switzerland

Switzerland abounds with superb cherries, especially around Zurich. *Cherry Bread Pudding,* known as "chriesibrägel," is the most famous and traditional of all the cherry desserts. It's a simple and excellent way to enjoy the flavor of cherries.

5 slices day-old firm-textured white bread, cut into 1-inch pieces (3¾ cups)
2¼ cups milk
¼ cup butter *or* margarine
¼ cup sugar
1 teaspoon vanilla
¾ teaspoon ground cinnamon
½ teaspoon finely shredded lemon peel
2 eggs
1 cup fresh *or* frozen pitted dark sweet cherries, halved *or* ½ of a 16-ounce can pitted dark sweet cherries, drained and halved

In a medium saucepan combine bread pieces and milk; bring to boiling, stirring constantly. Remove from heat. Let cool 5 to 10 minutes.

Meanwhile, in a mixer bowl beat butter or margarine on medium speed of electric mixer for 30 seconds. Add sugar, vanilla, cinnamon, and lemon peel and beat till fluffy. Add eggs, one at a time, beating on medium speed after each addition. Add bread mixture; beat till well combined. Fold in the cherries.

Turn into a well-greased 8x1½-inch round baking dish. Place dish in a 13x9x2-inch baking pan on oven rack. Carefully pour hot water into outer pan to depth of 1 inch. Bake, uncovered, in 350° oven for 45 to 50 minutes or till knife inserted near center comes out clean. Serve warm. Serves 6.

Jan Hagels
Holland

Dutch cooks are noted for their outstanding sweets. *Jan Hagels,* rich cookies topped with cinnamon sugar and almonds, are a favorite during the Christmas season.

2 cups all-purpose flour
⅛ teaspoon salt
1 cup butter *or* margarine
1 cup packed brown sugar
1 teaspoon vanilla
1 egg yolk
1 slightly beaten egg white
¼ cup sugar
½ teaspoon ground cinnamon
¾ cup sliced almonds

Stir together flour and salt. In a mixer bowl beat butter or margarine on medium speed of electric mixer for 30 seconds. Add brown sugar and vanilla and beat till fluffy. Add egg yolk and beat till well combined. Stir dry ingredients into brown sugar mixture, mixing well.

Pat batter evenly in an ungreased 15x10x1-inch baking pan. Brush top with beaten egg white. Combine sugar and cinnamon; sprinkle evenly over top. Sprinkle almonds over all.

Bake in a 350° oven for 15 to 18 minutes or till light brown. Cut into 1½-inch diamonds while warm. Cool in pan. Remove from pan with spatula. Makes about 48 cookies.

Bisschop   *pictured on the front cover*
Holland

On a cold winter's night, the Dutch traditionally serve *Bisschop.* This sweet spiced red wine punch, also called claret cup, is served hot to family and friends.

6 inches stick cinnamon, broken up
1 teaspoon whole cloves
1 medium orange, sliced
1 medium lemon, sliced
1 cup sugar
1 cup water
2 750-milliliter bottles dry red wine
Orange slices (optional)

Cut a small square from several thicknesses of cheesecloth; place stick cinnamon and whole cloves in center. Bring edges together to form a bag. Tie with string.

Place bag in a 3-quart saucepan along with orange and lemon slices, sugar, and water. Bring to boiling, stirring to dissolve sugar. Reduce heat.

Add the wine. Heat, covered, for 30 minutes but *do not boil.* Remove spice bag and citrus slices. Pour into a heat-proof punch bowl. Garnish the punch with additional orange slices, if desired. Makes 14 (4-ounce) servings.

Pâté Maison

"Pâté" is the French term for a finely ground mixture of meat or poultry and seasonings. "Pâté" is always served well chilled, traditionally at the beginning of the meal.

Every French cook has his own recipe, thus the name *Pâté Maison* ("pâté" of the house). A glass of wine and a slice of well-seasoned pâté are memorable before-the-meal delicacies.

½ **turkey breast, skinned and boned (2 pounds)**
3 **ounces pork fat** *or* **salt pork, cut up**
2 **beaten eggs**
⅓ **cup dry white wine**
¼ **cup brandy**
4 **teaspoons vinegar**
¾ **teaspoon salt**
½ **teaspoon dried thyme, crushed**
½ **teaspoon dried basil, crushed**
¼ **teaspoon dried savory, crushed**
⅛ **teaspoon dried oregano, crushed**
⅛ **teaspoon pepper**
¾ **pound ground pork**
¾ **pound ground veal**
4 **slices bacon**
3 **or 4 bay leaves**

Cut strips of turkey to make 1½ cups meat; set aside. Grind remaining turkey and pork fat or salt pork through fine blade of food grinder. Combine the eggs, wine, brandy, vinegar, salt, thyme, basil, savory, oregano, and pepper. Add ground turkey mixture, pork, and veal; mix well.

Lay bacon crosswise in bottom and up sides of 9x5x3-inch loaf pan. Press in *half* of the ground meat mixture; arrange turkey strips over. Spoon in remaining ground meat mixture. Top with bay leaves. Cover with foil. Bake in a 350° oven about 1¾ hours. Remove from oven. Drain off fat; replace the foil. Place another 9x5x3-inch pan atop the hot loaf. Press *very firmly* to compact mixture; fill the empty pan with dry beans. Chill overnight. Remove the bay leaves. Turn loaf out onto a serving plate and slice. Makes 10 to 12 servings.

Bitterballen

Crispy-fried spicy meatballs, *Bitterballen*, are served piping hot with mustard. This dish is a popular appetizer in Holland, and is usually served with glasses of ice-cold Dutch gin ("gen-ever") or beer.

3 **tablespoons butter** *or* **margarine**
¼ **cup all-purpose flour**
½ **cup beef** *or* **chicken broth**
⅓ **cup milk**
2 **tablespoons finely chopped onion**
2 **tablespoons snipped parsley**
1 **teaspoon Worcestershire sauce**
¼ **teaspoon salt**
⅛ **teaspoon ground nutmeg**
   Dash pepper
1½ **cups coarsely ground cooked beef** *or* **veal**
1 **cup fine dry bread crumbs**
2 **beaten eggs**
   Shortening *or* **cooking oil for deep-fat frying**
   Dijon-style mustard *or* **prepared mustard**

In a saucepan melt butter or margarine; stir in flour. Add beef or chicken broth and milk all at once; cook and stir till thickened and bubbly. Cook and stir 1 minute more. Remove from heat. Stir in onion, parsley, Worcestershire sauce, salt, nutmeg, and pepper.

Add ground cooked beef or veal; mix well. Cover and chill thoroughly.

With wet hands shape beef mixture into 1-inch balls. Roll in bread crumbs. Place beaten eggs in a shallow dish. Dip *each* meatball into eggs; roll again in crumbs. Cover and chill for 2 hours.

Fry meatballs, a few at a time, in deep hot fat (365°) for 2 to 3 minutes or till golden brown. Drain well on paper toweling. Keep warm in a 325° oven while frying remaining meatballs.

To serve, dip meatballs in Dijon-style mustard or prepared mustard. Makes about 40 appetizer meatballs.

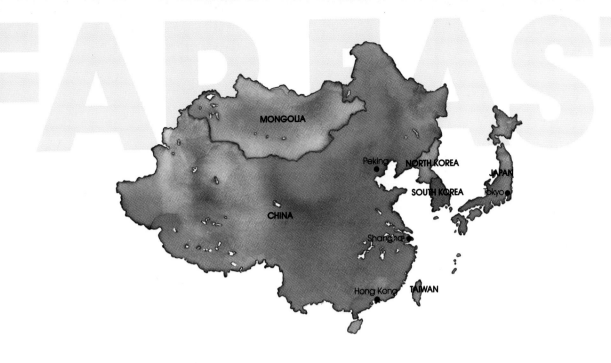

FAR EAST

The Far East combines simple cooking techniques with luxurious food presentation. Stir-frying, deep-frying, simmering, and steaming are age-old techniques for producing flavorful dishes from unusual ingredients.

Utensils are simple and few, too. The wok, bamboo steamer, and Mongolian hot pot are the "appliances" of the Far Eastern kitchen.

Cooking times are minimal. It is the preparation of the food that is time consuming since ingredients are cut into small shapes for fast cooking.

Separate courses are a rarity in the Far East. Instead, all dishes go on the table at once, and diners help themselves as they please. No meal is ever complete without the ever-present soup and a bowl of rice. Desserts are seldom served; sweets are reserved for between meal snacks. If available, fresh fruit provides the light ending to a meal.

In China, the presentation of the food is all important. Dishes must display a pleasing balance of contrasting tastes, textures, and colors. Regional specialties include the hotly seasoned dishes of Szechuan, the sugar-sweetened favorite foods of Shanghai, the fresh, natural flavors of Cantonese cooking, and the mildly seasoned but exquisite Mandarin entrées of Peking.

China's neighbor, Korea, uses many of the same ingredients for cooking — garlic, soy sauce, and ginger — but adds a spicy touch by using hot chili peppers.

Japanese cooking emphasizes the beautiful presentation of foods, too. Exotic vegetables such as daikon (a large white radish), burdock, spinach, mushrooms, and lotus root are common ingredients. Seaweed is an important ingredient in many dishes including "dashi," a flavorful cooking stock.

The finale to any Far Eastern meal is the customary cup of tea. In China, it is black tea; in Japan, green; and in Korea, it is ginseng.

Pictured clockwise from top right
Vegetable-Beef Stir-Fry (see recipe page 90), Omelet-Wrapped Sushi (see recipe, page 101), Kujol Pan (see recipe, page 100), and Kowloon Duckling with Plum-Orange Sauce (see recipe, page 92)

FAR EAST

Vegetable-Beef Stir-Fry  *pictured on page 88* — Korea

Like the Chinese and Japanese, Koreans slice fresh ingredients incredibly thin for stir-frying. This technique conserves cooking fuel since the small, uniform pieces need minimal frying time.

Vegetable-Beef Stir-Fry ("chap chae") typifies Korean cooking — a distinctive cuisine of bold, spicy flavors. "Chap chae" consists of beef strips marinated in a mixture of soy sauce, green onion, sesame, and garlic.

Bean threads are traditionally served with this stir-fry. Also called cellophane noodles, bean threads are fine, transparent noodles made from the starch of green mung beans.

½ **pound boneless beef sirloin *or* top round steak**
¼ **cup thinly sliced green onion**
¼ **cup soy sauce**
2 **cloves garlic, minced**
2 **tablespoons sesame oil *or* cooking oil**
1 **tablespoon sesame seed, crushed**
1 **tablespoon sugar**
½ **teaspoon pepper**
2 **dried mushrooms**
1 **ounce bean threads (cellophane noodles)**
⅓ **cup cold water**
1 **tablespoon cornstarch**
2 **tablespoons cooking oil**
¾ **cup carrots cut into julienne strips**
1 **cup bok choy cut into julienne strips**
1 **cup sliced broccoli flowerets**

Partially freeze meat; thinly slice across the grain into paper-thin bite-size strips. For marinade, combine green onion, soy sauce, garlic, sesame oil or cooking oil, sesame seed, sugar, and pepper; add meat. Marinate 30 minutes at room temperature.

Soak dried mushrooms in enough warm water to cover for 30 minutes; squeeze to drain well. Cut into julienne strips.

Cut or break bean threads into 4-inch lengths; cook in boiling water for 5 minutes or till tender. Drain well and keep warm.

Drain meat, reserving marinade. Add water and cornstarch to reserved marinade; mix well. Preheat a wok or large skillet over high heat; add oil. Add carrots and stir-fry 3 minutes. Add bok choy, broccoli, and mushrooms; stir-fry 2 minutes or till vegetables are crisp-tender. Remove vegetables. (Add more oil, if necessary.)

Add *half* the beef to hot wok or skillet; stir-fry 2 to 3 minutes or till brown. Remove beef. Stir-fry remaining beef 2 to 3 minutes. Return all meat to wok or skillet. Stir reserved marinade mixture and stir into beef. Cook and stir till thickened and bubbly. Stir in carrots, bok choy, broccoli, and mushrooms; cover and cook 1 minute.

To serve, place bean threads on one end of platter. Place stir-fried mixture on remaining portion of platter. Makes 4 servings.

Szechwan Dry-Fried Shredded Beef — China

Szechwan food, one of the major styles of Chinese cooking, is peppery and richly flavored. *Szechwan Dry-Fried Shredded Beef* uses hot bean sauce and Szechwan pepper to give it a hot and spicy flavor.

The meat is cut parallel to the grain, rather than across it. This technique cuts the meat fibers so they can be easily pulled apart into shreds.

1 **pound beef flank steak**
2 **tablespoons soy sauce**
1 **tablespoon hot bean sauce**
1 **tablespoon dry sherry**
2 **teaspoons grated gingerroot**
1 **teaspoon sesame oil *or* cooking oil**
½ **teaspoon crushed Szechwan pepper *or* pepper**
 Cooking oil for deep-fat frying
2 **green onions, thinly sliced**
1 **medium carrot, thinly bias sliced**
1 **cup finely chopped celery**

Partially freeze beef; thinly slice *parallel* to the grain into paper-thin bite-size strips. Cut or pull strips apart into shreds.

Stir together soy sauce, hot bean sauce, dry sherry, gingerroot, sesame oil or cooking oil, and Szechwan pepper or pepper. Set aside.

Pour cooking oil into a wok or large skillet to depth of ½ inch; heat oil. Fry beef shreds in hot oil, a small amount at a time, for 3 minutes or till the meat is brown and crispy. Using a slotted spoon or a wire strainer, remove beef shreds; set aside. Pour off all but *1 tablespoon* of the oil.

Stir-fry onions and carrot for 1½ minutes. Add celery; stir-fry for 1½ minutes more.

Add the beef to wok or skillet; stir in soy mixture. Cook and stir for 1 to 2 minutes or till heated through. Serve at once. Makes 4 servings.

Grilled Marinated Short Ribs   Korea

One of the most popular dishes in Korea is "bulgalbi," marinated beef ribs grilled over charcoal. In Korea, beef is very expensive, so it's reserved for special occasions.

For a spicy side-dish accompaniment, serve Korea's famous *Kimchi* (see recipe, page 95).

3 **pounds beef chuck short ribs, cut into 2½-inch lengths**
½ **cup soy sauce**
½ **cup water**
¼ **cup sliced green onion**
1 **clove garlic, minced**
2 **tablespoons sesame seed, toasted**
2 **tablespoons sesame oil *or* cooking oil**
1 **tablespoon sugar**
1 **tablespoon rice vinegar *or* vinegar**
½ **teaspoon dry mustard**
¼ **teaspoon pepper**
   Kimchi (see recipe, page 95)

Trim excess fat from ribs. With bone side down, cut each piece halfway to bone at ½-inch intervals; at right angles to first cuts, cut ½ inch deep at ½-inch intervals.

For marinade, combine soy sauce, water, green onion, garlic, sesame seed, sesame oil or cooking oil, sugar, rice vinegar or vinegar, dry mustard, and pepper. Place meat in a plastic bag; set in large bowl. Pour marinade into bag. Close bag; chill 4 to 5 hours, turning bag occasionally. Remove meat; wipe dry. Reserve marinade.

Place ribs on grill, bone side down; cover grill. Grill over *medium* coals. (Hold hand, palm-side down, just above coals. Count "one thousand one, one thousand two," etc. If you need to withdraw your hand after four counts, the coals are medium.) Grill about 15 minutes or till meat is brown, brushing with marinade frequently. Turn ribs, meaty side down; grill 30 minutes more, brushing with marinade frequently. Serve with Kimchi. Serves 6.

Teppanyaki   Japan

In Japan, an artful presentation of food is considered almost as important as a balance of textures and flavors.

When serving this dish, capture the feeling of Japan by artistically assembling the meat, shrimp, and desired vegetables on a large platter.

The Japanese would cook this dish on a "teppan," an extra-large griddle; but an electric griddle makes an excellent substitute.

Teppanyaki is cooked tableside so the host can stir-fry the ingredients a little at a time as they are needed.

12 **fresh *or* frozen large shrimp**
½ **pound boneless beef sirloin *or* top round steak**
1 **whole medium chicken breast, skinned, halved lengthwise, and boned**
3 *or* 4 desired vegetables*
   Cooking oil
   Soy-Ginger Sauce (see recipe, page 97)
   Hot Mustard Sauce (see recipe, page 100)
   Hot cooked rice

Thaw shrimp, if frozen. Shell and devein shrimp. Partially freeze beef and chicken. Thinly slice beef and chicken across the grain into bite-size strips. Toss beef and chicken separately with a little oil to keep pieces from sticking together. Arrange the beef and chicken, shrimp, and the desired vegetables on a large platter.

Heat electric griddle at the table; brush on some oil (about 2 tablespoons). To cook vegetables, start with those that take longer (carrot, leeks, green pepper) and end with vegetables requiring the least time (mushrooms, pea pods, bean sprouts). Before stir-frying, be sure vegetables are drained and patted dry with paper toweling. Cook *half* of each vegetable, one at a time, stir-frying till vegetable is crisp-tender; add oil as needed. Push cooked vegetables to side of griddle. Transfer vegetables to platter when all are cooked.

Add *half* the beef, chicken, and shrimp to griddle; stir-fry, keeping ingredients separate, 1 to 3 minutes or till meat is desired doneness and shrimp are pink. Transfer to platter and serve at once. Repeat, cooking remaining vegetables and meat after first portion has been eaten. Serve with Soy-Ginger Sauce, Hot Mustard Sauce, and hot cooked rice. Makes 6 servings.

***Note:** For vegetables, choose 3 or 4 of the following: 2 cups cut-up Chinese cabbage or spinach; 1 cup thinly sliced carrot; 2 leeks, sliced crosswise; 1 cup green pepper cut into strips; 1 cup sliced water chestnuts; 1 cup sliced fresh mushrooms; 1 cup fresh pea pods; 1 cup fresh bean sprouts.

FAR EAST

Fuji Chicken in Miso Japan

The distinctive flavor of *Fuji Chicken in Miso Sauce* comes from its blend of seasonings. Finely chopped pieces of chicken simmer in chicken broth flavored with red miso, sake, rice vinegar, and soy.

Miso is a paste made from cooked, fermented soy beans. Japanese use miso in many dishes to give a characteristic flavor.

3 **tablespoons red miso (red bean paste)**
2 **tablespoons chicken broth**
2 **tablespoons sake** or **dry sherry**
2 **teaspoons sugar**
2 **teaspoons rice vinegar** or **vinegar**
1 **teaspoon soy sauce**
2 **whole medium chicken breasts**
1 **teaspoon cornstarch**
2 **cups desired vegetables***

In a saucepan stir red miso into broth; stir in sake or dry sherry, sugar, rice vinegar or vinegar, and soy sauce. Bring to boiling, stirring to dissolve sugar. Reduce heat.

Skin, halve lengthwise, and bone chicken; finely chop. Sift cornstarch over chicken; toss to coat. Add chicken to broth mixture. Simmer, covered, about 8 minutes or till chicken is done.

To serve, spoon chicken mixture into individual rice bowls. Arrange ½ *cup* of the desired vegetables around edge of *each* bowl. Makes 4 servings.

*Note: For vegetables, choose any of the following: sliced mushrooms, sliced bamboo shoots, sliced water chestnuts, crisp-cooked bias-sliced carrot, crisp-cooked bias-sliced crookneck squash, or crisp-cooked pea pods.

Kowloon Duckling pictured on page 88 China

Hickory chips
2 **tablespoons soy sauce**
½ **teaspoon grated gingerroot**
⅛ **teaspoon pepper**
1 **4- to 5-pound domestic duckling** or **capon**
6 **to 8 green onions, cut up**
6 **sprigs parsley**
1 **clove garlic**
½ **cup soy sauce**
2 **tablespoons honey**
2 **tablespoons lemon juice**
Plum-Orange Sauce

About 1 hour before cooking, soak hickory chips in enough water to cover. Drain chips. Combine the 2 tablespoons soy sauce, gingerroot, and pepper; brush over inside cavity of duckling or capon. Stuff cavity with onions, parsley, and garlic. Skewer neck and body cavity closed; tie legs to tail securely with cord. In a saucepan combine the ½ cup soy sauce, honey, and lemon juice; bring just to boiling.

In a covered grill arrange *slow* coals around edge of grill. (Hold hand, palm-side down, just above coals. Count "one thousand one, one thousand two," etc. If you need to withdraw your hand after five or six counts, the coals are *slow*.) Sprinkle coals with some dampened hickory chips. Center heavy foil drip pan on grill, not directly over coals. Place bird, breast-side up, in foil pan. Lower grill hood. Grill for 2¼ to 2½ hours or till done. Sprinkle chips over coals every 30 minutes. Brush bird often with soy-honey mixture. Remove drippings from pan as necessary. Serve with Plum-Orange Sauce. If desired, garnish platter with orange slices and sprigs of Chinese parsley or parsley. Makes 3 servings.

Plum-Orange Sauce: Drain one 16-ounce can whole, unpitted *purple plums*, reserving ¼ cup syrup. Force plums through a sieve, removing pits and skins. In a saucepan combine sieved plums, reserved plum syrup, ¼ teaspoon finely shredded *orange peel*, 3 tablespoons *orange juice*, 4 teaspoons *sugar*, 1 teaspoon *Worcestershire sauce*, 1 teaspoon *rice vinegar or vinegar*, and ¼ teaspoon *ground cinnamon*. Bring to boiling; reduce heat and boil gently, uncovered, about 20 minutes or till reduced to ½ cup.

FAR EAST

Lobster Cantonese   China

Lobster Cantonese is a Chinese classic. A subtle combination of garlic, onion, soy, and fermented black beans enhances the delicate flavors of lobster and pork.

Fermented black beans are made from soy beans and are heavily salted. Store any unused beans, covered, in the refrigerator.

½   **pound boneless pork**
2   **6- to 8-ounce frozen lobster tails, thawed**
1   **cup chicken broth**
1   **tablespoon cornstarch**
2   **tablespoons soy sauce**
1   **tablespoon dry sherry**
2   **tablespoons cooking oil**
2   **cloves garlic, minced**
¼   **cup sliced green onion**
1   **tablespoon chopped fermented black beans**
    Hot cooked rice

Partially freeze pork; slice thinly into bite-size strips. Remove lobster meat from shells and cut into bite-size pieces; set aside. Combine chicken broth and cornstarch; stir in soy sauce and sherry. Set aside.

Preheat a wok or large skillet over high heat; add the cooking oil. Stir-fry garlic in hot oil for 30 seconds. Add the green onion and black beans and stir-fry 1½ minutes. Add the pork and stir-fry for 2 minutes. (Add more oil, if necessary.) Add the lobster and stir-fry 2 to 3 minutes or till the lobster and the strips of pork are done.

Stir chicken broth mixture; stir into pork and lobster. Cook and stir till thickened and bubbly. Cook and stir 2 minutes more. Serve at once with hot cooked rice. Makes 4 servings.

Pork-Vegetable Soup   China

Soups play an important role in the Chinese cuisine. A hot, light soup is a welcomed dish in a traditional Chinese meal.

Pork-Vegetable Soup features noodles, a food for the Chinese second in importance only to rice. Noodles signify longevity in the Chinese culture, and eating them is thought to ensure a long life.

½   **pound boneless pork**
1   **tablespoon soy sauce**
2   **teaspoons cornstarch**
1½   **cups fine noodles (3 ounces)**
4½   **cups chicken broth**
1   **cup thinly sliced Chinese cabbage**
1   **small cucumber, seeded and cut into julienne strips**

Partially freeze pork; slice thinly into bite-size strips. Combine soy sauce and cornstarch; add to the pork, stirring to mix well. Let stand for 30 minutes.

Meanwhile, cook noodles according to package directions; drain well. Set aside. In a large saucepan bring chicken broth to boiling. Stir in pork, Chinese cabbage, and cucumber. Return to boiling; reduce heat. Simmer, uncovered, for 10 to 15 minutes. Stir in the cooked noodles; heat through. Ladle soup into individual serving bowls. Makes 6 to 8 side-dish servings.

Beef Dumpling Soup   Korea

1   **beaten egg**
½   **cup finely chopped bok choy or cabbage**
½   **cup fresh bean sprouts, chopped**
2   **tablespoons finely chopped onion**
1   **clove garlic, minced**
1   **teaspoon sesame oil or cooking oil**
1   **teaspoon sesame seed, toasted**
    Dash salt
    Dash pepper
½   **pound ground beef**
30 **to 32 wonton skins**
8   **cups beef broth**
2   **green onions, thinly sliced**
1   **tablespoon soy sauce**

For filling, in a mixing bowl combine egg, bok choy or cabbage, bean sprouts, onion, garlic, sesame or cooking oil, sesame seed, salt, and pepper. Add ground beef; mix well.

For dumplings, place one scant tablespoon of the filling in center of each wonton. Moisten the edges lightly with water. Fold wonton skins in half diagonally to form triangular-shaped dumplings. Pinch edges to seal.

In a large saucepan or Dutch oven combine beef broth, green onions, and soy sauce; bring to boiling. Drop dumplings, one at a time, into boiling water; reduce heat. Simmer, uncovered, for 10 minutes. Ladle soup into individual serving bowls. Makes 6 to 8 side-dish servings.

Kimchi

In Korea, *Kimchi* — a peppery-hot, fermented pickled cabbage relish — is served daily with rice. During winter, Koreans store *Kimchi* underground in earthen pots; but through summer, they prepare it fresh.

1½ **to 2 pounds Chinese cabbage**
   ***or* bok choy, cut into 1½-inch**
   pieces
4 **cups water**
½ **cup salt**
4 **ounces daikon (Japanese**
   white radish), peeled and cut
   into julienne strips (¾ cup)
¼ **cup carrot, cut into julienne**
   strips
3 **green onions, bias sliced into**
   1½-inch lengths
2 **teaspoons shrimp paste *or***
   anchovy paste
2 **cloves garlic, minced**
½ **teaspoon ground red pepper**
½ **teaspoon grated gingerroot**
¼ **teaspoon sugar**

In a large bowl combine cabbage or bok choy, water, and salt. Let stand 4 hours. Rinse well; drain, leaving some water clinging to the leaves. Stir in daikon, carrot, green onions, shrimp paste or anchovy paste, garlic, red pepper, gingerroot, and sugar; mix well.

Press into a 1-quart jar. Secure lid. Let stand in cool place (60° to 70° F) for 2 to 3 days. If desired, serve with Grilled Marinated Short Ribs (see recipe, page 91) and hot cooked rice. To store, cover and refrigerate. Makes 4 cups.

Green Beans with Miso Dressing

3 **cups fresh green beans, bias**
   sliced into 1-inch pieces *or*
   two 9-ounce packages
   frozen cut green beans
Miso Dressing
Toasted sesame seed
Lemon peel strips

In a covered saucepan cook cut green beans in a small amount of boiling water 20 to 30 minutes or till crisp-tender. (If using frozen green beans, cook according to package directions, omitting salt in cooking water.) Drain well. Toss with Miso Dressing; chill well. Remove from refrigerator about ½ hour before serving time to bring to room temperature. Pass toasted sesame seed and lemon peel strips. Makes 6 servings.

Miso Dressing: In a small bowl combine 1 *egg yolk* with ¼ cup *white miso* (white bean paste). Stir in 1 tablespoon *sake or dry sherry*, 1 tablespoon *water*, and 1 teaspoon *sugar*; mix well. Makes about ½ cup sauce.

Vegetarian Fried Rice

8 **dried mushrooms**
1 **beaten egg**
3 **tablespoons soy sauce**
3 **tablespoons dry sherry**
⅛ **teaspoon pepper**
2 **tablespoons cooking oil**
1½ **cups green beans bias sliced**
   into 1½-inch lengths
1 **medium onion, halved and**
   sliced
½ **cup bias-sliced celery**
½ **cup bamboo shoots**
2 **cups cooked rice, chilled**
¼ **cup chopped peanuts**

In a small bowl soak dried mushrooms in enough warm water to cover for 30 minutes; squeeze to drain well. Chop mushrooms, discarding stems. In a small mixing bowl combine beaten egg, soy sauce, dry sherry, and pepper; set aside.

Preheat a wok or large skillet over high heat; add cooking oil. Stir-fry green beans, onion, and celery in hot oil for 3 minutes or till crisp-tender. Remove vegetables. Add mushrooms and bamboo shoots; stir-fry 1 minute. Add green beans, onion, celery, and cooked rice. Cook and stir 6 to 8 minutes. (Add more oil if necessary.)

While stirring rice mixture constantly, drizzle egg mixture over rice mixture. Cook and stir till eggs are set. Sprinkle chopped peanuts atop. Makes 4 to 6 side-dish servings.

FAR EAST

Chicken and Crab Pot Stickers China

Chicken and Crab Pot Stickers first are fried then simmered and cooked in hot steam. Pot stickers — little dumplings — stick to the pot, hence their name.

Pot stickers are delicately seasoned and make a savory first course. A specialty on the menu in many Chinese restaurants, now you can make them at home for an international dinner party.

1 cup finely chopped cooked chicken
1 7½-ounce can crab meat, drained, flaked, and cartilage removed
¾ cup finely chopped celery
¾ cup finely chopped bok choy *or* cabbage
¼ cup finely chopped green onion
1 tablespoon soy sauce
1 tablespoon dry sherry
2 teaspoons cornstarch
1 teaspoon sesame oil *or* cooking oil
½ teaspoon salt
½ teaspoon sugar
3 cups all-purpose flour
½ teaspoon salt
1 cup boiling water
⅓ cup cold water
¼ cup all-purpose flour
6 tablespoons cooking oil
1⅓ cups water
Soy-Ginger Sauce
Chinese Mustard Sauce

Combine chicken, crab meat, celery, bok choy or cabbage, and green onion. Stir soy sauce and sherry into cornstarch; stir in sesame or cooking oil, ½ teaspoon salt, and sugar. Add to chicken-crab meat mixture. Cover and refrigerate.

To prepare the dumplings, stir together the 3 cups flour and the ½ teaspoon salt. Pour the 1 cup boiling water slowly into flour mixture, stirring constantly. Stir till well-combined. Stir in the ⅓ cup cold water. When cool enough to handle, knead dough on a well-floured surface, kneading in the ¼ cup flour till dough is smooth and elastic (8 to 10 minutes total). Shape dough into a ball. Place dough back in bowl; cover with a damp towel. Let stand at room temperature for 15 to 20 minutes.

Turn dough out onto a lightly floured surface. Divide dough into 4 equal portions. Roll *each* portion to ⅛-inch thickness. Cut *each* portion into ten rounds, 3 inches in diameter, with a cookie cutter (reroll dough as needed).

Spoon about *1 tablespoon* of the filling in center of one dough round. Fold the round in half across filling; moisten and pinch edges to seal. Set pinched edge of dumpling upright and press gently to slightly flatten bottom. Transfer dumpling to a floured baking sheet. Cover with a dry towel. Repeat with the remaining filling and rounds.

In a large skillet heat *2 tablespoons* of the cooking oil about 1 minute or till very hot. Set *half* of the dumplings upright in skillet (making sure dumplings do not touch each other). Cook in hot oil about 1 minute or till bottoms are lightly brown.

Carefully add ⅔ *cup* of the water to skillet. Reduce heat; cover and cook about 10 minutes. Uncover and cook 3 to 5 minutes or till all water evaporates. Add *1 tablespoon* of the cooking oil to skillet; lift and tilt skillet to spread oil. Cook dumplings, uncovered, for 1 minute more. Using a wide spatula gently remove dumplings from skillet. Keep warm in a 250° oven. Repeat to cook the remaining dumplings using remaining oil and remaining water. Serve with Soy-Ginger Sauce and Chinese Mustard Sauce. Makes 40 appetizers.

Soy-Ginger Sauce: Combine 3 tablespoons *soy sauce*, 2 tablespoons *rice vinegar or white vinegar*, and ⅛ teaspoon *ground ginger.*

Chinese Mustard Sauce: In a small saucepan bring ¼ cup *water* to boiling. Combine ¼ cup *dry mustard*, 2 teaspoons *cooking oil*, and ½ teaspoon *salt.* Stir boiling water into mustard mixture.

Pictured clockwise from top
Steamed Buns with Sweet Filling (see recipe, page 99), Soy-Ginger Sauce, Chinese Mustard Sauce, Chicken and Crab Pot Stickers, and Steamed Pork Dumplings (see recipe, page 98)

FAR EAST

Steamed Pork Dumplings   *pictured on page 96*   China

Of China's many regional varieties of cooking, Cantonese is the best known in America and Europe. That's because thousands of Chinese from Canton, a region in southern China, introduced their cooking to Westerners when they immigrated to Western countries in the 1800s. Cantonese cooking became very popular then and remains so today.

Cantonese cooking features tasty, bite-size stuffed dumplings known as "dim sum." Translated, "dim sum" means heart's delight. After sampling *Steamed Pork Dumplings* or *Steamed Buns with Sweet Filling* (see recipe, page 99), you'll understand why the Chinese so named these delicious steamed dumplings.

2	**cups all-purpose flour**
⅔	**cup boiling water**
¼	**cup cold water**
6	**dried mushrooms**
½	**pound ground pork**
1½	**cups finely chopped cabbage**
¾	**cup finely chopped water chestnuts**
2	**tablespoons thinly sliced green onion**
2	**tablespoons soy sauce**
1½	**teaspoons cornstarch**
1	**teaspoon sugar**
1	**teaspoon grated gingerroot Cabbage leaves**

For dough, combine flour and boiling water, stirring constantly with fork or a chopstick. Add cold water; mix with hands till dough forms ball (dough will be sticky). Cover; set aside.

For filling, soak dried mushrooms in enough warm water to cover for 30 minutes; squeeze to drain well. Discard stems; chop mushrooms. Combine mushrooms, pork, 1½ cups chopped cabbage, water chestnuts, and green onion. Stir soy sauce into cornstarch; stir in sugar and gingerroot. Stir into meat mixture. Set aside.

Divide dough in half. Return *half* of dough to covered bowl. Divide other half into 15 balls. On a well-floured surface, roll *each* ball into a circle 3 inches in diameter. Place about *1 tablespoon* of the meat mixture in center of *each*. Bring dough up around filling, pleating dough to fit around meat mixture. Press dough firmly around filling. Gently flatten bottom of dumpling so that dumpling stands upright by itself. Repeat shaping with the remaining dough and filling.

Over high heat bring water for steaming to boiling. Place cabbage leaves to cover bottom of lightly greased steamer rack. Place dumplings, pleated side up, on steamer rack so dumplings don't touch. (If all dumplings won't fit on steamer rack, refrigerate while others steam.) Place steamer rack over boiling water. Cover steamer; steam dumplings 15 to 17 minutes. Makes 30.

Pork and Shrimp Wontons   China

¾	**pound boneless pork, finely chopped**
1	**clove garlic, minced**
1	**tablespoon cooking oil**
1	**cup finely chopped bok choy *or* cabbage**
½	**cup finely chopped celery**
½	**cup thinly sliced green onion**
2	**tablespoons thinly sliced bamboo shoots**
2	**tablespoons soy sauce**
1	**tablespoon water**
1	**teaspoon cornstarch**
1	**egg**
1	**4½-ounce can shrimp, drained and finely chopped**
40	**wonton skins *or* 10 egg roll skins, quartered**
	Shortening *or* cooking oil for deep-fat frying
	Soy-Ginger Sauce (see recipe, page 97)
	Chinese Mustard Sauce (see recipe, page 97)

To make filling, in a wok or skillet stir-fry pork and garlic in the 1 tablespoon hot oil 3 to 4 minutes. Add bok choy, green onion, and bamboo shoots; stir-fry about 3 minutes more. Stir soy and water into cornstarch; stir in the egg. Add to pork. Cook and stir till thickened; remove from wok or skillet. Add shrimp to pork-vegetable mixture. Cool slightly.

To wrap wontons, place a wonton skin with one point toward you. Spoon *1 rounded teaspoon* of the filling just off center of skin. Fold bottom point of wonton skin over the filling; tuck point under filling. Roll wonton once to cover filling, leaving about 1 inch unrolled at the top of skin. Moisten the right-hand corner of skin with water. Grasp the right- and left-hand corners of skin; bring these corners toward you below the filling. Overlap the corners; press to seal. Repeat with the remaining wonton skins and filling.

Fry wontons, a few at a time, in deep hot fat (365°) for 2 to 3 minutes or till golden brown. Use a slotted spoon or wire strainer to remove wontons. Drain on paper toweling. Serve warm with Soy-Ginger Sauce and Chinese Mustard Sauce. Makes 40 appetizers.

Steamed Buns with Sweet Filling *pictured on page 96* China

Steamed Buns with Sweet Filling are called "ma yung bao" in China. The filling uses sweet bean paste, which is made from soy beans and sugar. Sweet steamed buns are considered a treat to the Chinese, just as cookies are to Westerners.

1¼ to 1½ cups all-purpose flour
 1 package active dry yeast
 ½ cup milk
 2 tablespoons cooking oil
 1 tablespoon sugar
 ¼ teaspoon salt
 ¼ cup canned sweet red bean paste
 ¼ cup chopped pitted dates
 ¼ teaspoon vanilla

For dough, in a mixer bowl combine ½ cup of the flour and the yeast. In a saucepan heat together milk, oil, sugar, and salt just till warm (115° to 120°). Add to flour mixture. Beat at low speed of electric mixer ½ minute, scraping sides of bowl constantly. Beat 3 minutes at high speed. Stir in as much of the remaining flour as you can mix in with spoon. Turn out on a lightly floured surface. Knead in enough of the remaining flour to make a moderately stiff dough (6 to 8 minutes total). Place in a lightly greased bowl; turn once to grease surface. Cover; let the dough rise in warm place till nearly double (about 1 hour).

Punch dough down; turn out onto a lightly floured surface. Cut into 12 portions; shape each into a ball. Cover; let rest 5 minutes.

For filling, in a small bowl combine sweet red bean paste, dates, and vanilla.

On a lightly floured surface, roll each ball of dough to a circle 3 inches in diameter. Place 2 *teaspoons* of the filling mixture in center of *each* dough circle. Bring edges of dough up around filling, stretching a little till edges *just* meet; pinch to seal in center, forming a small ball. Cover filled buns and let rise 10 minutes.

Meanwhile, over high heat, bring water for steaming to boiling. Place buns, seam side down, on a lightly greased steamer rack so buns don't touch; do not let rise. (If all buns won't fit on steamer rack, refrigerate while others steam.) Place the steamer rack over boiling water. Cover steamer; steam rolls for 20 minutes. Makes 12.

Fried Zucchini Appetizers   Korea

 3 medium zucchini
 2 cups ground cooked chicken
 1 slightly beaten egg
 2 tablespoons finely chopped onion
 1 clove garlic, minced
 1 teaspoon sesame oil *or* cooking oil
 1 teaspoon sesame seed
   Dash salt
   Dash pepper
   Cooking oil for deep-fat frying
 1 slightly beaten egg
 1 cup all-purpose flour
 1 cup ice water
 2 tablespoons cooking oil
 ½ teaspoon sugar
 ½ teaspoon salt
 1 or 2 ice cubes
   Soy sauce (optional)

Slice zucchini into ½-inch-thick slices. Combine chicken, 1 egg, onion, garlic, the 1 teaspoon sesame or cooking oil, sesame seed, the dash salt, and pepper till well combined. Spread *each* zucchini slice with *1 teaspoon* of the chicken mixture.

Using a wok or a skillet at least 3 inches deep, pour in cooking oil to depth of 1 inch. Heat to 365°.

For batter, combine egg, flour, ice water, the 2 tablespoons oil, sugar, and the ½ teaspoon salt. Beat just till moistened (a few lumps should remain). Stir in 1 or 2 ice cubes. *Use at once.*

Dip zucchini-chicken slices in batter. Fry in hot oil, several slices at a time, zucchini side down for 2 to 3 minutes or till light brown. Turn and fry on the other side for 2 to 3 minutes or till light brown. Drain on paper toweling, chicken-mixture side up. Keep warm while frying the remaining slices. Serve with soy sauce, if desired. Makes 32 appetizers.

FAR EAST

Kujol Pan   *pictured on page 88*   Korea

The literal translation of this traditional Korean dish, *Kujol Pan,* is "nine varieties." For this dish, small pancakes, thin slices of omelet, pieces of meat, and fine strips of vegetables are stacked on a tray. Each person selects the desired ingredients and puts them in the center of a pancake. The pancake is then rolled around the filling and dipped in either *Hot Mustard Sauce* or *Soy Dipping Sauce.*

Kujol Pan is an ideal participation dish to start off an Oriental dinner. Or, serve it as a snack at a cocktail party. Guests will enjoy getting involved and selecting their own combinations of tasty ingredients.

½ **pound beef top round steak** *or* **boneless pork**
3 **eggs**
1 **tablespoon cooking oil**
1 **medium zucchini, cut into julienne strips**
6 **green onions, cut into julienne strips**
1 **cup Chinese cabbage sliced into julienne strips**
3 **medium carrots, cut into julienne strips**
  Korean Pancakes
  Hot Mustard Sauce
  Soy Dipping Sauce

Partially freeze beef or pork; slice thinly across the grain into bite-size strips. Slice again into julienne strips. Set aside.

Separate egg yolks from whites. In separate bowls slightly beat egg yolks and egg whites. In a lightly greased 10-inch skillet cook the beaten egg yolks, without stirring, till set but not brown. Invert skillet over a baking sheet to remove cooked yolks. Cook egg whites, half at a time, the same as for the yolks. Cut cooked egg yolks and egg whites into julienne strips. Set aside.

Preheat a wok or large skillet over high heat; add cooking oil. Stir-fry meat for 2 to 3 minutes or till brown. Remove meat. Add the zucchini; stir-fry 1 minute. Remove the zucchini. (Add more oil, if necessary.) Add the onions; stir-fry 1 minute. Remove the onions. Add the Chinese cabbage; stir-fry 1 minute. Remove the cabbage. Add the carrots; stir-fry 2 minutes. Remove the carrots.

To serve, arrange the meat, egg yolk, egg white, and vegetable strips in separate piles around a plate of stacked Korean Pancakes. Select fillings as desired. Place in the center of a pancake and roll up. Dip in Hot Mustard Sauce or Soy Dipping Sauce. Makes about 36 appetizers.

Korean Pancakes: Combine 1 cup all-purpose *flour,* 1 cup *milk,* ½ cup *beef broth,* 2 *eggs,* 1 tablespoon *sugar,* and ⅛ teaspoon *salt.* Beat with a rotary beater till well combined. Heat a lightly greased skillet or griddle. For *each* pancake, spoon in about *1 tablespoon* of the batter; spread with back of spoon into a circle 3 inches in diameter. Lightly brown both sides. Remove from pan. Allow to cool. Repeat with remaining batter, greasing skillet as needed. Makes about 36 pancakes.

Hot Mustard Sauce: Combine ¼ cup *dry mustard* and 1½ teaspoons *sugar.* Stir in 2 tablespoons *water* and 2 tablespoons *soy sauce* till smooth.

Soy Dipping Sauce: Combine ¼ cup *soy sauce,* 2 tablespoons *white vinegar,* 1 tablespoon *sliced green onion,* and 2 teaspoons *sesame seed,* toasted.

Omelet-Wrapped Sushi   *pictured on page 88*   Japan

"Sushi" is hot cooked rice flavored with rice vinegar, sake, and sugar. The rice mixture is compressed tightly till the rice sticks together.

The Japanese snack on "sushi" much like Westerners munch chips. There are many ways to serve "sushi"; this variation wraps the "sushi" in a tender omelet.

 1 **cup short, medium, *or* long grain rice**
 3 **tablespoons sugar**
 3 **tablespoons rice vinegar *or* white vinegar**
 2 **tablespoons sake, mirin, *or* dry sherry**
 1 **4½-ounce can shrimp, rinsed and drained**
 ⅓ **cup fresh *or* frozen peas, cooked**
    Japanese Omelets

For sushi, cook rice according to package directions. In a small saucepan combine sugar, vinegar, and sake, mirin, or dry sherry; bring to boiling. Stir vinegar mixture into hot cooked rice. Add shrimp and peas; stir together.

Line an 8x8x2-inch pan with waxed paper. Spread the rice mixture in the pan and cover with waxed paper. Place a second 8x8x2-inch pan atop and press very firmly to compact mixture. Remove top pan. Chill several hours. Remove top waxed paper and invert rice mixture onto a cutting board. Remove remaining waxed paper. Cut into sixteen 2-inch squares.

Place one sushi square in the center of a Japanese Omelet. Fold in two opposite sides of omelet, then remaining two sides. Place, seam side down, and slice into ½-inch slices. Repeat with remaining sushi squares and omelets. Makes 64 appetizers.

Japanese Omelets: In a bowl beat together 8 *eggs*, ¼ cup *water*, and ½ teaspoon *salt* till well combined. In a lightly greased 6-inch skillet add about *2 tablespoons* of the egg mixture; lift and tilt skillet to spread batter. Cook the omelet 1½ to 2 minutes. Do not turn. (Omelet should be cooked but not brown.) Remove; set aside. Continue with the remaining egg mixture, greasing skillet as needed. Cool the omelets completely. Makes 16 omelets.

Sweet Rice Eggs   Japan

Sweet Rice Eggs aren't eggs at all. A rice mixture is formed into an egg shape, hence the name. In Japan, these tasty snacks are called "ohasi."

1½ **cups short, medium, *or* long grain rice**
 ½ **cup sugar**
 2 **tablespoons black sesame seed, toasted**
 1 **cup canned sweet red bean paste**

Cook rice according to package directions. Let cool 10 minutes. Mash till the consistency of mashed potatoes. Cool. Combine sugar and toasted sesame seed. Set aside.

Using *1 tablespoon* of the bean paste, shape paste into a ball. Cover each bean paste ball with about ¼ *cup* of the mashed rice paste and form into an egg shape. Roll *each* rice egg in the sugar-sesame seed mixture. Cover; chill thoroughly. Makes 16.

Walnut Tea   China

In China, *Walnut Tea* is a popular dessert served at banquets. Its consistency is similar to a hot, creamy soup, but it is known in China as "tea."

If you own Chinese tea cups, use them instead of small bowls.

 ¾ **cup broken walnuts**
    Water
 ½ **cup water**
 ¼ **cup sugar**
 1 **tablespoon rice flour *or* cornstarch**
1½ **cups water**

In a saucepan bring walnuts and enough water to cover to boiling; cook 2 minutes. Drain walnuts; discard water.

In a blender container or food processor bowl combine walnuts and the ½ cup water. Cover; blend or process till smooth. In a saucepan combine sugar and rice flour or cornstarch; add the 1½ cups water and the walnut mixture. Cook and stir over medium heat till thickened and bubbly. Cook and stir 2 to 3 minutes longer. Serve as a dessert soup in 6 small cups or bowls. Makes 6 servings.

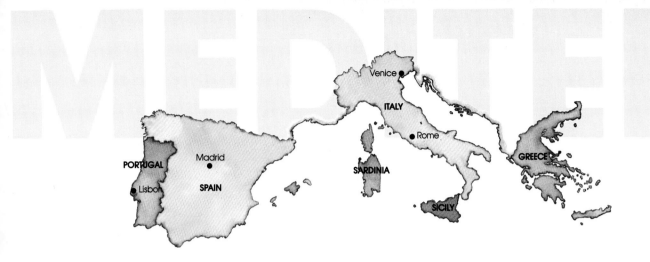

MEDITERRANEAN

The characteristic flavors of garlic and olive oil, the foods of Spain's New World colonies, and the influences of Turkish and Arab invaders have combined to produce the similar yet distinctive cuisines found in Greece, Italy, Portugal, and Spain.

Oldest by far of these four nations is Greece where, for centuries, olive trees have provided the oil so essential to Mediterranean cooking. As part of the Ottoman Empire for years, Greece was greatly influenced by the Turks, and both Greece and Turkey share credit for baklava, moussaka, and dolmas (stuffed vegetables).

In the neighboring country of Italy, world-renowned pasta and pizza have overshadowed other national specialties such as sausages, prosciutto, and a variety of cheeses including Gorgonzola, Bel Paese, Parmesan, and ricotta.

Two basic cooking styles are prevalent in Italy. In the north, butter, meat, and flat pasta are essential ingredients. Beans, rice, and a cornmeal mush known as polenta often serve as pasta substitutes. In the south, sea-food, tubular-shaped noodles, and olive oil are more frequently used.

Farther south in Sicily, Arab invaders passed on their love of sweet desserts as well as the art of making ice creams and sherbets.

Spain, too, was not immune from Arab influence. African Moors, who dominated southern Spain in the Middle Ages, brought rice, figs, citrus fruits, and spices. They also planted groves of almond trees. Their legacy of confections was left behind to enhance Spain's peasant-style cuisine. Tomatoes, red and green peppers, and chocolate came from Spain's Latin American conquests and also serve as reminders of its past.

The Portuguese, who share the Iberian Peninsula with the Spanish, are great lovers of salt-dried cod (often referred to as the poor man's meat), and are said to have over 350 official ways to prepare it. For over 400 years, Portugal—home to some of the greatest explorers of all time—has sent fishermen almost 3,000 miles away to Newfoundland to bring back this treasured food.

Pictured clockwise from left
Straw and Hay (see recipe, page 113), Pork Alentejana (see recipe, page 104), and Lamb-Eggplant Avgolemono (see recipe, page 104)

MEDITERRANEAN

Pork Alentejana *pictured on page 102* Portugal

This pork and clam dish originated in the Alentejo region of Portugal, where pork is served almost daily.

To prepare clams in shell for cooking: Thaw clams, if frozen. Cover clams with salted water (3 tablespoons to 8 cups water); let stand 15 minutes. Repeat this process twice.

1½ cups dry white wine
4 teaspoons paprika
2 cloves garlic, minced
2 bay leaves
1 teaspoon salt
2 pounds lean boneless pork, cut into 1-inch pieces
¼ cup olive oil *or* cooking oil
2 medium onions, thinly sliced
¼ cup chopped pimiento
24 fresh *or* frozen small clams in shell (see copy at left)
½ teaspoon salt
¼ teaspoon pepper

For marinade, combine wine, paprika, garlic, bay leaves, the 1 teaspoon salt, and dash *pepper*. Add pork. Cover; marinate 2 hours or overnight in refrigerator, stirring occasionally. Drain pork, reserving marinade. Pat meat dry. In skillet brown pork in *half* of the hot oil. Add reserved marinade. Bring to boiling; reduce heat. Simmer, uncovered, about 45 minutes or till liquid is almost evaporated. Skim off fat and remove bay leaves.

Meanwhile, cook onions and pimiento in the remaining hot oil till onion is tender. Add the clams, the ½ teaspoon salt, and the ¼ teaspoon pepper. Cover and cook 5 to 7 minutes or till shells open (discard any that do not open). Add pork mixture to clam mixture; heat through. Serves 8.

Lamb-Eggplant Avgolemono *pictured on page 102* Greece

Though prepared in numerous ways throughout the year in Greece, for the Easter feast lamb traditionally is roasted over a spit.

"Avgolemono" is Greece's most popular sauce, "avgo" meaning egg, and "lemono," lemon. Superstitious villagers make a kissing sound as the broth is stirred into the eggs to prevent the mixture from curdling.

6 lamb shoulder chops, cut ¾ inch thick
2 tablespoons olive oil *or* cooking oil
1 medium onion, chopped
2 cups beef broth
½ teaspoon dried dillweed
1 large eggplant, peeled and cut into 12 strips
1 cup sliced celery
2 eggs, separated
¼ teaspoon finely shredded lemon peel
2 tablespoons lemon juice
2 tablespoons snipped parsley
Lemon slices
Shredded lemon peel

Sprinkle lamb with salt and pepper. Slowly brown chops, *half* at a time, on both sides in hot oil. Remove; set aside. Add onion; cook till tender. Drain off fat. Stir in beef broth and dillweed. Return all meat. Bring to boiling; reduce heat. Cover; simmer 20 minutes. Add eggplant; cook 15 minutes more. Add celery; cook 10 minutes more. Drain, reserving ¾ cup liquid. Transfer to serving platter; keep warm.

In mixer bowl beat egg yolks about 5 minutes or till thick and lemon colored. Thoroughly wash beaters; beat egg whites to stiff peaks. Fold egg yolks into whites. Gradually stir the reserved liquid, ¼ teaspoon lemon peel, and the lemon juice into eggs. Cook and stir for 7 minutes or till thickened. *Do not boil.* Pour over meat. Garnish with parsley, lemon slices, and additional lemon peel. Serves 6.

Chicken in Pepitoria Spain

The saffron, chicken, and rice flavor combination of *Chicken in Pepitoria* is reminiscent of the famous Spanish paella. In paella, however, rice cooks together with all the meats and vegetables in a special shallow, round paella pan.

1 2½- to 3-pound broiler-fryer chicken, cut up
¼ cup all-purpose flour
2 tablespoons cooking oil
3 cloves garlic, minced
½ cup sliced green onion
½ cup sliced fresh mushrooms
1 cup chicken broth
1 cup dry white wine
1 tablespoon dried parsley flakes
1 bay leaf
2 hard-cooked eggs, sieved
¼ cup ground almonds
¼ cup soft bread crumbs
⅛ teaspoon ground saffron
Hot cooked rice

Rinse chicken pieces; pat dry. In a paper or plastic bag combine flour, 1 teaspoon *salt*, and ¼ teaspoon *pepper*. Add chicken, a few pieces at a time; shake to coat. In a skillet brown chicken on all sides in hot oil about 15 minutes. Remove and set aside; reserve oil. Cook garlic, onion, and mushrooms in reserved hot oil till onion is tender. Drain off fat. Stir chicken broth, wine, parsley, and bay leaf into onion mixture. Return chicken to skillet. Bring to boiling; reduce heat. Cover and simmer 45 minutes or till chicken is tender. Transfer chicken to platter; keep warm. Remove bay leaf; skim fat.

For sauce, combine eggs, almonds, bread crumbs, and saffron; stir into skillet. Cook and stir till thickened and bubbly. Pour sauce over chicken. Serve with hot cooked rice. Makes 6 servings.

Chicken in Phyllo

1 cup chopped celery
¾ cup chopped onion
1 tablespoon butter *or* margarine
2 cups chopped cooked chicken *or* turkey
2 tablespoons chicken broth
2 teaspoons dried parsley flakes
½ teaspoon salt
½ teaspoon ground nutmeg
⅛ teaspoon pepper
1 beaten egg
8 ounces frozen phyllo dough, thawed (10 to 12 sheets)
6 tablespoons butter *or* margarine, melted
2 tablespoons butter *or* margarine
2 tablespoons all-purpose flour
¼ teaspoon salt
1¼ cups chicken broth
2 beaten egg yolks
4 teaspoons lemon juice

Cook celery and onion in the 1 tablespoon butter till tender. Add chicken or turkey and the 2 tablespoons broth. Cook, uncovered, till broth is evaporated, stirring occasionally. Stir in parsley, the ½ teaspoon salt, nutmeg, and pepper. Remove from heat. Stir in beaten egg. Set aside.

For *each* roll, stack *half* the sheets of phyllo dough, brushing between *each* layer with *some* of the 6 tablespoons butter or margarine. Spread *1¼ cups* of the chicken mixture over *each* phyllo stack to within 1 inch of edges. Fold in one short side and long sides. Roll as for jelly roll, starting with folded short side. Place, seam side down, on a lightly greased 13x9x2-inch baking dish. Brush with remaining melted butter; score with a sharp knife. Bake in 350° oven for 40 minutes.

For sauce, melt the 2 tablespoons butter. Stir in flour and the ¼ teaspoon salt. Add the 1¼ cups broth. Cook and stir till thickened and bubbly. Cook and stir 1 minute more. Combine beaten egg yolks and lemon juice. Stir about *half* of the hot mixture into egg yolk mixture. Return all to saucepan. Cook and stir 2 minutes more. Spoon sauce atop rolls. Makes 6 to 8 servings.

Cod and Potato Casserole

1 pound salt cod
1 cup chopped onion
2 tablespoons olive oil *or* cooking oil
1 10½-ounce can tomato puree
1 cup chicken broth
¼ cup snipped parsley
⅛ teaspoon pepper
3 medium potatoes (1 pound), peeled and sliced

In a bowl cover cod with cold water; soak 12 hours or overnight, changing water 3 or 4 times. Rinse cod. In a saucepan cover cod with cold water. Bring to boiling; reduce heat. Simmer, covered, for 20 minutes. Drain. Meanwhile, in saucepan cook onion in hot oil till tender but not brown. Stir in tomato puree, chicken broth, parsley, and pepper. Bring to boiling; reduce heat. Simmer, uncovered, for 15 minutes. Flake drained cod with a fork; gently stir cod and potatoes into tomato mixture. Turn into an ungreased 1½-quart casserole. Bake, covered, in 350° oven for 1¼ to 1½ hours, stirring once or twice. Makes 4 servings.

Linguine with White Clam Sauce

Clam recipes in Italy usually call for the vongole clam, a tiny clam found on the shores of the Adriatic Sea. A good substitute is a small clam, such as the cherrystone or littleneck clam.

24 fresh *or* frozen small clams in shell (see copy at left, page 104)
1 cup dry white wine
1 large clove garlic, minced
2 tablespoons olive oil *or* cooking oil
2 tablespoons butter *or* margarine
8 ounces hot cooked linguine
¼ cup snipped parsley
Grated Parmesan cheese

Place clams on rack in Dutch oven. Add wine. Cover tightly and steam for 5 to 7 minutes or till shells open. Strain broth through cheesecloth; reserve broth. Remove clams from shell (discard any that do not open). Cut up clams; set aside.

In large saucepan cook garlic in hot oil and butter or margarine. Stir in the reserved clam broth and dash *pepper.* Bring to boiling; reduce heat. Simmer, uncovered, for 10 to 15 minutes or till ½ cup liquid remains. Stir in clams; heat through. Toss clam mixture with linguine and parsley till well coated. Sprinkle with Parmesan. Serves 4.

MEDITERRANEAN

Huevos a la Flamenca

In Spain eggs appear in many forms and at different times of the day. They are scrambled, fried, stuffed, poached, or made into tortillas (paper-thin omelets).

Huevos a la Flamenca is an egg cassoulet native to Andulasia, home of the flamenco dance. The eggs are baked atop a thick, spicy "sofrito" sauce.

"Sofritos" are widely used in Spanish cookery. For "sofrito" (which means lightly fried), garlic, onion, and green pepper are sautéed in olive oil. Tomatoes, spices, and sometimes meats are added to make the sauce thick.

½ **pound chorizo** *or* **Italian sausage links, sliced**
1½ **cups diced fully cooked ham**
1 **medium onion, chopped**
1 **clove garlic, minced**
3 **large tomatoes, seeded, chopped, and drained**
1 **large sweet red** *or* **green pepper, chopped**
½ **cup tomato puree**
1 **tablespoon sliced pimiento**
½ **teaspoon dried thyme, crushed**
½ **teaspoon dried oregano, crushed**
⅛ **teaspoon ground red pepper**
6 **eggs**
1 **cup frozen cut asparagus, thawed**
¼ **cup frozen peas, thawed**

In skillet cook sausage, ham, onion, and garlic till onion is tender and sausage is brown. Drain off fat. Stir in tomatoes, red or green pepper, tomato puree, pimiento, thyme, oregano, and red pepper. Bring to boiling; reduce heat. Simmer, uncovered, about 15 minutes or till liquid is almost evaporated. Spoon sauce into six 8- or 10-ounce individual casseroles. Carefully break *one* egg at a time into a small dish; slide *one* into each casserole. Arrange asparagus and peas around eggs. Bake, uncovered, in a 350° oven about 20 minutes or till eggs are set. Sprinkle with paprika, if desired. Makes 6 servings.

Cheese-Filled Manicotti

¾ **pound ground beef**
¼ **pound bulk pork sausage**
2 **cups water**
1 **6-ounce can tomato paste**
½ **cup chopped onion**
1 **3-ounce can sliced mushrooms, drained**
1 **clove garlic, minced**
2 **teaspoons dried oregano, crushed**
1 **teaspoon sugar**
½ **teaspoon salt**
8 **manicotti shells**
1 **beaten egg**
1½ **cups ricotta** *or* **cream-style cottage cheese, drained**
¼ **cup grated Parmesan cheese**
2 **tablespoons snipped parsley**
½ **teaspoon salt**

In a large saucepan brown beef and sausage; drain off fat. Stir in water, tomato paste, onion, mushrooms, garlic, oregano, sugar, and the ½ teaspoon salt. Bring to boiling; reduce heat. Simmer, uncovered, for 20 minutes, stirring occasionally.

Meanwhile, cook manicotti shells in boiling salted water about 20 minutes or till tender; drain well. Combine egg, ricotta or cottage cheese, Parmesan cheese, parsley, and ½ teaspoon salt. Using small spoon, stuff about 3 *tablespoons* of the cheese mixture into *each* shell. Pour *half* of the meat sauce into a 12x7½x2-inch baking dish. Arrange stuffed manicotti in a row in the dish. Spoon remaining sauce atop. Bake, covered, in a 350° oven for 30 to 35 minutes. Pass additional Parmesan cheese, if desired. Makes 4 to 6 servings.

Spaghetti with Four Cheeses

6 **tablespoons butter** *or* **margarine**
3 **ounces fontina cheese, cubed**
3 **ounces gorgonzola cheese, cubed (¾ cup)**
3 **ounces Bel Paese cheese, cubed (¾ cup)**
¼ **teaspoon white pepper**
1 **cup whipping cream**
½ **cup grated Parmesan cheese**
Hot cooked spaghetti

In saucepan melt butter or margarine. Stir in fontina cheese, gorgonzola cheese, Bel Paese cheese, and white pepper. Cook and stir over low heat till cheeses are melted. *Do not boil.* Stir in whipping cream and Parmesan cheese. Heat through. Serve over spaghetti. Makes 4 or 5 servings.

In Italy, especially the southern portion, a main meal would be incomplete without pasta.

Pasta has been the national dish of Italy for so long that it is difficult to trace its origin. Some say Marco Polo brought it with him from the Orient. Others say it was around even earlier as it is mentioned in ancient Greek and Roman literature.

Until the latter part of the 18th century, all pastas were shaped for stuffing. Then noodles came into vogue in court circles. The debut of the three-pronged fork followed shortly, enabling diners to eat the new form of pasta politely.

The invention of a spaghetti-making machine made dried pasta available to the masses. The machine so impressed Thomas Jefferson during his European travels that he introduced it to North Americans in 1790, involving the United States in a love affair with pasta that's lasted ever since.

Made from durum wheat flour and water, pasta can be yellow or, if spinach is added, green. Its many shapes each serve a specific purpose. Ravioli, manicotti, conchiglione, and cappelletti are usually stuffed. Long, thin pastas such as spaghetti, fettucine, vermicelli, and linguine are often topped with sauces. Lasagna noodles are used exclusively for lasagna, a layered casserole.

MEDITERRANEAN

Caldeirada Fish Stew

Portugal

Appropriately named "caldeirada a fregateira" (frigate cauldron), this spicy fish chowder usually is concocted aboard fishing boats from the day's catch. Since the ingredients depend so much upon the type of seafood available, the recipe varies from north to south. *Caldeirada Fish Stew* can include eel, swordfish, or squid as well as whitefish and shellfish. This chowder is often served over fried bread triangles.

¾ **pound fresh *or* frozen fish fillets**
½ **large green pepper, cut into ½-inch squares**
2 **tablespoons chopped onion**
2 **cloves garlic, minced**
1 **tablespoon olive oil**
1 **16-ounce can tomatoes, cut up**
½ **cup dry white wine**
¼ **cup tomato paste**
¼ **cup snipped parsley**
1 **bay leaf**
¾ **teaspoon ground coriander**
½ **teaspoon ground nutmeg**
¼ **teaspoon ground red pepper**
1 **8-ounce can whole oysters**
1 **7-ounce can crab meat, flaked and cartilage removed**
½ **lemon, sliced**
6 **slices French bread, toasted**

Thaw fish, if frozen. With a sharp knife cut the fish fillets into 1-inch pieces; set aside.

In a 3-quart saucepan cook green pepper, onion, and garlic in hot oil till tender but not brown. Add *undrained* tomatoes, wine, tomato paste, parsley, bay leaf, coriander, nutmeg, red pepper, and 1 cup *water.* Bring to boiling; reduce heat. Cover and simmer 20 minutes.

Add fish pieces, *undrained* oysters, *undrained* crab meat, and lemon slices to tomato mixture. Return to boiling; reduce heat. Cover and simmer 5 to 7 minutes or till fish flakes easily when tested with a fork. Remove bay leaf. To serve, ladle the soup over the toast in individual serving bowls. Serves 6.

Garbanzo Bean Soup

Italy

Dried beans and lentils have been popular in Italy since the days of Pompeii, when garbanzo beans or chick-peas and bacon were sealed in clay pots for exportation all over the Roman Empire.

This *Garbanzo Bean Soup* from Tuscany calls for rice, but other versions specify pasta.

2 **cups dry garbanzo beans**
16 **cups water**
1 **8-ounce can tomato sauce**
2 **cloves garlic, minced**
2 **teaspoons salt**
1 **teaspoon dried rosemary, crushed**
¼ **teaspoon pepper**
3 **cups cooked rice**
¼ **cup snipped parsley**

Rinse beans. In a Dutch oven combine beans and *8 cups* of the water. Bring to boiling; reduce heat and simmer 2 minutes. Remove from heat. Cover; let stand 1 hour. (Or, soak beans in water overnight in a covered pan.) Drain beans and rinse. Combine rinsed beans and remaining 8 cups of water. Stir in tomato sauce, garlic, salt, rosemary, and pepper. Bring to boiling; reduce heat. Cover and simmer 1½ to 2 hours or till beans are tender.

With slotted spoon transfer *2 cups* of the cooked beans to blender container; add *2 cups* of the cooking liquid. Cover and blend till smooth; return to Dutch oven. Add cooked rice and parsley. Heat through. Makes 8 to 10 side-dish servings.

Caldo Gallego

Spain

The Galacian version of the Spanish "cocido" or stew, *Caldo Gallego,* is generally flavored with cured pork shoulder and aged salt pork. Some like to serve the thin dark broth or "caldo" alongside the pork shoulder and turnip greens.

¾ **cup dry great northern beans**
8 **cups water**
½ **pound chorizo *or* Italian sausage links, sliced**
¼ **pound salt pork *or* bacon, diced**
2 **turnips, peeled and sliced**
1 **medium red onion, sliced**
1 **clove garlic, minced**
1 **teaspoon salt**
¼ **teaspoon pepper**
1 **10-ounce package frozen turnip greens *or* chopped spinach**
1 **cup chopped cabbage**

In a 4-quart Dutch oven combine beans and *4 cups* of the water. Bring to boiling; reduce heat and simmer 2 minutes. Remove from heat. Cover; let stand 1 hour. (Or, soak beans in the water overnight in a covered pan.) Drain beans and rinse. In same Dutch oven or kettle combine rinsed beans and remaining 4 cups water. Bring to boiling; reduce heat. Cover and simmer 30 minutes.

Meanwhile, cook sausage and salt pork till brown. Drain off fat. Add sausage, salt pork, turnips, red onion, garlic, salt, and pepper to beans. Return to boiling; reduce heat. Cover and simmer 20 minutes. Add turnip greens and cabbage; return to boiling. Reduce heat and simmer, uncovered, 10 minutes more. Makes 6 side-dish servings.

Caldo Verde   Portugal

Authentic *Caldo Verde* recipes call for "couve" cabbage, a large green cabbage grown in Portugal. Instead of "couve," use green cabbage, kale, spinach, or lettuce.

- **2 medium potatoes, peeled and quartered**
- **1 tablespoon olive oil**
- **4 cups chicken broth**
- **½ small head cabbage, shredded (3 cups)**
- **⅓ cup chopped onion**
- **¼ teaspoon pepper**

In a saucepan cook potatoes in boiling salted water for 20 to 25 minutes or till tender; drain. Add olive oil and mash; set aside.

In a saucepan bring chicken broth to boiling; stir in cabbage, onion, and pepper. Cook, uncovered, for 5 minutes or till cabbage is tender.

To serve, spoon potatoes into 4 individual serving bowls. Ladle soup atop. Makes 4 servings.

Gazpacho   Spain

Although the most popular version of *Gazpacho* is chilled fresh tomato soup, it can be more than that. Some versions are served hot, with meatballs or chicken or even grapes. Others exclude tomatoes entirely and call for very little liquid. Regardless of the differences, all gazpachos do contain vegetables and garlic.

- **4 medium tomatoes**
- **1 cup chopped cucumber**
- **¼ cup chopped green pepper**
- **¼ cup finely chopped onion**
- **¼ cup sliced pitted ripe olives**
- **1 small clove garlic, minced**
- **1 cup cold water**
- **2 tablespoons wine vinegar**
- **1 tablespoon olive oil *or* salad oil**
- **½ teaspoon sugar**
- **½ teaspoon salt**
- **⅛ teaspoon ground cumin**
- **⅛ teaspoon pepper**
- **Croutons *or* sieved hardcooked egg (optional)**

Plunge tomatoes into boiling water for 30 seconds to loosen skins; remove and immerse in cold water. With a knife, remove the loosened skin. Coarsely chop tomatoes (should have about 1½ cups).

In a mixing bowl combine chopped tomatoes, cucumber, green pepper, onion, olives, and garlic. Stir in cold water, vinegar, oil, sugar, salt, cumin, and pepper. Cover and chill thoroughly. Garnish *each* serving with croutons or sieved egg, if desired. Makes 6 to 8 servings.

Peasant Salad   Greece

Also called summer, village, or Greek salad, *Peasant Salad's* character changes subtly as you substitute different fresh vegetables during the summer.

- **1 clove garlic, halved**
- **1 small head romaine, torn**
- **1 head escarole *or* bibb lettuce, torn (3 cups)**
- **3 medium tomatoes**
- **1 medium cucumber, sliced**
- **1 medium green pepper, cut into thin rings**
- **1 small onion, thinly sliced and separated into rings**
- **1 cup crumbled feta cheese**
- **½ cup pitted ripe olives**
- **⅓ cup snipped parsley**
- **Greek Dressing**

Rub wooden salad bowl with cut clove of garlic; discard garlic. Combine torn greens in bowl. Cut tomatoes into wedges. Add tomato, cucumber, green pepper, and onion rings. Top with feta cheese, olives, and parsley. Cover and chill. Just before serving, pour Greek Dressing over salad. Toss to coat vegetables. Makes 8 to 12 servings.

Greek Dressing: In screw-top jar combine ½ cup *olive oil;* ¼ cup *red wine vinegar;* ½ teaspoon *salt;* ¼ teaspoon dried *oregano,* crushed; and ¼ teaspoon freshly ground *pepper.* Cover and shake well to mix. Chill thoroughly. Shake again just before serving.

MEDITERRANEAN

Pisto

Spain

Families in central and northwestern Spain savor this peppery potpourri of braised vegetables. Some regional versions contain eggs, either scrambled or poached on top.

1 small onion, chopped
1 clove garlic, minced
2 tablespoons olive oil *or* cooking oil
2 medium tomatoes, peeled and chopped
1 medium zucchini, sliced
1 small eggplant, unpeeled and cubed
1 small green pepper, cut into strips
1 small sweet red pepper, cut into strips
½ cup diced fully cooked ham
¼ cup dry sherry
½ teaspoon dried basil, crushed
¼ teaspoon salt
¼ teaspoon pepper

In a large skillet cook onion and garlic in hot oil till tender but not brown. Stir in tomatoes, zucchini slices, eggplant cubes, green pepper strips, red pepper strips, ham, sherry, basil, salt, and pepper. Cover and cook 5 minutes or till eggplant and zucchini are tender. Makes 6 servings.

Fresh Vegetable Marinade

Italy

3 medium tomatoes, sliced
1 small red onion *or* mild white onion, thinly sliced and separated into rings
1 medium cucumber, sliced
1 medium green pepper, cut into rings
¼ cup chopped pitted ripe olives
⅓ cup vinegar
2 tablespoons dry red wine
1 tablespoon sugar
1 tablespoon salad oil
½ teaspoon dried basil, crushed
¼ teaspoon salt
Dash pepper
Lettuce leaves (optional)

In a bowl combine tomato slices, onion rings, cucumber slices, green pepper rings, and chopped olives. In a screw-top jar combine vinegar, red wine, sugar, salad oil, basil, salt, and pepper. Cover and shake well to mix. Pour dressing over vegetables. Cover and chill several hours or overnight; spoon dressing over vegetables occasionally. Lift vegetables from dressing with slotted spoon. Serve on lettuce leaves, if desired. Makes 6 to 8 servings.

Stuffed Escarole

Italy

2 cups soft bread crumbs
¼ cup Romano cheese
¼ cup grated Parmesan cheese
1 clove garlic, minced
2 tablespoons raisins
2 tablespoons pine nuts
1 tablespoon snipped parsley
Dash pepper
2 small heads escarole
1 clove garlic, minced
1 tablespoon olive oil *or* cooking oil
1 cup water

For stuffing, in a mixing bowl combine bread crumbs, Romano cheese, Parmesan cheese, 1 clove minced garlic, raisins, pine nuts, parsley, and pepper; set aside. Spread leaves of escarole gently to wash thoroughly, leaving head intact. Turn upside down and drain well. Open head; spreading leaves till center is exposed. Place *half* the stuffing in center of *each* head; close and tie with string. In large saucepan cook 1 clove garlic in hot oil till golden. Add water. Place escarole in pan. Cover tightly and cook over medium heat about 8 minutes. Turn escarole over; cook, covered, 5 minutes more or till escarole is tender. To serve, slice escarole crosswise. Makes 6 to 8 servings.

Ensalada de Esparragos

Both green and white asparagus varieties are native to Spain. Ancient Romans used to import the fresh spears for their feasts from what was then called Hispania.

This vegetable arrangement with its eye-catching garnishes exemplifies the typical Spanish salad.

Pictured
Ensalada de Esparragos, Bolillo Rolls (see recipe, page 116)

18 **stalks fresh asparagus**
    ***or* one 10-ounce package frozen asparagus spears**
⅓ **cup olive oil *or* salad oil**
⅓ **cup wine vinegar**
2 **tablespoons sliced green onion**
½ **teaspoon salt**
    Lettuce leaves
3 **medium tomatoes, halved and sliced crosswise**
12 **pimiento-stuffed olives, sliced**
1 **small sweet red *or* green pepper, cut into strips**

For fresh asparagus, wash stalks and scrape off scales. Break off woody bases at point where stalks snap easily. In a 10-inch skillet place whole asparagus spears in small amount of boiling salted water. To avoid overcooking, prop tips out of water with crumpled foil. Cover and cook about 10 minutes or till crisp-tender. (Or, cook frozen asparagus according to package directions.) Drain and cool.

For dressing, in a screw-top jar combine olive oil or salad oil, vinegar, green onion, and salt. Cover and shake. Chill thoroughly. On a lettuce-lined salad plate, arrange asparagus, halved tomato slices, sliced olives, and pepper strips. Shake dressing again just before serving. Pour over salad. Serves 6.

111

MEDITERRANEAN

Spaghetti with Marinara Sauce   Italy

Perhaps because this meatless tomato sauce is commonly found in seaside Naples, it has been dubbed "marinara" or sailors' sauce.

2 **medium carrots, finely chopped**
1 **large onion, chopped**
2 **cloves garlic, minced**
2 **tablespoons cooking oil**
2 **28-ounce cans tomatoes, cut up**
1 **teaspoon sugar**
1 **teaspoon salt**
1 **teaspoon dried oregano, crushed**
   Dash pepper
   Dash ground red pepper
   Hot cooked spaghetti, linguine, or fine noodles
   Grated Parmesan cheese (optional)

For sauce, in a 3-quart saucepan cook carrots, onion, and garlic in hot cooking oil till tender but not brown. Stir in *undrained* tomatoes, sugar, salt, oregano, pepper, and red pepper. Bring to boiling; reduce heat. Simmer, uncovered, for 45 to 60 minutes or till desired consistency.

Serve sauce over the hot pasta. Pass Parmesan cheese, if desired. Makes 6 side-dish servngs.

Lemon-Basil Carrots   Greece

1 **pound tiny new carrots *or* medium carrots, cut into 2½-inch pieces**
2 **tablespoons butter *or* margarine**
1 **tablespoon lemon juice**
½ **teaspoon garlic salt**
½ **teaspoon dried basil, crushed**
   Dash pepper

In a saucepan cook carrots in boiling salted water for 10 to 20 minutes or till tender. Drain. In a saucepan melt butter or margarine. Stir in lemon juice, garlic salt, basil, and pepper. Add carrots; toss gently to coat. Makes 4 to 6 servings.

Spinach-Stuffed Conchiglioni   *pictured on back cover*   Italy

4 **ounces large-shell macaroni (conchiglioni) *or* manicotti shells**
1 **pound fresh spinach *or* one 10-ounce package frozen chopped spinach**
1 **tablespoon finely chopped onion**
1 **tablespoon butter *or* margarine**
1 **beaten egg**
⅔ **cup ricotta cheese**
⅓ **cup grated Parmesan cheese**
⅔ **cup light cream**
⅔ **cup dairy sour cream**
¼ **cup chopped prosciutto, mortadella, *or* fully cooked ham**
⅛ **teaspoon white pepper**
   Dash ground nutmeg

Cook pasta in large amount of boiling salted water for 23 to 25 minutes or till tender; drain well.

For filling, thoroughly wash fresh spinach leaves. In a large covered saucepan cook fresh spinach in a small amount of boiling salted water for 3 to 5 minutes. (Or, cook frozen spinach according to package directions.) Drain well. To remove excess moisture, squeeze spinach between several layers of paper toweling. Chop spinach.

In a skillet cook onion in hot butter or margarine till tender but not brown. In a mixing bowl combine spinach, egg, ricotta, Parmesan, and onion mixture.

To stuff, place *one rounded tablespoon* of the filling in *each* conchiglioni shell or ¼ *cup* of the filling in *each* manicotti shell. Place the shells in a 12x7½x2-inch baking dish. Cover; bake in a 350° oven for 15 minutes.

For sauce, stir together light cream and sour cream; add prosciutto, mortadella, or ham and white pepper; pour over pasta. Sprinkle with nutmeg. Bake, uncovered, in a 350° oven for 10 minutes or till heated through. Makes 4 side-dish servings.

Straw and Hay   *pictured on page 102*   Italy

Yellow pasta and green spinach pasta combine to give this exquisite Italian dish the appearance of "straw and hay."

¾ **pound fresh asparagus, bias sliced into 1-inch pieces,** *or* **one 8-ounce package frozen cut asparagus**
¼ **cup sliced green onion**
1 **tablespoon butter** *or* **margarine**
1 **cup light cream**
¼ **teaspoon salt**
⅛ **teaspoon ground nutmeg**
⅛ **teaspoon pepper**
1 **tablespoon lemon juice**
5 **ounces hot cooked linguine** *or* **fettucine**
5 **ounces hot cooked green linguine** *or* **fettucine**

In a covered saucepan cook fresh asparagus in small amount of boiling salted water for 8 to 10 minutes or till crisp-tender. (Or, cook frozen asparagus according to package directions.) Drain well.

In a saucepan cook green onion in hot butter or margarine till tender, but not brown. Stir in cream, salt, nutmeg, and pepper. Cook, uncovered, about 5 minutes or till slightly thickened. Stir in asparagus and lemon juice; heat through.

Combine pasta. Pour asparagus mixture over pasta. Toss to coat. Makes 6 to 8 side-dish servings.

Risotto with Giblets   Italy

Risotto in northern Italy involves a special technique to cook the rice. The rice simmers, tightly covered, in a seasoned broth until the mixture is creamy and the rice is "al dente" (slightly chewy).

Italians use arborio wide-grain rice when making "risotto"; but long grain rice is a good substitute.

½ **pound chicken** *or* **turkey giblets, chopped**
1 **cup sliced fresh mushrooms**
⅓ **cup chopped green pepper**
3 **tablespoons butter** *or* **margarine**
¾ **cup water**
¼ **cup dry sherry**
2 **tablespoons tomato paste**
¼ **teaspoon salt**
¼ **teaspoon dried sage, crushed Dash pepper**
1 **cup chicken broth**
⅔ **cup short, medium,** *or* **long grain rice Grated Parmesan cheese**

In a skillet cook giblets, mushrooms, and green pepper in butter or margarine till giblets are brown. Stir in water, sherry, tomato paste, salt, sage, and pepper. Simmer, uncovered, for 15 minutes, stirring occasionally. Stir chicken broth and rice into giblet mixture. Bring to rolling boil; reduce heat. Cover tightly and simmer for 15 minutes; *do not lift cover.* Remove from heat. Let stand, covered, for 10 minutes. Serve immediately. Sprinkle with Parmesan cheese. Makes 6 side-dish servings.

MEDITERRANEAN

The influences of the Greek Orthodox church pervade Grecian holiday food traditions.

Easter and its preparation period is the most important time of the Greek Orthodox calendar. A three-week period known as "Aprokries" (from meat) precedes the 40-day Lenten fast. Throughout "Aprokries," Greeks feast to rid their pantries of all the foods forbidden during Lent.

Fasting, which commences on Clean Monday (two days before Ash Wednesday), is meatless with the exception of two days — on Palm Sunday and on the Annunciation of the Virgin Mary (March 25, also Greece's Independence Day).

On Holy Thursday, three days before Easter, Greek homemakers bake "lambropsomo" bread (also known as "tsourki") and *Koulourakia Cookies* (see recipe, page 117).

Though they are now associated with a Christian holiday, *Koulourakia Cookies* were first baked during pagan times. Ancient Minoans believed that the snake-coil-shaped cookies held healing powers.

The fast is broken on Easter. A tender spring lamb is roasted over a spit and a soup, "maryerista," is made from its internal organs. The Greeks eat the "lambropsomo" bread, *Koulourakia Cookies*, and red-dyed eggs, rejoicing at the resurrection of their Savior.

Massa Sovada Bread

Portugal

The recipe for *Massa Sovada Bread* (pictured opposite) is the basic dough for many Portuguese sweet breads. Originally from Azores, this bread is now eaten on "Natal a Portugesa" the twelfth night after Christmas. A cross scored on top of the bread signifies Christ, the Savior.

4 to 4½ cups all-purpose flour
2 packages active dry yeast
¾ cup sugar
¾ cup milk
6 tablespoons butter *or* margarine
½ teaspoon salt
2 eggs
1 beaten egg

In a large mixer bowl combine *1½ cups* of the flour and the yeast. In a saucepan heat together sugar, milk, butter or margarine, and salt just till warm (115° to 120°); stir constantly. Add to flour mixture; add the 2 eggs. Beat at low speed of electric mixer for ½ minute, scraping bowl. Beat 3 minutes at high speed. Stir in as much of the remaining flour as you can mix in with a spoon.

On a lightly floured surface, knead in enough of the remaining flour to make a moderately stiff dough that is smooth and elastic (8 to 10 minutes total). Shape into a ball. Place in a lightly greased bowl; turn once. Cover; let rise in warm place till double (2¼ to 2½ hours). Punch down. Cover; let rest 10 minutes. Shape into a round loaf. Place on a greased baking sheet. Pat or roll to a circle 8 inches in diameter. Cover; let rise till double (about 50 minutes). With a sharp knife, cut a cross on top of the loaf. Brush with 1 beaten egg. Bake in a 350° oven 20 minutes. Cover with foil. Bake 25 to 35 minutes more. Cool on wire rack. Makes 1 loaf.

Christopsomo Bread *pictured on front cover*

Greece

A Byzantine cross studded with whole walnuts decorates *Christopsomo Bread,* or Christ's bread, which is customarily served at Christmas.

The cross is a reminder of the Byzantine Empire which cradled the Eastern Orthodox doctrine when the Christian church split in 1054.

2¾ to 3 cups all-purpose flour
1 package active dry yeast
⅔ cup milk
¼ cup butter *or* margarine
3 tablespoons sugar
½ teaspoon salt
2 eggs
5 unshelled walnuts
1 beaten egg
1 teaspoon sesame seed

Stir together *1½ cups* of the flour and the yeast. Heat together milk, butter or margarine, sugar, and salt just till warm (115° to 120°); stir constantly. Add to flour mixture; add the 2 eggs. Beat at low speed of electric mixer ½ minute, scraping bowl. Beat 3 minutes at high speed. Stir in as much of the remaining flour as you can mix in with a spoon.

On a lightly floured surface, knead in enough of the remaining flour to make a moderately soft dough that is smooth and elastic (3 to 5 minutes total). Shape into a ball. Place dough in lightly greased bowl; turn once. Cover; let rise in warm place till double (1¼ to 1½ hours). Punch dough down; divide dough into thirds. Cover; let rest 10 minutes. Remove *one-third* of the dough; divide into 8 pieces. Roll each piece to a 12-inch rope. Twist 2 ropes together; repeat with remaining ropes, making 4 twisted ropes in all. Place *two* of the twisted ropes around inside edge of greased 9-inch round cake pan. Set aside remaining twists. Shape remaining *two-thirds* of dough into ball; flatten to an 8-inch round loaf. Fit inside the twists in cake pan. Make a cross atop loaf of bread with reserved twisted ropes. Press an unshelled walnut in center of cross and at ends of ropes. Cover; let rise in warm place till nearly double (30 to 45 minutes). Brush top with 1 beaten egg. Sprinkle with sesame seed. Bake in a 350° oven for 30 to 35 minutes or till bread tests done. Cover with foil last 15 minutes of baking. Remove from pan; cool on wire rack. Makes 1 loaf.

MEDITERRANEAN

King's Cake
Portugal

With candied pineapple, cherries, and walnuts adorning it, *King's Cake* resembles a royal crown. Symbolic of the crowns of the three wise kings, *King's Cake* is served on "Natal a Portugesa" — January 6 — the date chosen to celebrate the wise men's arrival in Bethlehem to visit the Christ Child.

5½ **to 6 cups all-purpose flour**
2 **packages active dry yeast**
1¼ **cups milk**
1 **cup sugar**
½ **cup butter** *or* **margarine, cut up**
1 **teaspoon salt**
3 **beaten eggs**
½ **cup raisins**
½ **cup diced mixed candied fruits and peels**
½ **cup chopped walnuts**
2 **cups sifted powdered sugar**
2 **to 3 tablespoons milk**
   Candied pineapple *or*
      candied cherries
   Walnut halves

In a large mixer bowl combine *2 cups* of the flour and the yeast. In a saucepan heat milk, sugar, butter or margarine, and salt till warm (115° to 120°) and butter or margarine is almost melted; stir constantly. Add to flour mixture; add eggs. Beat at low speed of electric mixer for ½ minute, scraping bowl. Beat 3 minutes at high speed. Stir in raisins, fruits and peels, and ½ cup chopped walnuts. Stir in as much of the remaining flour as you can mix in with a spoon. Turn out onto a lightly floured surface. Knead in enough of the remaining flour to make a moderately stiff dough that is smooth and elastic (3 to 5 minutes total). Shape into a ball. Place dough in a greased bowl; turn once to grease surface. Cover; let rise till double (2 to 2½ hours). Punch dough down; divide in half. Cover; let rest 10 minutes. Shape each *half* into a roll about 18 inches long. Join ends to form a ring about 8 inches in diameter. Place *each* ring in a greased 10-inch tube pan. Cover; let rise till almost double (about 1 hour).

Bake in a 350° oven 25 to 30 minutes or till golden brown. Remove from pan. Cool on wire rack. For icing, stir together powdered sugar and 2 to 3 tablespoons milk to make an icing of drizzling consistency. Drizzle icing over cake. Garnish with candied pineapple or candied cherries and walnut halves. Makes 2 cakes.

Bolillo   *pictured on page 111*
Spain

7 **to 7¼ cups all-purpose flour**
2 **packages active dry yeast**
2½ **cups water**
1 **tablespoon sugar**
1 **tablespoon salt**
1 **tablespoon shortening**
   Yellow cornmeal
1 **egg white**
1 **tablespoon water**

In a mixer bowl combine *3 cups* of the flour and the yeast. Heat the 2½ cups water, sugar, salt, and shortening just till warm (115° to 120°) and shortening is almost melted; stir constantly. Add to flour mixture. Beat at low speed of electric mixer for ½ minute, scraping sides of bowl constantly. Beat 3 minutes at high speed. Stir in as much of the remaining flour as you can mix in with a spoon.

Turn out onto a lightly floured surface. Knead in enough remaining flour to make a moderately soft dough that is smooth and elastic (3 to 5 minutes total). Shape into a ball. Place in greased bowl; turn once to grease surface. Cover; let rise in warm place till double (1 to 1½ hours).

Punch down; divide dough into 18 portions. Cover; let rest 10 minutes. Shape each portion into an oval 5 inches long. Pull and twist ends slightly. Place on greased cornmeal-sprinkled baking sheets. Make a lengthwise cut ¼-inch deep on top of each roll. Beat the egg white and the 1 tablespoon water just till foamy; brush rolls. Cover; let rolls rise till double (about 1 hour).

Bake in a 375° oven for 20 minutes. Brush again with egg white mixture. Bake 10 to 15 minutes longer or till golden. Makes 18 rolls.

Koulourakia Cookies

Greece

Pictured
King's Cake

3 cups all-purpose flour
2 teaspoons baking powder
½ teaspoon baking soda
¼ teaspoon salt
¼ teaspoon ground cinnamon
¼ teaspoon ground nutmeg
½ cup unsalted butter
¼ cup shortening
½ cup sugar
1 egg
1 teaspoon vanilla
½ cup whipping cream
1 beaten egg
1 teaspoon water
Sesame seed

Stir together flour, baking powder, baking soda, salt, cinnamon, and nutmeg. In a mixer bowl beat butter and shortening on medium speed of electric mixer for 30 seconds. Add sugar and beat till fluffy. Add 1 egg and vanilla; beat well. Add dry ingredients and whipping cream alternately to butter mixture and beat till well mixed. Cover and chill 1 hour.

On a floured surface, using *1 tablespoon* of the dough for each cookie, roll dough into 6-inch lengths. Shape into coils or spirals. (*Or,* into wreaths, pressing to seal ends together.) Place on a greased cookie sheet. Combine beaten egg and the water. Brush cookies with egg mixture; sprinkle with sesame seed. Bake in a 325° oven for 20 minutes. Cool on a wire rack. Makes 2½ to 4 dozen cookies.

117

MEDITERRANEAN

Melamakárona Cookies

*Melamakárona
Cookies,* also known as
"phoenékia," date
back to the 14th cen-
tury. They're named for
the Phoenician mer-
chants who introduced ·
these honey-dipped
cookies to Greece.·
Make these traditional
New Year's Eve treats
fancier by imprinting
them with a cookie
stamp.

⅓ cup cooking oil
½ cup unsalted butter, softened
⅓ cup sugar
1 tablespoon orange juice
1 teaspoon baking powder
½ teaspoon baking soda
1¾ to 2 cups all-purpose flour
¾ cup sugar
½ cup water
⅓ cup honey
⅓ cup finely chopped walnuts

In a mixer bowl beat cooking oil into butter on
medium speed of electric mixer for 30 seconds.
Add the ⅓ cup sugar and beat till fluffy. Add
orange juice, baking powder, and baking soda;
beat well. Gradually add enough flour to make a
medium-soft dough; shape into ovals 2 inches long.
Bake on ungreased cookie sheet in a 350° oven for
20 to 25 minutes. Cool.

Meanwhile, in a saucepan combine the ¾ cup
sugar, the water, and honey. Bring to boiling; reduce heat. Simmer, uncovered, 5 minutes. Dip
cooled cookies into warm syrup. Sprinkle immediately with nuts. Dry on a wire rack. Makes 2½
to 3 dozen.

Galaktoboúreko Pastry

Galaktoboúreko Pastry
represents the family of
sweet phyllo pastries
that Grecian cooks
adopted from the
Middle East.

One famous phyllo
dough recipe is bak-
lava, a spiced nut-
filled pastry drenched
with honey syrup.
Called the sweet of
1,000 layers, baklava is
usually served in the
midafternoon with cof-
fee or cold water rather
than as a dessert.

Spread a damp
cloth over phyllo sheets
whenever working with
them. This prevents
them from drying out
before being used.

2 cups milk
¼ cup quick-cooking farina
½ cup butter *or* margarine
⅓ cup sugar
3 tablespoons brandy *or* peach
    brandy (1½ ounces)
1 teaspoon finely shredded
    orange peel
½ teaspoon vanilla
5 egg yolks
⅓ cup sugar
5 egg whites
8 ounces frozen phyllo dough,
    thawed (10 to 12 sheets)
¼ to ½ cup butter *or* margarine,
    melted
¾ cup sugar
½ cup water
1 teaspoon finely shredded
    orange peel
4 inches stick cinnamon
3 whole cloves
3 tablespoons brandy *or* peach
    brandy (1½ ounces)
½ teaspoon vanilla

In a saucepan bring milk to a gentle boil. Stir in
farina. Cook and stir till mixture is thickened and
smooth. Add the ½ cup butter or margarine and ⅓
cup sugar; stir till butter is melted. Remove from
heat; stir in 3 tablespoons brandy, 1 teaspoon
orange peel, and ½ teaspoon vanilla. Cover surface with waxed paper; cool. Beat egg yolks with
⅓ cup sugar about 5 minutes or till thick and lemon
colored. Thoroughly wash beaters. Beat egg whites
till stiff peaks form. Fold egg yolks into whites. Fold in
farina mixture. Place *1 sheet* of the phyllo in bottom
of a greased 13x9x2-inch baking pan; cut and
patch to fit. Brush with *some* of the ¼ to ½ cup
melted butter or margarine. Repeat with phyllo and
butter till you've used *half* of the phyllo. Pour egg
mixture over. Cover with remaining phyllo, brushing
butter between each layer. Score top layer of
phyllo into 2-inch diamonds. Bake in a 350° oven for
45 to 50 minutes or till golden.

Meanwhile for syrup, in a saucepan combine
the ¾ cup sugar, water, 1 teaspoon orange peel,
cinnamon, and cloves. Bring to boiling; reduce
heat. Simmer, uncovered, for 15 minutes. Remove
from heat. Remove cinnamon and cloves; discard.
Stir in 3 tablespoons brandy and ½ teaspoon vanilla. Cool. Gradually pour cooled syrup over
phyllo. Cool. Makes 16 servings.

Limonada

Limonada is a refreshing wine beverage popular in the unique Basque region of northern Spain. There, men look upon eating and drinking with such gusto they have formed exclusive all-male gastronomic societies. Members share with each other their latest culinary ventures, upholding the Basque belief that the kitchen is a man's place.

3 to 4 lemons
2 cups dry red wine
2 cups dry white wine
⅓ cup sugar
Ice cubes

For lemon spirals, thinly peel seven 6-inch long strips of lemon peel; set aside. Squeeze lemons to measure about 1 cup juice. Stir together lemon juice, red wine, white wine, and sugar. Chill the mixture thoroughly. To serve, pour over ice cubes in glasses. Garnish *each* serving with a lemon spiral. Makes about 7 (6-ounce) servings.

Coconut Tarts

Tart Pastry
3 beaten eggs
1½ cups sugar
6 tablespoons butter *or* margarine, melted
1 tablespoon lemon juice
⅛ teaspoon salt
1 3½-ounce can (1⅓ cups) flaked coconut

Prepare Tart Pastry. On a floured surface, roll pastry to ⅛-inch thickness. Cut into circles 3½ inches in diameter. Line 2½-inch fluted tart pans with pastry circles. Combine eggs, sugar, butter or margarine, lemon juice, and salt; stir in coconut. Spoon about *2 tablespoons* of the filling into each shell. Place filled tart shells on baking sheet or in shallow baking pan. Bake in a 400° oven for 20 minutes or till golden. Cool. Remove tarts from pans. Makes 24.
  Tart Pastry: In a medium mixing bowl stir together 2 cups all-purpose *flour* and 1 teaspoon *salt*. Cut in ⅔ cup *shortening or lard* till pieces are the size of small peas. Sprinkle with 6 to 7 tablespoons cold *water*, one tablespoon at a time. Gently toss with a fork till all is moistened.

Vitello Tonnato

1 2- to 2½-pound boneless veal roast
2 tablespoons olive oil *or* cooking oil
1 cup dry white wine
2 medium carrots, chopped
2 stalks celery, chopped
1 medium onion, chopped
1 clove garlic, minced
1 bay leaf
1 tablespoon snipped fresh thyme *or* 1 teaspoon dried thyme, crushed
1 teaspoon salt
1 3¾-ounce can tuna, drained
2 to 3 anchovy fillets
2 tablespoons lemon juice
1 egg yolk
¾ cup olive oil
1 tablespoon capers
Lemon slices
Sliced pitted ripe olives
Capers
Snipped parsley

In a Dutch oven brown meat on all sides in 2 tablespoons hot oil. Add wine, carrots, celery, onion, garlic, bay leaf, thyme, salt, ¼ teaspoon *pepper,* and 1 cup *water*. Bring to boiling; reduce heat. Cover; simmer for 1½ to 2 hours or till meat is tender. Remove meat from pan. Cool; cut into ¼-inch slices. (If desired, strain wine mixture; reserve for later use.)
  In a blender container combine tuna, anchovies, lemon juice, and egg yolk. Cover; blend till well mixed. With blender running slowly, gradually pour ¾ cup olive oil into blender container. (When necessary, stop blender and use rubber spatula to scrape down sides.) Blend till mixture is fairly smooth. Transfer tuna mixture to mixing bowl. Stir in the 1 tablespoon capers.
  Spread half of tuna mixture on serving platter. Place veal slices on tuna. Cover completely with remaining tuna mixture. Cover and chill overnight. Before serving as the first course, garnish with lemon slices, olives, capers, and parsley. Serves 18 to 20.

MEXICO

The Spanish conquest of Mexico left Spain richer not only in gold and silver, but also in new and delicious foods. To Spain, along with precious metals, went corn, tomatoes, peppers, and cacao beans from land long cultivated by Mayans, Toltecs, and Aztecs. Spain, in return, introduced new foods to the cuisines of Mexico. Rice, pork and dairy products, and Spanish favorites inherited from the years of Moorish conquest — almonds, citrus fruits, and sweet desserts — all found their way to Mexico.

Spanish and native Indian cooking styles melded to enhance Mexican cookery. To the traditional corn tortillas were added the wheat tortillas favored by the Spanish. Frying foods in lard, unheard of before the Spanish arrived with their pork supplies, became a standard cooking technique. Native Indians adopted the Spanish method of frying meat to complement their customary roasting and stewing preparations.

Mexican meals are characterized by the ever-present table sauces such as guacamole or "salsa cruda" (tomato sauce). And the characteristic flavor of Mexican dishes — not always hot — is derived from the blending of vegetables and finely ground dried chilies, herbs, and spices.

Though for numerous Mexicans a meal may consist of tortillas and beans, the elegant tradition of the Spanish "comida," the large midday dinner, still continues. The "comida" is characterized by its many courses, including: a soup; a pasta course; a poultry, meat, or fish main course; then cooked beans followed by dessert. And it all ends with a "siesta"!

Even a Mexican beverage reflects the nation's Indian-Spanish heritage. Hot chocolate, a worldwide favorite, was once an Aztec specialty reserved for royalty only. The Spanish sweetened it with sugar and cinnamon and introduced the world to a unique taste treat.

Pictured clockwise from back
Tequila Sunrise (see recipe, page 128), Shredded Beef Tostadas (see recipe, page 122), Sausage-Stuffed Zucchini (see recipe, page 125), Ceviche (see recipe, page 129), Tortilla Casserole (see recipe, page 125), and Custard and Fruit Dessert (see recipe, page 128).

MEXICO

Shredded Beef Tostadas   *pictured on page 120*

Mexican cooks use the tortilla in many interesting ways, and it's an absolute basic in their cookery. Wrapped around a variety of fillings, a tortilla can become a taco, an enchilada, a burrito, chimichanga, or flauta.

Large tortillas fried flat till crisp, then sprinkled with shredded cheese, bits of vegetables, and seasoned cooked meat are called tostadas.

1 **pound cooked beef chuck pot roast**
½ **cup water**
2 **tablespoons finely chopped onion**
1 **clove garlic, minced Cooking oil**
6 **8-inch flour tortillas**
2 **cups shredded lettuce**
2 **medium potatoes, cooked, peeled, chilled, and diced**
2 **tablespoons salad oil**
1 **tablespoon lemon juice**
1 **tablespoon vinegar**
2 **cups Refried Beans (see recipe, page 125)** *or* **one 16-ounce can refried beans**
2 **cups Guacamole con Tomatillos (see recipe, page 129)** *or* **two 6-ounce containers frozen avocado dip, thawed**
¾ **cup shredded cheddar** *or* **Monterey Jack** *or* **grated Parmesan cheese**

For shredded beef, in a skillet combine meat, water, onion, and garlic; cover and cook for 30 minutes or till most of the liquid is absorbed and meat will shred easily. Remove skillet from heat. Using two forks, pull meat apart into shreds.

In a heavy skillet heat ¼ inch cooking oil. Fry tortillas, one at a time, in hot oil for 20 to 40 seconds on each side or till crisp and golden. Drain on paper toweling. Wrap fried tortillas in foil and keep warm in a 250° oven.

In a mixing bowl combine shredded lettuce and diced potatoes. Stir together salad oil, lemon juice, and vinegar; toss with potato mixture.

Place tortillas on 6 dinner plates. Dividing ingredients equally among tortillas, layer ingredients for tostadas in the following order: beans, shredded beef, lettuce mixture, guacamole or avocado dip, and cheese. Makes 6 servings.

Stuffed Peppers with Walnut Sauce

When the Treaty of Cordoba was signed in 1821, it signified the end of Spanish domination of Mexican territories. To celebrate their independence, the loyal people of Puebla (now a Mexican state) created many dishes whose ingredients were chosen to match the colors of the Mexican flag — green, white, and red. One of the festive dishes served at the victory banquet was *Stuffed Peppers with Walnut Sauce*. This famous Mexican dish uses green peppers, a white walnut-cream cheese sauce, and red pomegranate seeds.

Walnut Sauce
1 **pound ground beef**
½ **cup chopped onion**
1 **clove garlic, minced**
1 **10½-ounce can tomato purée**
1 **medium apple, peeled, cored, and chopped**
½ **cup raisins**
¼ **cup snipped cilantro** *or* **parsley**
¼ **cup slivered almonds, toasted**
1 **tablespoon vinegar**
¾ **teaspoon salt**
¼ **teaspoon ground cinnamon**
¼ **teaspoon ground cumin**
⅛ **teaspoon pepper**
6 **large green peppers Pomegranate seeds (optional)**

Prepare Walnut Sauce; chill. For meat filling, in a skillet cook ground beef, onion, and garlic till meat is brown and onion is tender. Drain off fat. Stir in tomato purée, apple, raisins, cilantro or parsley, almonds, vinegar, salt, cinnamon, cumin, and pepper. Cover; simmer 10 minutes.

Cut tops from the peppers; discard seeds and membranes. Cook the green pepper shells, uncovered, in a large amount of boiling salted water for about 5 minutes or till crisp-tender; invert peppers to drain well. Sprinkle insides of peppers lightly with salt. Spoon meat filling into peppers; place in a 10x6x2-inch baking dish. Bake, covered, in 350° oven for 30 to 35 minutes or till heated through.

To serve, spoon chilled Walnut Sauce over peppers. Sprinkle with pomegranate seeds, if desired. Makes 6 servings.

Walnut Sauce: In a blender or food processor container combine ½ cup *walnuts;* one 3-ounce package *cream cheese,* softened; ¼ cup *milk;* ¼ teaspoon *salt;* and ¼ teaspoon ground *cinnamon.* Cover; blend or process till smooth. Chill thoroughly.

Chicken Mole   *pictured on page 127*

The national holiday dish of Mexico is "mole poblano de guajolote," a complicated recipe for turkey with a "mole" or sauce. And its origin is as legendary as the dish is delicious.

Folklore has it the nuns of the convent of Santa Rosa in Puebla, Mexico, expected a visit from their archbishop. Unfortunately they had nothing elegant enough to serve such a dignitary. So they prayed, and while they prayed they also put everything on hand — including tomatoes, bananas, sesame seeds, raisins, and chocolate — into a sauce pot. They also made a great sacrifice: They killed and cooked their only turkey to serve with the sauce. Was it prayers or culinary skills that made the dinner such a smashing success?

Mexican cooks, relying on their rich tradition, have developed several delightful variations of that time-honored dish, as the recipe for *Chicken Mole* demonstrates.

1 2½- to 3-pound broiler-fryer chicken, cut up
2 tablespoons butter *or* margarine
¼ cup finely chopped onion
¼ cup finely chopped green pepper
1 clove garlic, minced
1 7½-ounce can tomatoes, cut up
½ cup beef broth
2 teaspoons sugar
¼ of a square (¼ ounce) unsweetened chocolate
½ teaspoon chili powder
¼ teaspoon salt
⅛ teaspoon ground cinnamon
⅛ teaspoon ground nutmeg
 Dash ground cloves
 Dash bottled hot pepper sauce
2 tablespoons cold water
1 tablespoon cornstarch

In a large skillet brown chicken pieces in hot butter or margarine for 15 minutes. Season chicken with a little salt and pepper. Remove from skillet; set chicken pieces aside.

In the same skillet cook onion, green pepper, and garlic in pan drippings till vegetables are tender. Add *undrained* tomatoes, beef broth, sugar, chocolate, chili powder, salt, cinnamon, nutmeg, cloves, and hot pepper sauce; stir to combine ingredients and melt chocolate. Add chicken; cover and reduce heat. Cook about 45 minutes or till chicken is tender.

Transfer chicken to a heated serving platter; keep warm. Combine cold water and cornstarch; stir into sauce. Cook and stir till thickened and bubbly. Cook and stir 2 minutes more. Pour sauce over chicken. Serves 6.

Chicken Enchiladas   *pictured on page 127*

1 16-ounce can tomatoes
1 4-ounce can green chili peppers, rinsed and seeded
½ of a 6-ounce can (⅓ cup) tomato paste
1 teaspoon ground coriander
½ teaspoon salt
¼ to ½ teaspoon ground red pepper
½ cup finely chopped onion
1 tablespoon cooking oil
1 tablespoon all-purpose flour
1 cup dairy sour cream
2 cups finely chopped cooked chicken
2 tablespoons cooking oil
12 6-inch flour tortillas
1 cup shredded Monterey Jack cheese

In a blender container place tomatoes, chili peppers, tomato paste, coriander, salt, and red pepper. Cover; blend till smooth.

In a small saucepan cook the chopped onion in the 1 tablespoon hot oil till tender but not brown. Stir flour into sour cream. Stir together onion, sour cream mixture, and chicken.

In a skillet heat the 2 tablespoons cooking oil. Fry tortillas, one at a time, in hot oil for 10 seconds or just till limp. Drain on paper toweling. Spoon chicken mixture onto tortillas; roll up.

Place filled tortillas, seam side down, in 13x9x2-inch baking dish. Pour blended tomato mixture atop. Cover with foil; bake in a 350° oven for 30 minutes. Remove foil; sprinkle with the Monterey Jack cheese. Return to the oven for 5 minutes or till the cheese is melted. Makes 6 servings.

MEXICO

Lime Soup

From Yucatán, a Mexican state, comes a distinctively flavored dish called "sopa de lima," *Lime Soup.* On the Yucatán peninsula grows a species of lime indigenous to that area only. These limes taste bitter and have a fragrant aroma. Fortunately, the soup loses very little of its authentic flavor when it is made with limes from your local market plus a little grapefruit peel.

6   **cups chicken broth**
4   **chicken gizzards**
4   **chicken livers *or* 2 small
      chicken breasts**
1   **medium onion, chopped**
1   **clove garlic, minced**
1   **tablespoon cooking oil**
1   **large tomato, chopped**
⅓   **cup chopped green pepper**
½   **teaspoon dried oregano,
      crushed**
3   **tablespoons lime juice**
4   **pieces grapefruit peel, cut into
      1x½-inch slices**
3   **6- or 7-inch corn *or* flour
      tortillas**
      Cooking oil
      Lime slices
      **Pickled serrano *or* jalapeño
      peppers, rinsed, seeded, and
      chopped**

In a 3-quart saucepan combine chicken broth and chicken gizzards; simmer, covered, 1 hour. Add livers; cook 5 minutes more. (If using breasts, simmer, covered, about 30 minutes more or till meat is tender.) Remove meat from broth. Cool. Finely chop gizzards and livers. (If using chicken breasts, skin, bone, and shred.) Strain broth.

In a small skillet cook onion and garlic in hot oil till tender but not brown. Add the tomato, green pepper, and oregano. Cook over medium heat for 5 minutes. Remove from heat and stir into chicken broth. Add lime juice and grapefruit peel. Simmer, covered, for 30 minutes; add chicken and heat through. Remove grapefruit peel just before serving. Meanwhile, cut tortillas in half and then into ½-inch-wide strips. Fry strips, about ⅓ at a time, in ½-inch hot oil for 40 to 50 seconds or till crisp and light brown. Drain on paper toweling. Divide fried tortilla strips among 6 soup bowls. Ladle soup over. Serve immediately. Garnish with thin slices of lime. Pass pickled peppers. Makes 6 side-dish servings.

Refried Beans

Beans, known as "frijoles," are an important food in the Mexican cuisine. Several varieties — red kidney, ink, speckled, yellow, pinto, and black beans — combine with chili peppers and other seasonings in many favorite dishes.

Mexican cooks consider no meal complete without beans. For the first meal, the beans are rather soupy and traditionally are served in individual bowls. For the next meal, leftover beans are mashed, then cooked with lard to a smooth paste. Served this way, they are "frijoles refritos" or *Refried Beans*.

½ **pound dry black beans** *or* **dry pinto beans (1¼ cups)**
3 **cups water**
4 **cups water**
1 **medium onion, chopped (½ cup)**
2 **tablespoons lard** *or* **bacon drippings**
1 **4-ounce can green chili peppers, rinsed, seeded, and chopped**
½ **teaspoon salt**

Rinse beans. In a large saucepan combine black or pinto beans and the 3 cups water. Bring to boiling; simmer 2 minutes. Remove from heat. Cover; let stand 1 hour. (Or, soak beans in water overnight in a covered pan.) Drain beans and rinse. In the same saucepan combine rinsed beans and the 4 cups water. Bring to boiling; reduce heat. Simmer beans about 1½ hours or till very tender. Drain beans, reserving cooking liquid.

In a large skillet cook chopped onion in hot lard or bacon drippings till tender but not brown. Stir in beans and ¾ cup of the cooking liquid, chili peppers, and the salt. Mash beans in skillet. Cook, uncovered, over medium heat for 5 minutes or till thickened (like mashed potatoes). Season to taste. Serve with enchiladas, burritos, tacos, or as a side dish. Makes about 4 cups.

Sausage-Stuffed Zucchini   *pictured on page 120*

4 **medium zucchini (1½ pounds)**
½ **pound bulk chorizo** *or* **Italian sausage**
2 **tablespoons chopped onion**
1 **3-ounce package cream cheese, softened**
1 **8¾-ounce can whole kernel corn, drained**
1 **tomato, peeled, seeded, and chopped**
½ **cup shredded cheddar cheese (2 ounces)**

Cut the ends off *each* zucchini; halve zucchini lengthwise. In a covered skillet cook zucchini, cut side down, in a small amount of boiling salted water for 5 to 10 minutes or till crisp-tender. Drain. Scoop out pulp, leaving ¼-inch shell. Discard pulp.

In a skillet cook sausage and onion till meat is brown and onion is tender. Drain off fat. Add cream cheese; cook and stir till cream cheese is melted. Stir in corn, tomato, and cheddar cheese. Place the zucchini halves in a 13x9x2-inch baking dish. Fill *each* zucchini half with some of the sausage mixture. Bake in a 350° oven about 25 minutes. Makes 8 side-dish servings.

Tortilla Casserole   *pictured on page 120*

10 **6-inch corn tortillas**
1 **medium onion, chopped**
1 **clove garlic, minced**
2 **tablespoons cooking oil**
3 **medium tomatoes, peeled, seeded, and chopped**
1 **teaspoon dried oregano, crushed**
½ **teaspoon sugar**
½ **teaspoon salt**
⅛ **teaspoon pepper**
1 **cup whipping cream**
¼ **cup grated Parmesan cheese**
¼ **cup shredded Monterey Jack cheese (1 ounce)**

Cut tortillas into strips about 3 inches long and ½ inch wide. In a medium saucepan cook onion and garlic in hot cooking oil till onion is tender but not brown. Add tomatoes, oregano, sugar, salt, and pepper. Bring to boiling; reduce heat. Cover and simmer 5 minutes. Remove from heat. Fold in tortilla strips, whipping cream, and Parmesan cheese.

Turn into an ungreased 1-quart casserole. Bake, uncovered, in a 350° oven about 30 minutes or till heated through. Sprinkle with Monterey Jack cheese. Bake for 2 to 3 minutes more or till cheese is melted. Garnish with a sprig of fresh cilantro or parsley and strips of chili pepper, if desired. Makes 6 side-dish servings.

MEXICO

Sopaipillas

Sopaipillas are an airy hot bread, similar to a fritter. Traditionally they're served in triangular or pillow-shaped pieces. These delicious puffs, when topped with guacamole, make an unusual appetizer. Or, served with honey, they can double as a satisfying dessert.

- **2 cups all-purpose flour**
- **1 tablespoon baking powder**
- **½ teaspoon salt**
- **1 tablespoon shortening**
- **⅔ cup warm water (110° to 115°)**
- **Shortening *or* cooking oil for deep-fat frying**
- **Honey, sugar and cinnamon, *or* Guacamole con Tomatillos (see recipe, page 129)**

In a bowl stir together flour, baking powder, and salt. Cut in the 1 tablespoon shortening till mixture resembles coarse crumbs. Gradually add water, stirring with fork. Turn dough out onto a lightly floured surface; knead into a smooth ball. Divide dough in half; let stand 10 minutes.

Roll *each* half to 12½x10-inch rectangle. Cut into 2½-inch squares. (Do not reroll or patch dough.) Fry, a few at a time, in deep hot fat (425°) till golden. Drain on paper toweling. Serve warm with honey, roll in sugar and cinnamon, or serve with Guacamole con Tomatillos as an appetizer. Makes 40.

Heavenly Cake

Desserts are quite important to Mexican cookery, perhaps because they soothe the palate from the bite of fiery foods.

A Mexican favorite is "Torta del Cielo," or *Heavenly Cake*. A popular dessert for special family occasions — birthdays, anniversaries, weddings, or engagement parties — its light, delicate texture is comparable to that of sponge cake.

- **2 cups finely ground almonds**
- **⅓ cup all-purpose flour**
- **¼ teaspoon salt**
- **6 egg yolks**
- **3 tablespoons brandy**
- **½ teaspoon vanilla**
- **⅓ cup sugar**
- **6 egg whites**
- **1 teaspoon cream of tartar**
- **⅓ cup sugar**
- **Whipped cream**
- **Fresh strawberries, orange sections, banana slices, *or* pineapple chunks**

Grease and flour the bottom of a 9-inch springform pan; attach sides. Stir together almonds, flour, and salt. In a small mixer bowl beat egg yolks at high speed of electric mixer for 6 minutes or till thick and light colored. Add brandy and vanilla. Gradually add ⅓ cup sugar, about 2 tablespoons at a time, beating till sugar is dissolved. Set aside. Wash beaters thoroughly.

In a large mixer bowl combine egg whites and cream of tartar; beat till soft peaks form. Gradually add ⅓ cup sugar, beating till stiff peaks form. Gently fold yolk mixture into whites. Gently fold flour mixture into egg mixture, about ⅓ at a time. Turn into prepared pan.

Bake in a 325° oven for 50 to 55 minutes or till cake tests done. Cool in pan for 15 minutes. Loosen sides; remove cake from pan. Cool thoroughly. Serve with whipped cream and fruit. Serves 12.

Churros *pictured on front cover*

- **1 cup water**
- **1 tablespoon sugar**
- **1 teaspoon salt**
- **1 cup all-purpose flour**
- **2 eggs**
- **Peel of ½ lemon**
- **Shortening *or* cooking oil for deep-fat frying**
- **Sugar *or* powdered sugar**

In a saucepan bring water, sugar, and salt to boiling. Remove from heat. Stir in flour all at once and beat till smooth. Beat in eggs, one at a time, till mixture is smooth. Spoon the batter into a pastry bag fitted with large star point. Pipe 3-inch strips onto small pieces of waxed paper or floured surface.

Add lemon peel to deep fat and heat to 375°. Using a wide spatula, tranfer strips to hot fat. Fry churros, a few at a time, for 3 to 4 minutes or till golden brown, turning as necessary. Roll in sugar or powdered sugar. Makes 24.

Pictured clockwise from top right
Chicken Mole (see recipe, page 123), Chicken Enchiladas (see recipe, page 123), and Sopaipillas.

MEXICO

Chocolate Mexicano

The Aztecs moved into southern Mexico during the 1300s. These highly civilized people, who dominated this area for 200 years, found uses for many native foods, especially the versatile cacao bean.

When Spanish explorer Hernando Cortés landed in Mexico in 1519, he was treated to a delicacy, "chocólatl" —a cold, bitter, syrupy beverage. To adapt it to their taste, Spaniards added sugar and sometimes vanilla and cinnamon, then served it as a hot beverage.

Chocolate Mexicano can be made with a rotary beater or a "molinillo," a carved wooden beater with discs that is twirled between the hands to make hot chocolate frothy. (See illustration at bottom right.)

6 **cups milk**
½ **cup sugar**
3 **squares (3 ounces) unsweetened chocolate, cut up**
1 **teaspoon ground cinnamon**
¼ **teaspoon salt**
2 **beaten eggs**
2 **teaspoons vanilla**
   Stick cinnamon (optional)

In a saucepan combine milk, sugar, chocolate, ground cinnamon, and salt. Cook and stir till chocolate is melted and milk is very hot. Gradually stir *1 cup* of the hot mixture into eggs; return to saucepan. Cook 2 to 3 minutes more over low heat. Remove from heat. Add vanilla; beat with rotary beater or *molinillo* till very frothy.

Pour into mugs; garnish with stick cinnamon, if desired. Makes 6 (8-ounce) servings.

Custard and Fruit Dessert   *pictured on page 120*

2 **cups milk**
½ **cup sugar**
2 **inches stick cinnamon or ½ of a vanilla bean**
4 **egg yolks**
2 **tablespoons finely ground almonds**
¼ **cup light rum**
1 **medium pineapple**
2 **medium bananas, sliced or 1 large papaya, peeled, seeded, and cut up**

For custard sauce, in a saucepan combine milk, sugar, and cinnamon or vanilla bean. Bring to boiling; reduce heat and simmer for 20 minutes. Remove the stick cinnamon or vanilla bean.

In a mixer bowl beat egg yolks at high speed of electric mixer about 5 minutes or till thick and lemon colored. Gradually add milk mixture and ground almonds to the egg yolks; beat at low speed to combine. Return mixture to saucepan; cook and stir over medium heat till mixture coats a metal spoon. Remove from heat and pour sauce into a bowl; set in a larger bowl filled with ice. Stir for 1 to 2 minutes to cool quickly. Add the rum; cover and chill thoroughly.

Halve pineapple lengthwise. Using a sharp knife, cut out the pineapple meat and slice into chunks. Turn pineapple shells, cut side down, on paper toweling to drain well. Combine pineapple chunks and sliced bananas or papaya; mound into pineapple shells. Pour some of the custard sauce over the fruit; pass remaining. Serves 4.

Tequila Sunrise   *pictured on page 120*

Mexican tequila is world famous. This intoxicating brew originated long ago in the Toltec civilization when women prepared a drink called "pulque," a beer-like substance made from the juice of the agave plant. When the Spaniards arrived, they refined the process and began distilling what we know today as tequila.

1½ **ounces tequila**
½ **ounce lime juice**
   Crushed ice
3 **ounces orange juice**
¼ **ounce grenadine syrup**
   Lime slice

Pour tequila and lime juice over crushed ice in a tall glass. Slowly pour in orange juice. Pour in grenadine syrup. Garnish with a lime slice. Stir before drinking. Makes 1 (5-ounce) serving.

Margarita   *pictured on front cover*

1½ **ounces tequila**
1 **ounce lime juice**
1 **ounce orange liqueur**
   Ice cubes
   Lime wedge
   Coarse salt

In a cocktail shaker combine tequila, lime juice, and orange liqueur. Add ice cubes and shake well. For salt-rimmed glass, rub the rim of a cocktail glass with a lime wedge to moisten. Invert glass into a dish of coarse salt. Strain mixture into the glass. Makes 1 (2½-ounce) serving.

Guacamole con Tomatillos

Tomatillos look like small green tomatoes with papery husks, although their character is very different from ordinary tomatoes. Also called Mexican green tomatoes, husk tomatoes, or ground cherries, they can grow in many North American gardens. Buy them fresh or (more often) canned at Mexican markets. Peel the husk, but not the skin, from fresh tomatillos, or rinse the canned variety before using them.

2 **medium avocados, seeded, peeled, and cut up**
½ **of an 11-ounce can tomatillos, drained, rinsed, and cut up (5 or 6)**
¼ **cup chopped onion**
2 **tablespoons lemon juice**
1½ **teaspoons ground coriander**
½ **teaspoon salt**
¼ **teaspoon ground red pepper**
¼ **teaspoon pepper**

In a blender or food processor container place avocados, tomatillos, onion, lemon juice, coriander, salt, red pepper, and pepper. Cover and blend or process till well combined. Makes 2½ cups. (Use as a dip for chips or as a sauce to serve with tacos.)

Salsa de Tomatillos

½ **of an 11-ounce can tomatillos, drained, rinsed, and cut up (5 or 6)**
½ **small onion, cut up**
1 *or* **2 pickled serrano** *or* **jalapeño peppers, rinsed, seeded, and chopped,** *or* **¼ to ½ teaspoon ground red pepper**
2 **tablespoons snipped fresh cilantro** *or* **parsley** *or* **2 teaspoons dried cilantro** *or* **parsley flakes**
1 **clove garlic, minced**
¼ **teaspoon pepper**

In a blender or food processor container place tomatillos, onion, peppers or ground red pepper, cilantro or parsley, garlic, and pepper. Cover and blend or process till well combined. Makes about ½ cup. (Use as a dip for chips or as a sauce to serve with main dishes.)

Ceviche *pictured on page 120*

Also known as "seviche," this delicate dish's characteristic flavor and texture come from lime or lemon juice that marinates the fish.

1 **pound fresh** *or* **frozen haddock fillets** *or* **other fish fillets**
1 **cup lime juice** *or* **lemon juice**
⅓ **cup olive oil** *or* **cooking oil**
¼ **cup sliced scallions** *or* **chopped onion**
1 **4-ounce can green chili peppers, rinsed, seeded, and chopped**
2 **tablespoons coriander** *or* **snipped parsley**
Dash salt
Dash pepper
1 **medium tomato, peeled, seeded, and chopped**
Lettuce leaves
Lime slices

Thaw fish, if frozen. Cut fish into ½-inch cubes. Put fish into a glass or earthenware bowl and cover with lime or lemon juice. Cover and chill for 6 hours or overnight or till fish is opaque; stir occasionally.

Drain fish. Combine olive or cooking oil, scallions or onions, chili peppers, coriander or parsley, salt, and pepper. Stir into fish; toss gently till well combined. Cover and chill thoroughly. Toss chopped tomato with chilled fish mixture. Turn mixture into 10 to 12 lettuce-lined cocktail cups or turn onto a serving platter. Garnish with lime slices. Makes 10 to 12 appetizer servings.

The map shows the following labels:
TURKEY, SYRIA, LEBANON, ISRAEL, JORDAN, IRAQ, Baghdad, KUWAIT, IRAN, AFGHANISTAN, SAUDI ARABIA, UNITED ARAB EMIRATES, OMAN, YEMEN

MIDEAST

In the Middle East, climate, culture, and culinary style link inextricably. Throughout this warm climate, wheat, the primary starch staple, is used to make the flat round pita bread. Cracked wheat or bulgur is a basic ingredient of the popular pilafs.

Other dietary staples in this region include rice, lentils, garbanzo beans, fava beans, eggplant, and yogurt. Common seasonings are cardamom and cinnamon — reminders that the Middle East was once center of the world's spice trade.

Clarified butter is used extensively in cooking. In this hot, arid land, butter, when stripped of its milk solids, keeps for months without refrigeration. Another familiar ingredient is sesame seed, made into cooking oil or crushed into a paste known as "tahini."

Three of the world's great religions — Christianity, Judaism, and Islam — originated in the Middle East and influence its cooking styles as much as the area's climate does. In the Arabic countries, Islamic beliefs prescribe eating patterns. A dignitary or head of the family always is served first and offered the most food. Alcohol and pork are forbidden.

In Israel, the Jewish kosher dietary laws integrate with the European-style cooking of its many immigrants. This young nation has also adopted some of its neighbors' culinary customs, such as cooking meat with fruit. But it has created its own classics. A favorite Israeli dish is "falafel" — a fried ground garbanzo bean mixture that is stuffed inside the pita bread so common throughout the Middle East.

To the east, Afghanistan's cookery is a mixture of Middle Eastern and Southeast Asian influences. Turkey, once the center of the Ottoman Empire, has a cuisine that combines both Greek and Arabic styles. But its own Turkish coffee is revered by the neighboring Middle Eastern nations as well as the rest of the world.

Pictured clockwise from left
Shish Kabob (see recipe, page 133); Pita Bread (see recipe, page 138); Tabouleh Salad (see recipe, page 134); Carrot Tzimmes (see recipe, page 135); and Savory Filled Triangles (see recipe, page 141).

131

MIDEAST

Baked Kibbeh

In Syria and Lebanon, a woman is considered blessed if she has long fingers, for she can use them to shape "kibbeh," the national dish of both countries. This mixture of ground lamb and pork takes many forms. Some "kibbeh" are served raw; others are baked in layers. Many are stuffed and rolled into balls.

½ cup bulgur wheat
2 cups hot water
¼ cup finely chopped onion
¾ teaspoon salt
½ teaspoon ground cinnamon
¼ to ½ teaspoon pepper
1½ pounds ground lamb or ground beef
¾ cup finely chopped onion
⅓ cup pine nuts or slivered almonds
1 teaspoon lemon juice
½ to 1 teaspoon salt
   Dash pepper
   Plain yogurt

Soak bulgur in water for 1 hour. Drain well; squeeze out excess water. Stir in the ¼ cup chopped onion, the ¾ teaspoon salt, cinnamon, and ¼ to ½ teaspoon pepper. Add 1 pound of the ground meat; mix well. Set aside.

In a skillet cook remaining meat, the ¾ cup chopped onion, and nuts till meat is brown. Drain off fat. Stir in lemon juice, the ½ to 1 teaspoon salt, and the dash pepper. In a 10x6x2-inch baking dish press half of the meat-bulgur mixture evenly over the bottom. Top with cooked meat-nut mixture. Cover with remaining meat-bulgur mixture, pressing down with hands. Bake in 350° oven about 25 minutes or till done. Drain off fat. Serve warm or chilled with yogurt. Makes 6 servings.

Dolmas

Dolmas, or stuffed vegetables, have both Turkish and Greek heritages. They are eaten cold (if stuffed with rice only) or warm (if chopped meat is added).

Vegetables suitable for stuffing include eggplants, tomatoes, sweet peppers, onion, zucchini, cabbage leaves, or grape leaves.

⅓ cup long grain rice
6 large tomatoes, cored
1 pound ground lamb or ground beef
1 medium onion, chopped
¼ cup pitted whole dates, finely snipped
¼ cup chopped walnuts
½ teaspoon dried mint, crushed
¼ teaspoon ground coriander
⅛ teaspoon ground cardamom
⅛ teaspoon ground cloves
⅛ teaspoon ground cumin
2 beaten eggs

Cook rice according to package directions; drain. Halve tomatoes lengthwise; scoop out pulp. Chop pulp; drain well in colander. Sprinkle the inside of tomato cups with salt. Set aside.

In a large skillet cook lamb or beef and onion till meat is brown and onion is tender. Remove from heat; drain off fat. Stir in cooked rice, chopped tomato pulp, dates, walnuts, mint, coriander, cardamom, cloves, cumin, ¼ teaspoon salt, and ¼ teaspoon pepper. Stir in beaten eggs.

Spoon about ½ cup of the mixture into each tomato cup. Place in a 12x7½x2-inch baking dish. Bake in 375° oven for 20 minutes. Garnish with snipped coriander or parsley, if desired. Serves 6.

Mansaf

When desert nomads feast on Mansaf, a lamb dish, they do it with decorum and ritual. Before the meal, men wash their hands, then pray to Allah. Women then bring the feast on a "shrak," a large bread round. Using right hands only, the men tear the lamb into bite-size pieces which they then coat with rice. Once the men have had their fill, the leftovers are given to the women and children.

4 lamb shoulder chops
1 tablespoon olive oil or cooking oil
½ of a medium onion, sliced and separated into rings
½ cup water
3 inches stick cinnamon
1 cup water
½ cup long grain rice
¼ cup light raisins
½ teaspoon salt
½ teaspoon ground turmeric
¼ teaspoon ground allspice
¼ teaspoon pepper
½ cup plain yogurt
2 tablespoons milk
2 tablespoons snipped parsley
1 tablespoon all-purpose flour
¼ cup pine nuts or slivered almonds

Season lamb chops with salt and pepper. In a large skillet brown lamb in hot oil; remove, reserving oil. Add onion to reserved oil in skillet; cook till tender but not brown, adding more oil if necessary. Drain off fat. Return meat to skillet; add the ½ cup water and stick cinnamon. Bring to boiling; reduce heat. Cover and simmer 30 minutes.

Meanwhile, in a saucepan combine the 1 cup water, uncooked rice, raisins, salt, turmeric, allspice, and pepper. Bring to boiling; reduce heat. Cover and simmer about 20 minutes or till rice is done. Let stand, covered, for 10 minutes.

For sauce, in saucepan stir together yogurt, milk, parsley, and flour. Cook and stir till thickened and bubbly. Cook and stir 1 minute more.

To serve, drain lamb mixture; transfer to serving platter. Remove stick cinnamon; discard. Stir nuts into rice mixture. Arrange rice mixture around lamb. Pour some of the yogurt sauce atop. Pass remaining sauce. Makes 4 servings.

Orange-Chicken Pilaf   Afghanistan

In a traditional pilaf, rice cooks together with various meats, fruits, nuts, herbs, or spices. Authentic pilaf recipes specify "basmati" rice, which is grown in Afghanistan and Iran. For this recipe, use long grain rice instead.

2   medium oranges
¼   cup sugar
½   cup shelled, undyed pistachio nuts *or* slivered almonds
2   tablespoons butter *or* margarine
3   whole medium chicken breasts, halved lengthwise
1   cup long grain rice
1   cup water
2   tablespoons snipped parsley *or* coriander
1   teaspoon salt
½   teaspoon ground ginger
¼   teaspoon thread saffron, crushed
¼   teaspoon pepper
    Shelled, undyed pistachio nuts *or* slivered almonds

With vegetable peeler, cut the peel from *half* of 1 orange; chop peel. Cook chopped peel in boiling water for 5 minutes. Rinse; drain and set aside. Squeeze juice from the 2 oranges; add water to measure 1 cup. For syrup, in same saucepan combine orange juice mixture and sugar. Bring to boiling; reduce heat. Simmer, uncovered, for 5 minutes, stirring occasionally. Remove from heat; set aside.

In a skillet cook the ½ cup nuts in butter till light brown, stirring constantly. Remove nuts and set aside, reserving butter. Sprinkle chicken with salt and pepper. Cook chicken in reserved butter or margarine about 15 minutes or till brown.

To syrup, add peel, nuts, *uncooked* rice, water, parsley or coriander, salt, ginger, saffron, and pepper. Bring to boiling; turn into a 12x7x2½-inch baking dish. Place chicken atop. Cover and bake in 325° oven about 1 hour or till chicken is tender and rice is done. Sprinkle with nuts. Serves 6.

Shish Kabob   *pictured on page 130*   Turkey

During the days of the Ottoman Empire, Turkish soldiers used to cook their meat and vegetables on skewers over campfires; thus the kabob was born.

Of the many different kabob recipes, the *Shish Kabob,* made with a leg of lamb, is the most famous.

Kabobs can be served over hot cooked rice or wrapped in unleavened bread. Sometimes a tomato or yogurt sauce can go atop.

½   cup olive oil
¼   cup lemon juice
2   cloves garlic, minced
2   whole black peppercorns, cracked
2   whole cardamom seeds, cracked
2   whole cloves
1   teaspoon dried thyme, crushed
2   pounds boneless lamb, cut into ¾-inch pieces
2   large green peppers, cut into 1-inch squares
2   medium onions, cut into wedges

For marinade, stir together olive oil, lemon juice, garlic, peppercorns, cardamom, cloves, thyme, and 1 teaspoon *salt;* add lamb. Cover; chill 6 to 8 hours, stirring occasionally. Remove lamb, reserving marinade.

Thread 6 skewers with lamb pieces, green pepper squares, and onion wedges. Broil kabobs about 4 inches from heat for 10 to 12 minutes or till desired doneness, brushing with marinade and giving a quarter turn every 3 minutes. Makes 6 servings.

Spicy Stewed Liver   Yemen

½   pound lamb *or* beef kidney
1   pound lamb *or* calf liver
1   large onion, chopped
2   cloves garlic, minced
2   tablespoons cooking oil
1   16-ounce can tomatoes, cut up
2   canned green chili peppers, rinsed, seeded, and chopped
1   teaspoon ground turmeric
½   teaspoon ground cumin
½   teaspoon caraway seed
¼   teaspoon ground cardamom
1   tablespoon snipped coriander *or* parsley

Remove membranes and hard portions from kidney; cut kidney crosswise into bite-size pieces. Rinse liver; cut into serving-size pieces. In large saucepan cook onion and garlic in hot oil till tender but not brown. Add kidney and liver; cook till brown. Drain off fat. Remove liver and chill. Stir tomatoes, chili peppers, turmeric, cumin, caraway, cardamom, ½ cup *water*, ½ teaspoon *salt*, and ¼ teaspoon *pepper* into kidney mixture. Bring to boiling; reduce heat. Cover and simmer over low heat about 1¾ hours or till kidney is tender. Add liver; simmer about 10 minutes or till done, adding more water if necessary. Before serving, stir in coriander or parsley. Serve over rice, if desired. Serves 4 to 6.

MIDEAST

Lamb and Garbanzo Soup
Iran

Lamb and Garbanzo Soup once was baked in a mud oven for three hours inside an earthware pot sealed with clay.

Today, if an Iranian hostess has unexpected company, she simply adds more water to this hearty soup. Some Iranians like to puree the solids before serving; others like to strain the broth and serve it alongside the meat and vegetables.

2 pounds boneless lamb, cut into ½-inch pieces
2 tablespoons butter *or* margarine
1 medium onion, chopped
1 16-ounce can tomatoes, cut up
1 15-ounce can garbanzo beans, drained
2 tablespoons lime juice
1 bay leaf
½ teaspoon ground turmeric
½ teaspoon paprika
½ teaspoon ground cinnamon
   Onion slices, separated into rings
   Radish slices

In a Dutch oven brown lamb, half at a time, in hot butter or margarine. Add chopped onion; cook till tender but not brown. Drain off fat. Stir in *undrained* tomatoes, beans, lime juice, bay leaf, turmeric, paprika, cinnamon, 4 cups *water,* and ½ teaspoon *salt.* Bring to boiling; reduce heat. Cover and simmer for 1 to 1½ hours or till meat is tender. Remove bay leaf. Ladle into serving bowls. Garnish each serving with onion rings and radish slices. Serves 6.

Tabouleh Salad   *pictured on 130*
Lebanon and Syria

Tabouleh Salad calls for bulgur wheat, one of the main cereal grains of the Middle East. Bulgur may be unavailable in a local supermarket, but health food shops usually have it.

1 cup bulgur wheat
½ cup snipped parsley
3 tablespoons lemon juice
2 tablespoons olive oil *or* cooking oil
2 tablespoons sliced green onion
1 teaspoon snipped mint
1 tomato, cubed and seeded
   Lettuce leaves

Soak bulgur wheat in 2 cups hot *water* for 1 hour. Drain well; squeeze out excess water. Stir in parsley, lemon juice, oil, onion, mint, and 1 teaspoon *salt.* Cover and chill several hours. Before serving, stir in tomato. Serve on lettuce-lined salad plates. Makes 6 to 8 servings.

Fish with Tahini Sauce
Lebanon and Syria

2 pounds fresh *or* frozen fish fillets
¼ cup olive oil *or* cooking oil
2 tablespoons sliced green onion
1 tablespoon lemon juice
½ teaspooon salt
½ teaspoon dried dillweed
¼ teaspoon pepper
   Homemade Tahini
⅓ cup water
3 tablespoons lemon juice
1 clove garlic, minced
   Pine nuts, toasted (optional)
   Lemon slices (optional)

Thaw fish, if frozen. Separate fish into 6 serving size portions. Place in a greased shallow baking pan. Combine olive oil or cooking oil, green onion, the 1 tablespoon lemon juice, salt, dillweed, and pepper. Pour over fish. Broil 4 inches from heat till fish flakes easily when tested with a fork. (Allow 5 minutes for each ½-inch thickness.) Baste occasionally with oil mixture during broiling. If fish is more than 1 inch thick, turn when fish is half done.

To make sauce, in a small saucepan stir together the Homemade Tahini, water, the 3 tablespoons lemon juice, and the garlic. Cook and stir till heated through. Spoon sauce over fish. Garnish with toasted pine nuts or lemon slices, if desired. Makes 6 servings.

Homemade Tahini: Place steel blade in food processor or use blender; add 1 cup lightly toasted *sesame seed.* Cover; process or blend 3 to 5 minutes or till butter forms, stopping to scrape sides of container occasionally. Add ¼ teaspoon *salt.* Process or blend about 2 minutes more, gradually adding 1 tablespoon *olive or cooking oil,* till mixture is the desired smoothness. Makes ½ cup. (Or, purchase commercial tahini at a specialty food store.)

Spinach-Yogurt Salad

Iran

According to legend, *Spinach-Yogurt Salad,* or "borani esfanaj," was named in honor of a queen who was obsessed with yogurt dishes. Yogurt, also called "laban" or "mâst," has long been a favorite throughout the Middle East.

8 cups torn fresh spinach
1 small onion, chopped
1 small clove garlic, halved
⅓ cup plain yogurt
1 tablespoon olive oil *or* cooking oil
1 teaspoon snipped mint
¼ teaspoon salt
¼ teaspoon ground turmeric
⅛ teaspoon pepper
½ cup broken walnuts
Lemon wedges (optional)

In a saucepan cook spinach and onion in a small amount of boiling water about 3 minutes or just till spinach starts to wilt; drain. Rub a wooden salad bowl with the garlic; discard garlic. Spoon spinach mixture into salad bowl. Combine yogurt, oil, mint, salt, turmeric, and pepper. Add to spinach; toss gently till well coated. Cover and chill several hours. Before serving, add broken walnuts and toss gently. Garnish the salad with lemon wedges, if desired. Makes 4 servings.

Carrot Tzimmes *pictured on page 130*

Israel

Jewish families traditionally eat *Carrot Tzimmes* on Rosh Hashanah, the beginning of their new year. The carrots promise prosperity, and the honey-apple combination, a sweet, joyful new year.

8 carrots, sliced ¾-inch thick (3¾ cups)
⅓ cup honey
1 tablespoon lemon juice
½ teaspoon salt
1 tablespoon butter *or* margarine, melted
1 tablespoon all-purpose flour
1 8¼-ounce can crushed pineapple, drained
½ cup raisins
½ cup peeled coarsely chopped, apple

In a heavy saucepan cook carrots, covered, in ½ cup *water* for 5 minutes. *Do not drain.* Stir in honey, lemon juice, and salt. Bring to boiling; reduce heat. Cover and simmer 20 minutes. Stir together butter or margarine and flour; stir into carrots along with pineapple, raisins, and apple. Cover and simmer 10 minutes more, stirring occasionally. Serves 6 to 8.

Okra in Oil

Saudi Arabia

In Arab states, it was once thought that vegetables were inhabited by "djinns," spirits whose personalities affected the flavor of their edible domain. The piquant character of *Okra in Oil,* however, stems more from vinegar, garlic, and green chili peppers than from any spirits.

2 medium onions, chopped
1 clove garlic, minced
2 tablespoons olive oil *or* cooking oil
3 medium tomatoes, chopped
1 10-ounce package frozen whole *or* cut okra
¼ cup water
2 tablespoons vinegar
2 canned green chili peppers, rinsed, seeded, and chopped
½ teaspoon salt
¼ teaspoon ground coriander
¼ teaspoon pepper

In a large skillet cook onions and garlic in hot oil till onion is tender but not brown. Stir in tomatoes, okra, water, vinegar, green chili peppers, salt, coriander, and pepper. Bring to boiling; reduce heat. Cover and simmer 20 minutes. Serve warm or chilled. Makes 6 servings.

Potato Latkes Israel

Jewish foot soldiers, during their war for freedom from Assyrians (Battle of Maccabees, 165 B.C.), had as one of their staples *Potato Latkes*. Today these pancakes remain part of the Hanukkah feast celebrating the Jewish victory.

7 to 8 medium potatoes (2½ pounds)
1 medium onion
2 beaten eggs
¼ cup all-purpose flour
¼ cup Matzo meal
1½ teaspoons salt
¼ teaspoon pepper
Cooking oil *or* shortening for frying
Applesauce (see recipe below)

Peel and shred the potatoes and onion; drain well. In a large mixing bowl stir together potatoes, onion, eggs, flour, Matzo meal, salt, and pepper (mixture should be thick).

In a large skillet heat about ¼ inch cooking oil over medium heat. For *each* latke, spoon about *2 tablespoons* of the batter into the hot oil. Spread to make a circle about 2½ inches in diameter. Fry latkes, 3 or 4 at a time, for 1½ to 2 minutes on each side or till brown. Drain on paper toweling. Serve with Applesauce. Makes about 24.

Sour Cream Latkes Israel

Many Israelis adhere to the "Kashrut," the Jewish code of spiritual fitness. They consume only Kosher or ritually prepared foods.

The "Kashrut" emphasizes four main points. The only flesh considered edible is that of clove-footed animals that chew cud, fish with fins and scales, and birds who do not prey. Animals must be killed only by a "shohet," a specially certified slaughterer. All meat should be "kashered," that is, cleansed by a process of soaking and salting. And, meat and dairy foods cannot be mixed in the same dish or meal. So, orthodox Jews maintain two separate sets of dishes: one for meat and one for dairy foods.

Other foods are neutral and can be eaten with dairy products or meat.

1 cup all-purpose flour
¾ teaspoon baking soda
½ teaspoon salt
1 cup milk
½ cup dairy sour cream
Applesauce (see recipe below)

In mixing bowl stir together the flour, baking soda, and salt. Add milk and sour cream; beat with rotary beater till smooth. For *each* latke, spoon about *2 tablespoons* batter onto a hot, lightly greased griddle or heavy skillet. Cook latkes, 3 or 4 at a time, about 1¼ minutes on each side or till brown. Drain on paper toweling. Serve with Applesauce. Makes about 18.

Applesauce Israel

8 medium cooking apples, cored, peeled, and quartered
½ cup water
4 inches stick cinnamon
¼ cup packed brown sugar
Apple slice (optional)

In a 3-quart saucepan combine apples, water, and stick cinnamon. Bring to boiling; reduce heat: Cover and simmer 20 minutes or till apples are very tender. Remove cinnamon. Press apples through a sieve or food mill. Stir in brown sugar. Garnish with an apple slice, if desired. Makes 3 cups.

Barley Kugel Israel

1 cup toasted barley (7 ounces)
9 cups water
2 teaspoons salt
2 medium onions, chopped
1 cup sliced fresh mushrooms
2 tablespoons butter *or* margarine
¼ teaspoon pepper
2 beaten eggs
Sliced fresh mushrooms
Snipped parsley

Rinse barley; soak in *4 cups* of the water for 2 hours. Drain. In a 3-quart saucepan combine barley, the remaining water, and the salt. Bring to boiling; reduce heat. Cover and simmer for 1¼ hours. Drain. In a saucepan cook onion and the 1 cup mushrooms in hot butter or margarine till tender. Stir in barley and pepper. Gradually stir about *1 cup* of the hot mixture into eggs; return all to pan. Turn into a 1½-quart casserole. Bake, covered, in 350° oven for 40 minutes. Before serving, fluff with a fork to separate grains of barley. Garnish with sliced fresh mushrooms and parsley. Makes 8 to 10 servings.

Pictured clockwise from top left
Sour Cream Latkes, Potato Latkes, Applesauce, and Doughnut Spheres (see recipe, page 138).

MIDEAST

Pita Bread *pictured on page 130 and on front cover* Regional

In the Middle East, bread is considered a gift from God, and is a vital element in the daily diet. Villagers make and shape their own loaves each day, and, to be assured of receiving their own loaves, mark them before sending them to the local baker.

Pita Bread represents the typical unleavened Middle Eastern bread. Into these bread pockets can go any combination of chopped fully cooked ham, beef, pr chicken; canned tuna, shrimp, or salmon; sliced hard-cooked eggs; sliced or shredded cheese; shredded carrots, lettuce, or cabbage; chopped celery, green pepper, or apple; raisins or nuts; sliced olives, mushrooms, tomatoes, or avocado; or bean or alfalfa sprouts.

- 1 **package active dry yeast**
- 1¼ **cups warm water (110° to 115°)**
- 3¼ **to 3¾ cups all-purpose flour**
- ¼ **cup shortening**
- 1½ **teaspoons salt**

In a large mixer bowl soften yeast in warm water. Add *2 cups* of the flour, the shortening, and salt. Beat at low speed of electric mixer for ½ minute, scraping sides of bowl. Beat 3 minutes at high speed. Stir in as much of the remaining flour as you can mix in with a spoon. Turn out onto a lightly floured surface. Knead in enough of the remaining flour to make a moderately soft dough that is smooth and elastic (3 to 5 minutes total). Cover; let rest in a warm place about 15 minutes. Divide into 12 equal portions. Roll *each* between floured hands into a *very* smooth ball. Cover with plastic wrap or a damp cloth; let rest 10 minutes. Using fingers, gently flatten balls without creasing dough. Cover; let rest 10 minutes. (Keep dough pieces covered till ready to use.)

On a well-floured surface lightly roll one piece of dough at a time into a circle 7 inches in diameter, *turning dough over once.* Do not stretch, puncture, or crease dough. (Work with enough flour so dough does not stick.) Place on a baking sheet.

Bake rounds, 2 at a time, in a 450° oven about 3 minutes or till dough is puffed and softly set. Turn over with a spatula; bake about 2 minutes more or till dough is light brown. Repeat with remaining dough, baking one batch before rolling and baking the next batch.

To serve, slice bread crosswise to form a pocket; generously fill each pocket with desired filling. (Allow any extra bread to cool before wrapping for storage.) Makes 12 pita rounds.

Doughnut Spheres *pictured on page 136* Israel

- 4½ **to 4¾ cups all-purpose flour**
- 2 **packages active dry yeast**
- 1 **cup water**
- ¾ **cup sugar**
- 6 **tablespoons butter or margarine, softened**
- 2 **eggs**
- 1 **teaspoon vanilla**
  Cooking oil or shortening for deep-fat frying
  Sugar
  Jelly or preserves (optional)

In mixer bowl combine *1½ cups* of the flour and the yeast. Heat water, sugar, and butter or margarine just till warm (115° to 120°) and butter or margarine is almost melted; stir constantly. Add to flour mixture; add eggs and vanilla. Beat at low speed of electric mixer ½ minute, scraping bowl. Beat 3 minutes at high speed. Stir in as much of the remaining flour as you can mix in with a spoon.

Turn out onto a lightly floured surface. Knead in enough of the remaining flour to make a moderately soft dough that is smooth and elastic (3 to 5 minutes total). Shape into a ball. Place in lightly greased bowl; turn once to grease surface. Cover; let rest 10 minutes. Roll to ½-inch thickness; cut with floured 2½-inch biscuit cutter. Cover; let rise in warm place till almost double (about 1 hour). Fry doughnuts, a few at a time, in deep hot fat (375°) for 3 minutes, turning once. Drain on paper toweling. Sprinkle with sugar. Serve with jelly or preserves, if desired. Makes 2 dozen.

Noah's Pudding Turkey

3 cups water
¾ cup bulgur wheat
½ cup short grain rice
1 teaspoon salt
1 cup milk
½ cup sugar
½ cup light raisins
¼ cup dried currants
¼ cup chopped pitted dates
¼ cup chopped dried apricots
¼ cup orange juice
Chopped walnuts *or*
  chopped almonds

In a medium saucepan combine water, bulgur wheat, *uncooked* rice, and salt. Bring to boiling; reduce heat. Cover and simmer for 20 minutes. Add milk, sugar, light raisins, currants, dates, apricots, and orange juice. Cook, uncovered, over low heat for 20 minutes. Spoon into serving bowls. Sprinkle each serving with walnuts or almonds. Serve warm or chilled. Makes 8 servings.

Figs in Syrup Saudi Arabia

½ lemon
  Water
¼ cup sugar
2 tablespoons honey
1 whole clove
18 walnut halves
18 fresh figs *or* one 17-ounce
  jar whole figs, drained
½ cup plain yogurt
¼ teaspoon vanilla
  Chopped walnuts

With vegetable peeler, cut a thin strip of peel about 2 inches long from lemon. Set aside. Squeeze juice from lemon; add water to measure ½ cup. In a small saucepan combine lemon peel strip, lemon juice mixture, sugar, honey, and clove. Bring to boiling; reduce heat. Cook and stir till syrup is thickened and bubbly. Remove from heat; discard clove and lemon peel. Cool slightly.

Insert *one* walnut half into *each* fig. Place stuffed figs in individual dessert dishes. Stir together cooled syrup, yogurt, and vanilla. Spoon yogurt mixture over figs. Cover and chill till serving time. Sprinkle each serving with chopped walnuts. Makes 6 servings.

Mamool Cookies Lebanon and Syria

Traditionally baked for Easter, these delicate, shaped cookies can be stuffed with fillings such as pistachios, almonds, and dates.

2 cups all-purpose flour
½ cup quick-cooking farina
¼ teaspoon ground nutmeg
  Dash ground cloves
1 cup butter *or* margarine,
  softened
2 tablespoons water
¼ teaspoon orange blossom
  water
¼ cup chopped walnuts
1 tablespoon sugar
  Powdered sugar

Stir together flour, farina, nutmeg, and cloves. In large mixer bowl beat butter or margarine on medium speed of electric mixer for 30 seconds. Add *half* of the flour mixture to butter; beat on low speed of electric mixer till well mixed. Add remaining flour mixture, water, and orange blossom water alternately to beaten mixture; beat till mixture is well mixed. Divide dough into 12 pieces.

On a lightly floured surface, pat *each* piece to a circle 2½ inches in diameter. Combine walnuts and sugar. Place about *1 teaspoon* of the nut mixture in center of *each* circle. Fold over and press edges together to seal. Place on an ungreased cookie sheet. Bake in a 350° oven for 30 to 35 minutes or till done. Cool on wire rack for 10 minutes. Roll in powdered sugar. Makes 12.

139

MIDEAST

Loukomi Candy

Loukomi Candy, otherwise known as Turkish delight, is a chewy confection traditionally flavored with orange flower water or rose water. Here, fresh orange juice makes a tasty substitute.

1½ cups sugar
3 envelopes unflavored gelatin
1 teaspoon finely shredded orange peel
1¼ cups orange juice
⅔ cup chopped pistachio nuts *or* chopped almonds
⅓ cup chopped candied cherries
Powdered sugar

In saucepan combine sugar, gelatin, and orange peel. Stir in orange juice. Cook and stir over low heat till mixture is slightly thickened. Chill till consistency of unbeaten egg whites (partially set); fold in nuts and candied cherries. Pour into 9x5x3-inch loaf pan. Chill about 1½ hours or till firm.

Remove from pan; cut into 1-inch cubes. Place cubes, about 1 inch apart, on a waxed paper-lined baking sheet; let dry at room temperature about 2 hours. Coat cubes with powdered sugar. Makes about 3 dozen candies.

Cheese-Filled Pastries

Turkey

Phyllo pastries, or "böreks," may contain either sweet or savory fillings. The phyllo dough is usually wrapped around the filling, forming small bundles of different shapes — triangles, crescents, or cubes.

In addition to bundles, a "börek" also can mean layers of phyllo dough and filling baked in a baking dish.

1 8-ounce package cream cheese, softened
½ cup feta cheese
¼ cup snipped parsley
1 tablespoon snipped fresh dill *or* 1 teaspoon dried dillweed
1 egg yolk
8 sheets frozen phyllo dough, thawed (8 ounces)
¼ cup butter *or* margarine, melted

For filling, beat cream cheese till creamy. Add feta cheese, parsley, and dill to cream cheese. Add egg yolk; beat just till combined.

Stack *2 sheets* of the phyllo dough. (Cover unused sheets with a damp cloth to prevent drying.) Brush stack of phyllo dough with *some* of the melted butter or margarine. Cut lengthwise into quarters. For *each* piece, spoon about *1½ tablespoons* of filling about 1 inch from end of one of the narrow sides. Fold end over filling at 45-degree angle. Continue folding to form a triangle that encloses the filling, using entire strip of 2 layers. See illustration below. Place on baking sheet; brush with butter or margarine. Bake in 375° oven 18 minutes. Serve warm or chilled. Makes 16.

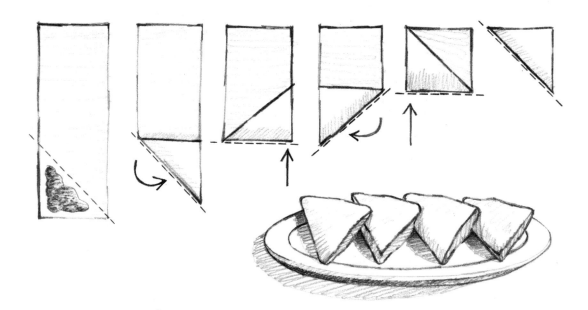

Knish

Knish, potato-filled pastries, are common fare in Israel, often available as snacks from street vendors. These pastries may double as appetizers at a bar mitzvah.

Pastry for Double-Crust Pie
- 6 **medium potatoes (2 pounds), peeled and cut up**
- 1 **medium onion, chopped (½ cup)**
- 2 **tablespoons butter** or **margarine**
- ½ **teaspoon salt**
  Dash pepper
- 1 **beaten egg**
- 1 **tablespoon cooking oil**

Prepare Pastry for Double-Crust Pie; form into ball. For filling, cook potatoes in boiling salted water for 20 to 25 minutes or till tender; drain. Cook onion in hot butter till tender. In mixer bowl combine potatoes, onion, salt, and pepper; beat with electric mixer till smooth. On lightly floured surface, roll pastry to ⅛-inch thickness. Cut into 16 circles 4 inches in diameter. Place ¼ cup of the potato mixture in center of each circle; bring edges of dough up over filling and pinch to seal. Place, seam side down, on ungreased baking sheet. Stir together egg and oil. Brush knish with egg mixture. Bake in 350° oven for 40 to 45 minutes or till brown. Makes 16.

Pastry for Double-Crust Pie: In bowl stir together 2 cups all-purpose flour and 1 teaspoon salt. Cut in ⅔ cup shortening or lard till pieces are the size of small peas. Sprinkle 6 to 7 tablespoons water over mixture, 1 tablespoon at a time; toss with a fork. Form dough into a ball.

Savory Filled Triangles *pictured on page 130*   Lebanon and Syria

Homemade Bread Dough or **2 loaves frozen bread dough**
- ½ **pound ground lamb** or **ground beef**
- 2 **tablespoons chopped onion**
- 1 **tablespoon snipped parsley**
- ½ **teaspoon salt**
  Dash pepper
- 1 **tablespoon lemon juice**
- 1 **10-ounce package frozen chopped spinach**
- 2 **tablespoons chopped onion**
- ½ **teaspoon salt**
  Dash pepper
- 1 **tablespoon lemon juice**
- 1 **tablespoon butter** or **margarine**
  Butter or **margarine, melted**

Prepare Homemade Bread Dough. (Or, thaw frozen bread dough in refrigerator overnight.) For meat filling, in skillet cook meat, 2 tablespoons onion, the parsley, ½ teaspoon salt, and dash pepper till meat is brown; drain off fat. Stir in 1 tablespoon lemon juice; cool. For spinach filling, in saucepan cook spinach with 2 tablespoons onion, ½ teaspoon salt, and dash pepper according to package directions. Drain well, squeezing out excess water. Stir 1 tablespoon lemon juice and the 1 tablespoon butter or margarine into spinach; cool.

Cut each loaf of bread dough into 8 pieces. Pat out each piece to form a triangle with 4-inch-long sides. Place 2 tablespoons of the meat or spinach filling in center of each triangle. Fold in corners, not quite to middle. Pinch corners. Cover; let rise till nearly double (about 45 minutes). Brush with melted butter. Bake on ungreased baking sheets in 350° oven for 25 minutes or till light brown. Makes 16.

Homemade Bread Dough: In a mixer bowl combine 1 cup all-purpose flour and 1 package active dry yeast. In saucepan heat ½ cup milk, 3 tablespoons sugar, 3 tablespoons butter or margarine, and ½ teaspoon salt just till warm (115° to 120°); stir constantly. Add to flour mixture; add 1 egg. Beat at low speed of electric mixer for ½ minute, scraping bowl. Beat 3 minutes at high speed. Stir in as much of 1 to 1½ cups all-purpose flour as you can mix in with a spoon. On floured surface, knead in enough of the remaining flour to make a moderately stiff dough that is smooth and elastic (6 to 8 minutes total). Shape into a ball. Place in greased bowl; turn once. Cover; let rise in warm place till double (about 1 hour). Punch down; divide in half. Cover; let rest 10 minutes. Shape into 2 loaves.

GREENLAND

ICELAND

FINLAND

SWEDEN

Helsinki

NORWAY

Oslo

Stockholm

Godthab

DENMARK

SCANDINAVIA

Scandinavia is the land of the Vikings. Centuries ago, these pirates sailed and explored the North Atlantic, feasting on mussels, mutton, cheese, cabbage, apples, onion, berries, and nuts. Their descendants even today appreciate these delicious native foods.

Wholesome, hearty fare still characterizes Scandinavian cuisine. Carrots, potatoes, rutabagas, and turnips are familiar vegetables. They grow well in the cool, short summers and can be kept over the long winters. Rye, too, is suited to the Scandinavian climate. It is used for the bread flour that is made into substantial loaves or the wafer-thin flatbread.

Scandinavian cooks take advantage of the plentiful dairy products. Butter, cheese, and cream are used lavishly in country-style dishes. Also favored are the flavorings cardamom, dill, and caraway.

Most dearly prized by the Scandinavian palate is the abundant seafood — especially herring. In Sweden, the traditional first course of the smör-gasbord is a multitude of herring dishes. But cod, salmon, and crayfish are popular, too. The Norwegian favorite is "lutefisk," salt cod soaked in lye before cooking.

A national Danish treat is the "smørrebrød." These open-faced sandwiches, eaten with a knife and fork, offer endless possibilities. Any combination of meat, poultry, fish, eggs, cheese, pickles, and vegetables can top the customary rye bread. "Smør-rebrød" is a popular lunchtime entrée, whether one is at school, home, work, or in a restaurant.

Unlike her neighbors whose cuisines show little influence from other countries, Finland's food preferences combine Swedish and Russian tastes. Finnish restaurants serve their versions of the Swedish smörgasbord as well as the Russian "blini" (small pancake) and "borsch" (beet soup). And Finland has adopted vodka as its national drink. But unique to Finland are their reindeer sausages.

Pictured clockwise from top right
Sweet Raisin Bread (see recipe, page 148), Sandbakkelse (see recipe, page 149), Almond Braid (see recipe, page 146), Lucia Buns (see recipe, page 148), and Apple Cake (see recipe, page 150)

SCANDINAVIA

Frikadeller Meatballs

Denmark

Frikadeller Meatballs are the Danish answer to Swedish meatballs. Buttermilk or yogurt gives these fine-textured meatballs a slight tang. Though usually served hot with gravy and potatoes, leftover *Frikadeller Meatballs* can be sliced and served cold on buttered bread.

1 beaten egg
¼ cup buttermilk *or* plain yogurt
¾ cup soft bread crumbs (1 slice)
1 small onion, chopped (¼ cup)
½ teaspoon salt
¼ teaspoon pepper
⅛ teaspoon ground nutmeg
½ pound ground pork
½ pound ground beef
1 tablespoon butter *or* margarine

In a mixing bowl combine egg and buttermilk or yogurt. Stir in bread crumbs, onion, salt, pepper, and nutmeg. Add ground meat; mix well.

Shape meat into 6 or 8 ovals about 3 inches long. In a skillet cook meatballs, uncovered, in hot butter or margarine over medium heat about 20 minutes or till done, turning occasionally. Drain on paper toweling. Makes 4 to 6 servings.

Lamb with Cabbage

Regional

1½ pounds boneless lamb, cut into 1-inch pieces
2 tablespoons butter *or* margarine
1 medium onion, sliced and separated into rings
1 cup water
10 whole peppercorns
2 bay leaves
1 tablespoon snipped fresh dill *or* 1 teaspoon dried dillweed
1 teaspoon salt
1 head cabbage, cut into wedges
Dairy sour cream (optional)

In a Dutch oven brown the meat, half at a time, in hot butter or margarine. Add onion; cook till onion is tender but not brown. Drain off fat. Return all meat to Dutch oven. Stir in water, peppercorns, bay leaves, dill, and salt. Bring to boiling; reduce heat. Cover and simmer for 20 minutes.

Add cabbage; cook, uncovered, for 10 minutes. Cover and simmer 30 minutes more. Remove from heat; discard bay leaves and peppercorns. Pass sour cream, if desired. Makes 6 to 8 servings.

Liver and Raisin Bake

Finland

"Maksalaatikko" or *Liver and Raisin Bake* is frequently served warm with melted butter and homemade lingonberry or cranberry preserves.

1 cup water
1 cup milk
1 cup brown rice
1 pound pork liver *or* beef liver
¼ pound salt pork *or* bacon, sliced
1 medium onion, chopped
⅓ cup raisins
2 beaten eggs
2 tablespoons dark corn syrup
1 teaspoon salt
½ teaspoon dried marjoram, crushed
¼ teaspoon pepper
⅛ teaspoon ground cloves
3 slices salt pork *or* bacon

In a saucepan bring water and milk to boiling. Add *uncooked* rice; cover and cook about 50 minutes or till rice is tender. Grind liver with food grinder; *do not drain*. Set aside.

In a skillet cook the ¼ pound salt pork or bacon till crisp, remove, drain on paper toweling, and crumble; reserve drippings in skillet. To drippings add onion; cook till tender but not brown.

Stir together cooked rice mixture, liver, salt pork or bacon pieces, onion, raisins, eggs, corn syrup, salt, marjoram, pepper, and cloves. Turn into a greased 8x8x2-inch baking pan. Arrange the 3 slices salt pork or bacon atop meat mixture. Bake, uncovered, in a 350° oven for 25 to 30 minutes. Makes 6 servings.

Fiskeboller

Seafood was standard fare of the seafaring Vikings. And, over the years Scandinavians have developed ingenious methods of preparing fish.

One example is Norwegian fish pudding, a fluffy fish batter that can be baked as a custard or fried in the shape of balls called *Fiskeboller.* Often topping *Fiskeboller* is a mushroom, shrimp, or oyster sauce.

1 pound fresh *or* frozen cod fillets
½ medium onion, cut up
¼ cup whipping cream
3 eggs
¼ cup all-purpose flour
½ teaspoon salt
¼ teaspoon pepper
⅛ teaspoon ground nutmeg
Cooking oil *or* shortening for deep-fat frying
Mushroom Sauce

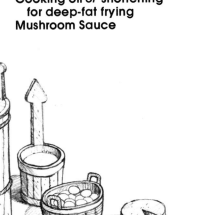

Thaw fish, if frozen. Pat fish dry with paper toweling; cut up. In a blender or food processor container combine ½ cup of the fish and the onion. Cover and blend or process till finely chopped. Remove and repeat with remaining fish. In a blender or food processor container combine all chopped fish and onion, whipping cream, eggs, flour, salt, pepper, and nutmeg. Cover and blend or process till mixture is nearly smooth.

In a saucepan or deep-fat fryer heat about 2 inches cooking oil or shortening to 365°. Carefully drop fish batter from a tablespoon into hot oil. Fry the fish balls, several at a time, about 3 minutes or till golden brown. Remove the fish balls; drain well on paper toweling. Keep warm. Prepare Mushroom Sauce. To serve, spoon sauce over fish balls. Makes 4 to 6 servings.

Mushroom Sauce: In a saucepan cook 1½ cups sliced fresh *mushrooms* in 2 tablespoons hot *butter or margarine* about 5 minutes or till tender. Stir in 2 tablespoons all-purpose *flour* and ⅛ teaspoon *pepper.* Add 1 cup *beef broth* all at once. Cook and stir till thickened and bubbly. Cook and stir 1 minute more. Stir in 2 tablespoons dry *sherry* and 1 tablespoon snipped *parsley.* Combine 1 slightly beaten *egg yolk* and 2 tablespoons *milk.* Slowly stir about *1 cup* of the hot mixture into egg yolks; return all to saucepan. Cook and stir over low heat 2 minutes more. Makes about 1½ cups.

Summer Vegetable Soup *pictured on page 150*

The growing season in the land of the midnight sun is extremely short, so Finns must make the most of their precious vegetable gardens. As soon as young and tender vegetables ripen, Finns prepare *Summer Vegetable Soup.* Often they serve open-faced sandwiches with this creamy soup.

2 cups fresh *or* frozen cauliflower flowerets
1 cup thinly sliced carrot
1 cup fresh *or* frozen peas
¼ cup sliced green onion
½ teaspoon dried dillweed
2 tablespoons butter *or* margarine
2 tablespoons all-purpose flour
½ teaspoon salt
¼ teaspoon white pepper
1 cup milk
1 cup light cream
1 slightly beaten egg yolk
1 cup torn fresh spinach
6 radishes, sliced (½ cup)

In a large covered saucepan cook cauliflower, carrot, peas, green onion, and dillweed in boiling salted water for 10 minutes. (Or, cook frozen vegetables according to package directions.) Drain, reserving cooking liquid; add water if necessary to measure 1 cup.

In a saucepan melt butter or margarine. Stir in flour, salt, and pepper. Add the reserved cooking liquid, the milk, and cream all at once. Cook and stir till thickened and bubbly. Cook and stir 1 minute more. Slowly stir about *1 cup* of the hot mixture into the egg yolk; return all to pan. Cook and stir over low heat 2 minutes more. Stir in cooked vegetables, spinach, and radishes. Heat through. Makes 6 side-dish servings.

SCANDINAVIA

Sweet and Sour Red Cabbage
Regional

In Denmark, *Sweet and Sour Red Cabbage* is part of the traditional Christmas Eve meal. It accompanies a pork roast, caramelized new potatoes, and smooth brown gravy.

4   cups shredded red cabbage
1   medium cooking apple, cored and chopped (1 cup)
¼   cup water
3   tablespoons dry red wine
1   tablespoon vinegar
1   tablespoon sugar
½   teaspoon salt
    Dash pepper
1   tablespoon butter *or* margarine

In a large, covered skillet cook cabbage and apple in the water about 10 minutes or till tender. *Do not drain.* Stir in wine, vinegar, sugar, salt, and pepper. Re-cover and simmer for 5 minutes. Stir in butter or margarine till melted. Makes 6 servings.

Carrot Custard
Finland

3   cups shredded carrot
2   cups water
⅓   cup pearl barley
¼   cup chopped onion
1   cup milk
4   beaten eggs
½   teaspoon salt
¼   teaspoon pepper
⅛   teaspoon ground nutmeg
2   tablespoons fine dry bread crumbs (optional)
2   teaspoons butter *or* margarine, melted (optional)

In a saucepan combine carrot, water, barley, and onion. Bring to boiling; reduce heat. Cover and simmer 20 minutes or till barley is just tender. Drain. Stir in milk, eggs, salt, pepper, and nutmeg. Turn into a greased 1½-quart casserole. Bake, uncovered, in a 325° oven about 65 minutes or till set. Let stand 10 minutes before serving. If desired, combine bread crumbs and melted butter. Top casserole with buttered crumbs. Makes 6 servings.

Almond Braid   *pictured on page 142*
Sweden

6½ to 7 cups all-purpose flour
2   packages active dry yeast
½   teaspoon ground cardamom
2   cups milk
¾   cup sugar
¾   cup butter *or* margarine
1½ teaspoons salt
1   egg
1   egg yolk
½   teaspoon almond extract
1   slightly beaten egg white
¼   cup slivered almonds
2   tablespoons sugar

In a large mixer bowl combine 3 *cups* of the flour, the yeast, and cardamom. In a saucepan heat milk, the ¾ cup sugar, butter or margarine, and salt just till warm (115° to 120°) and butter or margarine is almost melted; stir constantly. Add to flour mixture; add egg, egg yolk, and almond extract. Beat at low speed of electric mixer for ½ minute, scraping sides of bowl constantly. Beat 3 minutes at high speed. Stir in as much of the remaining flour as you can mix in with a spoon. Turn out onto lightly floured surface. Knead in enough of the remaining flour to make a moderately stiff dough that is smooth and elastic (6 to 8 minutes total). Shape into a ball. Place in a lightly greased bowl; turn once. Cover; let rise in a warm place till double (about 1 hour). Punch down; divide dough into 6 portions. Cover and let rest 10 minutes.

Roll *each* portion into a rope 24 inches long. On greased baking sheets shape into 2 braids, using 3 ropes for each. Curve each to form a horseshoe shape. Cover and let rise till nearly double (25 to 30 minutes). Brush with beaten egg white; sprinkle with almonds and sugar. Bake in a 350° oven 20 to 25 minutes or till done. Cool on wire rack. Makes 2.

The toast "skoal" is deeply entrenched in Scandinavian etiquette.

A host usually makes the first toast with a glass of "aquavit" to welcome his guests. Guests are then free to toast their hostess. Custom demands that the hostess return each "skoal," making eye contact with well-wishers as she raises her glass. Since this can require a lot of sips, she may toast several diners at a time if many are present.

"Aquavit," meaning water of life, is a clear, throat-burning liquor made from potatoes. It is usually served at a Danish luncheon along with beer.

Whether at home or in a sidewalk cafe, beer drinking is an extremely popular Scandinavian pastime. Denmark has done much for the beer drinkers of the world, its two largest breweries being credited with developing industrial processes for the pure cultivation of yeast and the pasteurization of beer. In addition to the light pilsner beers, Danish breweries also produce a sweet beer and a special lager for Christmas. Danes like the flavor of beer so much that they'll drink it warm as well as cold.

SCANDINAVIA

Lucia Buns   *pictured on page 142*   Sweden

Lucia Buns are so named because they traditionally are baked for Saint Lucia's day, December 13. The holiday commemorates a 10th century Catholic saint who was blinded rather than betray her faith in God.

This saint, also called the Queen of Light, is honored during the dark northern winter by young girls all over Sweden. On Saint Lucia's day, in households with girls, one daughter will don a white robe and a wreath crown of candles, and awaken her parents with the Lucia Buns and coffee before the dawn.

¼ **teaspoon thread saffron, crushed**
2 **tablespoons boiling water**
3½ **to 4 cups all-purpose flour**
1 **package active dry yeast**
1¼ **cups milk**
½ **cup butter *or* margarine**
⅓ **cup sugar**
1 **teaspoon salt**
1 **egg**
Raisins
1 **slightly beaten egg white**

In a small bowl dissolve saffron in boiling water. In a large mixing bowl combine *2 cups* of the flour and the dry yeast. In a medium saucepan heat together milk, butter or margarine, sugar, and salt just till warm (115° to 120°) and butter or margarine is almost melted; stir constantly. Add to flour mixture; add egg. Beat at low speed of electric mixer for ½ minute, scraping sides of bowl constantly. Beat 3 minutes at high speed.

Stir in as much of the remaining flour as you can mix in with a spoon. Turn out onto a lightly floured surface. Knead in enough of the remaining flour to make a moderately soft dough that is smooth and elastic (3 to 5 minutes total). Shape into a ball. Place in a lightly greased bowl; turn once to grease surface. Cover and let rise in warm place till double (about 1½ hours).

Punch down; divide dough into quarters. Cover; let rest 10 minutes. Divide *each* quarter into 12 equal pieces. Roll *each* piece of dough into a 12-inch-long rope. On a lightly greased baking sheet, form one rope into an S-shape, coiling the ends snail fashion. Repeat with remaining ropes. (Make double buns, if desired. Press the center of two of the S-shaped pieces together to form a cross.) Press *one* raisin into the center of *each* coil. Cover and let dough rise in a warm place till nearly double (about 40 minutes). Brush buns with beaten egg white and bake in 375° oven for 12 to 15 minutes. Makes 48 single or 24 double buns.

Sweet Raisin Bread   *pictured on page 142*   Norway

2 **packages active dry yeast**
1¼ **cups warm milk (110° to 115°)**
5½ **to 6 cups unbleached *or* all-purpose flour**
½ **cup sugar**
1 **tablespoon salt**
½ **teaspoon ground cloves**
½ **teaspoon pepper**
1 **12-ounce can (1½ cups) beer**
½ **cup light corn syrup**
2 **cups rye flour**
1 **cup raisins**

In a large bowl soften yeast in warm milk; let stand 5 minutes. Beat in *1 cup* of the unbleached flour, the sugar, salt, cloves, and pepper. Cover; let stand in warm place till dough becomes light and bubbly (about 40 minutes). Add beer and corn syrup. Stir in rye flour, raisins, and as much of the remaining unbleached or all-purpose flour as you can mix in with a spoon. Turn out onto floured surface. Knead in enough of the remaining unbleached or all-purpose flour to make a stiff dough that is smooth and elastic (8 to 10 minutes total). Shape into a ball. Place in a lightly greased bowl; turn once to grease surface. Cover; let rise till double (about 1 hour). Punch down; divide dough into thirds. Cover; let rest 10 minutes. Shape into 3 round loaves. Place on greased baking sheets. Cover; let rise till double (35 to 40 minutes). Bake in 375° oven for 40 minutes or till bread tests done. Cover each loaf with foil during last 20 minutes of baking time to prevent overbrowning. Cool on wire rack. Makes 3 loaves.

Lefse

There are as many recipes for *Lefse* as there are Norwegian cooks. In eastern Norway, potato *Lefse* recipes predominate. In other areas, *Lefse* is based on wheat flour.

Fresh *Lefse* can be served crisp, like crackers, or soft. Some Norwegians like soft *Lefse* filled with "gjetost" (goat cheese) and sour cream; others like it as a dessert, spread with butter and cinnamon-sugar or with lingonberry preserves and whipped cream.

For crisp *Lefse*, bake single layers in a 425° oven for about 3 minutes. For soft *Lefse*, moisten the "lefse" sheets slightly between layers of damp towels before using.

Tightly wrap any leftover *Lefse* and store it in the freezer until ready to use.

2 to 2½ cups all-purpose flour
1 tablespoon sugar
1 teaspoon salt
¼ cup butter *or* margarine
1 cup buttermilk

In a mixing bowl stir together *2 cups* of the flour, the sugar, and salt. Cut in butter or margarine till mixture resembles coarse crumbs. Add buttermilk; stir till just moistened. Cover; chill at least 1 hour.

Turn out onto a lightly floured surface. Knead in enough of the remaining flour to make a stiff dough (8 to 10 minutes total). Divide into 8 portions; shape into balls. Cover and let stand 10 minutes. On a floured surface roll *each* ball to a circle 10 inches in diameter. Roll around rolling pin; transfer to a hot lightly greased griddle or skillet. Cook over medium heat for 4 to 6 minutes or till light brown; turn once. (Should be limp.) Cover with plastic wrap to prevent drying out. Repeat with remaining dough. Makes 8.

Sandbakkelse   *pictured on page 142*

1⅓ cups all-purpose flour
2 tablespoons ground almonds
Dash ground cardamom
½ cup butter *or* margarine
½ cup sugar
1 egg yolk
2 teaspoons water
Fresh strawberries *or* fruit preserves (optional)

Stir together flour, almonds, and cardamom. In a mixer bowl beat butter or margarine on medium speed of electric mixer for 30 seconds. Add sugar and beat till fluffy. Add egg yolk and water; beat well. Add dry ingredients to beaten mixture and beat till well combined. Place about *2½ teaspoons* dough in center of a 2½-inch sandbakkelse mold or tiny foilware cup. With thumb, press dough evenly and very thinly over bottom and up sides. Repeat with remaining dough. Place molds on cookie sheet. Bake in 375° oven for about 10 minutes or till edges are light brown. Cool on wire rack. To remove, invert molds and tap lightly. If desired, fill with fresh strawberries or preserves. Makes about 30.

Napoleon's Hats

Marzipan, an almond paste, plays a prominent role in Scandinavian baking, especially around the yule season. This sweet paste not only acts as a filling in *Napoleon's Hats* and other cakes and cookies, but also is a candy in its own right. Children shape and decorate marzipan candies to stuff into heart-shaped paper baskets that hang on Christmas trees.

2 cups all-purpose flour
¼ teaspoon salt
¾ cup butter *or* margarine
½ cup sugar
2 egg yolks
1 teaspoon vanilla
2 egg whites
¼ teaspoon cream of tartar
⅓ cup powdered sugar
1 cup ground almonds (4 ounces)

Stir together flour and salt. In a mixer bowl beat butter or margarine on medium speed of electric mixer for 30 seconds. Add sugar and beat till fluffy. Add egg yolks and vanilla; beat well. Add dry ingredients to beaten mixture and beat till well combined. Cover and chill 1 hour.

For almond paste filling, in a small mixer bowl beat egg whites and cream of tartar till soft peaks form (tips curl over). Gradually add powdered sugar, beating till stiff peaks form (tips stand straight). Fold in ground almonds. Set aside.

On a lightly floured surface roll dough to ⅛-inch thickness. Cut into circles 3 inches in diameter. Place about *1 rounded teaspoon* of the almond filling in center of *each*. Fold up and pinch 3 sides to form a 3-cornered hat, leaving top of filling exposed. Place 2 inches apart on ungreased cookie sheet. Bake in a 375° oven for 10 to 12 minutes or till done. Remove from cookie sheet; cool on wire rack. Makes about 36 cookies.

SCANDINAVIA

Apple Cake *pictured on page 142* Denmark

A wonderful way to use up leftovers, the "smørrebrød," or open-faced sandwich, usually reflects what was served over the past few evenings for dinner. Leftover or not, it seems every lunch box contains at least one "smørrebrød" with *Liver Pâté,* the Danish answer to our American peanut butter.

Making attractive "smørrebrød" platters is a culinary art. Experts argue over which toppings agree with which garnishes. But real restrictions are few: The overall flavor is the final test. Some favorite combinations include *Frikadellar Meatballs* (see recipe, page 144) with cucumber slices, *Liver Pâté* with meat aspic cubes, and pickled herring with red onion rings.

6 **medium cooking apples, peeled and sliced (6 cups)**
¼ **cup sugar**
3 **inches stick cinnamon**
9 **soft macaroons, crumbled (1½ cups)**
½ **cup fine dry bread crumbs**
½ **cup butter *or* margarine, melted**
⅛ **teaspoon ground nutmeg**
1 **cup whipping cream**
Apple slices, whole almonds, *or* currant jelly (optional)

In a medium saucepan combine the 6 apples, sugar, cinnamon, and ½ cup *water.* Bring to boiling; reduce heat. Cover and simmer for 8 to 10 minutes or till apples are tender. Remove and discard cinnamon. Cool to room temperature.

In a mixing bowl stir together the macaroon crumbs, bread crumbs, the melted butter or margarine, and nutmeg. In a mixer bowl whip the cream till soft peaks form.

In a 2-quart glass bowl layer *half* of the crumb mixture, *half* of the cooled apple mixture, and *half* of the whipped cream. Repeat layers. Garnish with apple slices, whole almonds, or currant jelly, if desired. Chill till serving time. Makes 6 servings.

Pictured from front to back
Liver Pâté and Summer Vegetable Soup (see recipe, page 145)

Berry Soup Regional

Scandinavians consume *Berry Soup* as fast as the berries ripen. Some people eat this delightful soup with sour cream as an appetizer; others top it with whipped cream to make a dessert.

In winter when fresh fruits are scarce, soups are made of dried fruit.

2 cups fresh blueberries, blackberries, raspberries, strawberries, *or* one 16-ounce package frozen berries, *or* one 16-ounce can berries, drained
2 cups apple juice
6 inches stick cinnamon
2 whole cloves
1 tablespoon cornstarch
1 teaspoon vanilla
Whipped cream *or* dairy sour cream (optional)
4 rusks (optional)

Clean berries, if fresh. (*Or*, thaw berries, if frozen.) In a saucepan combine berries, *1¾ cups* of the apple juice, cinnamon, and cloves. Bring to boiling; reduce heat. Simmer, uncovered, for 10 minutes, stirring occasionally. Combine the remaining apple juice and the cornstarch; stir into berry mixture. Cook and stir till slightly thickened and bubbly. Cook and stir 2 minutes more. Remove from heat; stir in vanilla. Remove and discard stick cinnamon and cloves. Spoon into 4 individual serving bowls. Garnish with whipped cream or sour cream and serve with rusks, if desired. Makes 4 servings.

Liver Pâté Denmark

1 pound pork liver *or* beef liver
¼ pound boneless pork, cut up
1 medium onion, cut up
1 2-ounce can anchovy fillets, drained
3 beaten eggs
1¼ cups light cream *or* milk
¼ cup all-purpose flour
½ teaspoon salt
¼ teaspoon ground ginger
¼ teaspoon pepper
Light *or* dark rye bread, thinly sliced
Assorted garnishes*

Grind liver, pork, onion, and anchovies through fine blade of food grinder. In a mixing bowl combine eggs and cream or milk. Stir in flour, salt, ginger, and pepper. Add ground meat mixture; mix well. Pour mixture into a greased 8x4x2-inch loaf pan. Bake in a 350° oven for 1¾ to 2 hours. Remove from oven; drain off fat, if necessary. Cover and chill overnight. Serve on rye bread and garnish. Makes 10 to 12 servings.

*Note: For garnishes, choose any of the following: sliced cucumbers, radishes, hard-cooked eggs, tomatoes, red onions, or beets; halved green grapes, capers, pimiento, and fresh dill or parsley.

Herring Salad Norway

½ pound dressed, boned salt herring
1 16-ounce jar *or* can diced beets, drained and rinsed
2 small apples, peeled, cored, and diced (1½ cups)
1 large potato, cooked, peeled, and diced (1 cup)
1 tablespoon finely chopped onion
¼ cup white vinegar
2 tablespoons sugar
¼ teaspoon pepper
½ cup whipping cream

Cut fish into bite-size pieces. Soak in enough cold water to cover for 12 hours, changing water several times. Drain. In a large bowl carefully stir together herring, beets, apples, potato, and onion. Stir together vinegar, sugar, and pepper till sugar is dissolved. Stir into herring mixture. Cover and chill till serving time. Whip cream to soft peaks; fold into chilled herring mixture. Serve immediately. Makes 5½ cups.

Venezuela
Colombia
Ecuador
Peru
Lima
Bolivia
La Paz
Paraguay
Argentina
Chile
Venezuela
Guyana
Surinam
Brazil
Rio de Janeiro
Uruguay
Buenos Aires

SOUTH AMERICA

South America's most famous and popular contribution to the world's food stores is the potato. Long before the Spanish arrived in the 15th century, Incans had cultivated more than 100 varieties of potatoes. They ingeniously preserved the potatoes in the chilly Andean highlands using a process that yielded results very similar to those of freeze-drying. The potato remains a dietary staple in Ecuador, Bolivia, and Peru, and is still preserved by the centuries-old Indian method.

Because most of South America was under Spanish domination for almost 300 years, cooking is a combination of native Indian and Spanish. Venezuela and Argentina are known for excellent beef. Venezuelans serve it with avocados or a hot chili pepper sauce. In Argentina, beef fills "empanadas," pastries of Spanish origin.

The one exception to the Spanish-Indian cuisine in South America is in Brazil, which was settled by Portuguese. Its cuisine blends the tastes of the Portuguese with those of native

Indians as well as Africans imported as slaves for sugar plantations.

Throughout Brazil, black beans, cassava meal, and rice are the dietary mainstays. Hot chili pepper is an indispensable flavoring ingredient. Hearts of palm are popular in vegetable dishes or salads.

The African influence is apparent in the use of coconut milk, nuts, palm oil, and shrimp. The Portuguese contribution is a love for the sweets and desserts of the Iberian Peninsula.

The pride of South America is its coffee industry. It has come a long way since coffee was first planted there in the 1700s. Together, Brazil, Colombia, and Central America, now produce over half the world's coffee.

The best grades of coffee are exported, but South Americans still cherish the inferior coffee that stays at home. Brazilians call their demitasses of coffee "cafezino" or little coffee. These loyal coffee drinkers usually take it black with sugar. For breakfast, they might add milk.

Pictured clockwise from back center
Feijoada Bean Stew (see recipe, page 154), Potatoes Rellenos (see recipe, page 157), Ensalada Mixta (see recipe, page 156), and Puffed Corn Pies (see recipe, page 154)

153

Feijoada Bean Stew   *pictured on page 152*   Brazil

Originally created in sunny Rio de Janeiro, *Feijoada Bean Stew* has grown in popularity to become Brazil's national dish. This meaty black bean stew appears at "carnival" (the pre-Lenten festival) and other celebrations throughout the year.

It is traditionally served over rice and sprinkled with "farofa" (manioc flour).

2½ cups dry black beans
12 cups water
1 to 1½ pounds smoked beef tongue
½ pound beef stew meat, cut into ¾-inch pieces
1 pig's foot
3 cups water
1 pound pork spareribs, cut into 1-rib portions
½ pound fresh pork sausage links
½ pound smoked sausage links, cut into bite-size pieces
¼ pound Canadian-style bacon *or* ham, cubed (¾ cup)
½ cup chopped onion
1 medium tomato, peeled and chopped
2 tablespoons snipped parsley
2 cloves garlic, minced
¼ teaspoon crushed red pepper
Hot cooked rice
Farofa (manioc flour) *or* regular farina (optional)

Rinse beans. In a 4-quart Dutch oven or kettle combine beans and 6 *cups* of the water. Bring to boiling. Reduce heat; simmer 2 minutes. Remove from heat. Cover; let stand 1 hour. (*Or,* soak beans in water overnight in a covered pan.) Drain and rinse. In same Dutch oven or kettle combine rinsed beans and 6 *cups* of the water. Bring to boiling; reduce heat. Cover; simmer for 2 hours or till beans are nearly tender.

Meanwhile, in another large kettle combine tongue, stew meat, pig's foot, and the remaining 3 cups water. Bring to boiling; reduce heat. Cover; simmer 45 minutes. Add spareribs; simmer 30 minutes more. Add fresh sausage; simmer 15 minutes more. Remove meats, reserving cooking liquid. Skin tongue. Remove and discard all bones. Chop all cooked meat. Skim fat from reserved cooking liquid; add liquid to beans along with the cooked meat, smoked sausage, Canadian-style bacon or ham, onion, tomato, parsley, garlic, and red pepper. Cover and simmer 30 minutes more. Mash beans slightly. Season to taste with salt and pepper. Serve over rice and sprinkle with farofa or farina, if desired. Makes 10 to 12 servings.

Puffed Corn Pies   *pictured on page 152*   Chile

4 fresh ears of corn
1 cup milk
1 teaspoon sugar
½ teaspoon salt
¼ teaspoon dried basil, crushed
1 pound ground beef
1 large onion, chopped (1 cup)
¼ cup beef broth
¾ teaspoon salt
½ teaspoon ground cumin
¼ teaspoon crushed red pepper
¼ teaspoon pepper
⅛ teaspoon dried marjoram, crushed
3 tablespoons cold water
2 teaspoons all-purpose flour
2 egg whites
2 beaten egg yolks
½ cup chopped, pitted ripe olives
¼ cup raisins
1 hard-cooked egg, sliced
2 teaspoons sugar
Sliced, pitted ripe olives (optional)

With a sharp knife, cut lengthwise down center of each row of corn kernels. Cut off just the tips of kernels; scrape cob with dull edge of knife (should have 2 cups cream-style corn). In a saucepan combine corn, milk, the 1 teaspoon sugar, the ½ teaspoon salt, and the basil. Cover and simmer about 10 minutes or till corn is tender. *Do not boil.*

In a skillet cook beef and onion till onion is tender and meat is brown. Drain off fat. Stir in beef broth, the ¾ teaspoon salt, the cumin, red pepper, pepper, and marjoram. Bring to boiling; reduce heat. Cover and simmer for 30 minutes. Combine water and flour; stir into meat mixture. Cook and stir till thickened and bubbly. Cook and stir 1 minute more. Beat egg whites till stiff peaks form (tips stand straight). Gradually stir corn mixture into egg yolks; fold in egg whites.

To assemble pies, place hot ground meat mixture in four 12-ounce casseroles. Top each with *some* of the ½ cup olives, raisins, and sliced egg. Pour a scant *1 cup* of the corn mixture atop each. Sprinkle each with ½ *teaspoon* sugar. Bake in 400° oven for 15 to 18 minutes or till set. Garnish with additional sliced olives, if desired. Makes 4 servings.

Soufflé-Topped Shrimp

Brazilian cookery, especially that in northern Brazil, uses coconut milk extensively. This ingredient appears in *Soufflé-Topped Shrimp* and other seafood dishes typical of the northern coastal areas.

1 pound fresh *or* frozen shrimp in shells
2 medium onions, chopped
½ cup snipped parsley
2 tablespoons butter *or* margarine
4 medium tomatoes, peeled and chopped (2 cups)
¼ cup Coconut Milk (see recipe, page 170) *or* milk
4 teaspoons cornstarch
½ teaspoon salt
⅛ teaspoon ground red pepper
4 egg yolks
4 egg whites
¼ teaspoon salt
1 small onion, thinly sliced and separated into rings

Thaw shrimp, if frozen. Remove shells; devein. Halve shrimp lengthwise. Cook 2 chopped onions and parsley in hot butter or margarine till onion is tender but not brown. Add shrimp and tomatoes; cover and cook over medium heat for 10 minutes. Stir together Coconut Milk or milk, cornstarch, ½ teaspoon salt, and ground red pepper; stir into shrimp mixture. Cook and stir till thickened and bubbly. Cook and stir 2 minutes more. Reduce heat. Keep the mixture warm.

Beat egg yolks about 5 minutes or till thick and lemon colored. Wash beaters. Beat egg whites and the ¼ teaspoon salt till stiff peaks form (tips stand straight). Fold yolks into whites. Turn *hot* shrimp mixture into 8x8x2-inch baking dish. Spread or dollop egg mixture atop. Top with the 1 onion cut into rings. Bake in a 375° oven for 20 to 25 minutes or till knife inserted near center comes out clean. Serve immediately. Makes 4 servings.

Chicken Empadao

3 cups all-purpose flour
½ teaspoon salt
2 tablespoons lard *or* shortening
2 tablespoons butter *or* margarine
¾ cup milk
4 slightly beaten egg yolks
3 whole medium chicken breasts
1 cup water
¼ cup tomato sauce
¼ cup chopped onion
1 tablespoon vinegar
2 sprigs parsley
1½ teaspoons salt
⅛ teaspoon pepper
Milk
½ cup finely chopped onion
2 tablespoons butter *or* margarine
3 tablespoons cornstarch
2 beaten egg yolks
¼ cup snipped parsley

For pastry, in a large mixing bowl stir together flour and the ½ teaspoon salt. Cut in lard or shortening and 2 tablespoons butter or margarine till pieces are the size of small peas. Stir in milk and the 4 egg yolks. Form dough into ball. Cover and chill 1 hour.

For filling, rinse chicken breasts. In saucepan combine chicken, water, tomato sauce, the ¼ cup onion, vinegar, the 2 sprigs parsley, the 1½ teaspoons salt, and the pepper. Bring to boiling; reduce heat. Cover and simmer for 15 to 20 minutes or till chicken is tender. Remove chicken. When chicken is cool enough to handle, remove meat from bones. Cut chicken into bite-size pieces; set aside. Discard skin and bones. Strain broth; skim off fat. Measure broth; add enough milk to measure 2½ cups liquid. In saucepan cook the ½ cup onion in the 2 tablespoons hot butter or margarine till tender but not brown. Stir together milk mixture and cornstarch; add to onion all at once. Cook and stir till thickened and bubbly. Cook and stir 2 minutes more. Gradually stir thickened broth mixture into the 2 egg yolks. Stir in chicken and the ¼ cup snipped parsley. Season to taste with salt and pepper.

Divide dough in half. Roll out *half* of the dough to a circle 14 inches in diameter. Line a 10-inch pie plate with pastry; trim even with rim. Spread filling in pastry. For top crust, roll out the remaining dough. Cut slits for escape of steam. Top filling with top crust. Trim top crust ½ inch beyond edge of pie plate. Fold extra pastry under bottom crust; flute edge. Using pastry brush, brush with a little milk. Cover edge of crust with foil. Bake in 375° oven for 25 minutes. Remove foil; bake for 20 minutes more or till crust is golden. Makes 6 servings.

SOUTH AMERICA

Fish with Salsa Fria   *pictured on page 160*   Colombia

Salsa Fria in English means "cold sauce." This spicy cold tomato sauce serves as a refreshing accompaniment to the subtly flavored grilled fish. Prepare *Salsa Fria* far enough in advance to allow it time to chill.

1 3½- to 4-pound fresh *or* frozen dressed red snapper *or* other fish (with head and tail)
1 small fresh pineapple
   Salsa Fria
   Cooking oil
2 tablespoons lemon juice
   Salt
   Parsley sprigs

Thaw fish, if frozen. To prepare pineapple, remove crown. Wash and peel pineapple; remove eyes and core. Finely chop *1 cup* of the pineapple; reserve for Salsa Fria. Cut remaining pineapple into chunks; set aside. Prepare Salsa Fria. Brush fish with cooking oil; place in a well-greased wire basket over *slow* coals. Grill for 10 to 15 minutes. Turn fish and grill 10 to 15 minutes more or till fish flakes easily when tested with a fork, brushing occasionally with lemon juice. Sprinkle fish with salt. Transfer fish to a heated serving platter; garnish with parsley and the pineapple chunks. Pass Salsa Fria. Serves 8.

Salsa Fria: In saucepan simmer 4 cups peeled and cut up *tomatoes,* uncovered, 15 to 20 minutes or till most of the juice has evaporated. Add the reserved 1 cup finely chopped *pineapple,* ¾ cup chopped *green pepper,* ½ cup finely chopped *onion,* ¼ cup *lime or lemon juice,* 2 tablespoons *sugar,* 1 teaspoon *salt,* ⅛ teaspoon ground *cinnamon,* ⅛ teaspoon ground *cloves,* ⅛ teaspoon ground *ginger,* and a dash bottled *hot pepper sauce.* Cover and simmer 15 minutes more or till vegetables are tender. Cool; cover and chill till serving time. Makes 4 cups.

Ensalada Mixta   *pictured on page 152*   Venezuela

1 medium cucumber, peeled
   Lettuce leaves
2 large bananas, sliced
1 avocado, seeded, peeled, and sliced
1 large green pepper, cut into thin strips
1 red sweet pepper, cut into thin strips
½ small onion, thinly sliced and separated into rings
   Hot Pepper Dressing

Halve cucumber lengthwise; remove seeds and slice crosswise. In a lettuce-lined salad bowl arrange cucumber slices, banana slices, avocado slices, green and red sweet peppers, and onion rings. Pour Hot Pepper Dressing over salad. Cover and chill 1 to 2 hours. Toss before serving. Serves 8.

Hot Pepper Dressing: In a screw-top jar combine ⅓ cup *vinegar,* ¼ cup *salad oil or olive oil,* ½ teaspoon *salt,* and ¼ teaspoon bottled *hot pepper sauce.* Cover and shake to mix well.

Tomato Rice   Brazil

1 cup long grain rice
½ cup chopped onion
1 small clove garlic, minced
2 tablespoons cooking oil
2 cups water
1 large tomato, peeled and chopped
1 teaspoon salt

In a 2-quart saucepan cook *uncooked* rice, onion, and garlic in hot oil for 5 to 8 minutes or till rice is golden and onion is tender, stirring constantly. Remove from heat. Carefully stir in water, tomato, and salt. Return to heat. Bring to boiling; reduce heat. Cover and simmer 20 minutes or till rice is tender. Makes 8 servings.

Potatoes Rellenos *pictured on page 152* Chile

"Relleno" stems from the Spanish verb "rellenar," meaning to stuff or refill. Many South American vegetables lend themselves to stuffing. Avocados, potatoes, and peppers (as in the famous "chiles rellenos") are among the vegetable favorites.

6 medium potatoes (2 pounds), peeled and quartered
1 beaten egg yolk
½ cup all-purpose flour
½ pound ground beef
1 medium onion, finely chopped (½ cup)
1 hard-cooked egg, chopped
2 tablespoons raisins, chopped
2 tablespoons chopped, pitted ripe olives
½ teaspoon salt
¼ teaspoon dried oregano, crushed
¼ teaspoon pepper
⅛ teaspoon ground red pepper
Cooking oil *or* shortening for deep-fat frying

In covered saucepan cook potatoes in small amount of boiling salted water for 20 to 25 minutes or till tender. Drain and mash potatoes (should have about 3 cups). Cool, then chill potatoes.

Stir egg yolk and the flour into chilled potatoes; mix well. In a skillet cook beef and onion till meat is brown and onion is tender. Drain off fat. Stir in hard-cooked egg, raisins, olives, salt, oregano, pepper, and ground red pepper.

On a lightly floured sheet of waxed paper, pat out about ¼ *cup* of the potato mixture to a circle 4 inches in diameter; place about *2 tablespoons* of the meat mixture on *half* of the circle. Roll up, pressing sides and ends to seal. (Lift waxed paper to help fold potato mixture over meat.) Shape into a roll about 4 inches long. Repeat with remaining potato and meat mixtures. Fry, a few at a time, in deep hot fat (360°) about 3 minutes or till golden. Drain on paper toweling. Serve warm. Makes 12 side-dish servings.

SOUTH AMERICA

Potatoes with Hot Sauce
Bolivia

Once the highland Indians had learned the art of cheese making from the Spanish, they began sprucing up their boiled potatoes with creamy cheese sauces. *Potatoes with Hot Sauce* is a peppery version created by Bolivian Indians.

5 medium potatoes, peeled and quartered (5 cups)
1 hard-cooked egg
2 tablespoons finely chopped onion
2 teaspoons finely chopped fresh green chili pepper
1 tablespoon cooking oil
1 tablespoon all-purpose flour
¼ teaspoon salt
1 13-ounce can (1⅔ cups) evaporated milk
1 cup shredded mozzarella cheese (4 ounces)
1 teaspoon lemon juice
¼ cup chopped peanuts (optional)
¼ cup sliced, pitted ripe olives (optional)

In covered saucepan cook potatoes in a small amount of boiling salted water for 20 to 25 minutes or till tender. Transfer to serving bowl; keep warm. Meanwhile, separate egg yolk from white. Chop the yolk and chop the white; set both aside.

For sauce, in saucepan cook onion and chili pepper in hot oil till tender but not brown. Stir in flour and salt. Add evaporated milk all at once; cook and stir till thickened and bubbly. Cook and stir 1 minute more. Add egg yolk, cheese, and lemon juice, stirring till cheese is melted. Pour hot sauce over potatoes. Garnish with hard-cooked egg white, peanuts and olives, if desired. Serves 8.

Corn Soupbread
Paraguay

Called "sopa" (soup) in Spanish, this bread has a texture similar to spoon bread. It is normally served with steak.

1 medium onion, chopped (½ cup)
2 tablespoons butter or margarine
2 cups milk
1½ cups yellow cornmeal
3 beaten egg yolks
1 8½-ounce can cream-style corn
1 cup cream-style cottage cheese
1 cup shredded Muenster cheese (4 ounces)
½ teaspoon salt
3 egg whites
Butter or margarine

In a small saucepan cook onion in hot butter or margarine till tender but not brown. Set aside. In a medium saucepan stir milk into cornmeal. Cook, stirring constantly, till mixture is very thick and pulls away from sides of pan. Remove from heat.

In a mixing bowl combine onion mixture, egg yolks, corn, cottage cheese, Muenster cheese, and salt. Stir cornmeal mixture into cheese mixture; mix well. Beat egg whites till stiff peaks form (tips stand straight); fold into cornmeal and cheese mixture. Turn into a greased 2-quart casserole. Bake in a 350° oven for 50 minutes or till knife inserted near center comes out clean. Serve immediately with butter or margarine. Makes 8 servings.

Pumpkin Custard
Brazil

Pumpkin Custard is welcomed at the Saint John's day outdoor fiestas in June, Brazil's midwinter. The holiday honors not only Saint John (the matchmaking saint), but also the corn harvest. Corn, sweet potato, and pumpkin dishes make up the menu for the celebration.

3 slightly beaten eggs
1 cup mashed cooked pumpkin or canned pumpkin
1 cup light cream or milk
½ cup packed brown sugar
½ teaspoon ground cinnamon
¼ teaspoon ground ginger
¼ teaspoon ground nutmeg

In a mixing bowl stir together eggs, pumpkin, cream or milk, brown sugar, cinnamon, ginger, and nutmeg. Place an 8x1½-inch round baking dish or six 6-ounce custard cups in a shallow baking pan. Pour pumpkin mixture into baking dish or divide pumpkin mixture among the custard cups. Pour boiling water into pan around baking dish or custard cups to depth of 1 inch.

Bake in a 325° oven about 40 minutes or till knife inserted near center comes out clean. Serve warm or chilled. (To unmold chilled individual custards, first loosen edges with a spatula or knife. Invert onto a serving plate.) Makes 6 servings.

Coconut Quindins

Brazil

Portuguese nuns immigrating to Brazil carried with them their treasured candy recipes. Once in their new homeland they discovered they could adapt their recipes to a host of wonderful new candy ingredients.

Because sugar was such a prominent crop, the nuns profited by sending sweets back to the old country, where sugar was scarce. They used the extra income for their missions and other charities.

The presentation of these eye-catching sweets was of the utmost importance. The nuns experimented with different coatings such as nuts, coconut, and cocoa. Black slave women devised a new art form, creating intricate paper doilies to hold the sugary treats. Today these imaginative doilies have been replaced by dainty paper cups.

1 cup sugar
¾ cup water
1 7-ounce package (1¾ cups) flaked coconut
6 beaten egg yolks
2 teaspoons lemon juice
1 teaspoon butter *or* margarine

In 2-quart saucepan combine sugar and water. Bring to boiling. Cook and stir over medium heat till mixture reaches 234° on candy thermometer (soft-ball stage). Remove from heat; stir in coconut, egg yolks, lemon juice, and butter or margarine. Using about *1 tablespoon* in each, divide mixture among 24 buttered 1½-inch muffin cups. Place muffin pans in shallow pan; add boiling water to shallow pan to depth of ½ inch. Bake in a 375° oven for 30 minutes. Remove muffin pans from water; cool on wire rack. To unmold candies, first loosen edges with spatula or knife. Invert onto wire rack, tapping bottom of cups. Cool. Cover and chill to store. Makes 3 dozen.

Peanut Balls

Brazil

2½ cups shelled, roasted peanuts, ground (about 3 cups)
1 14½-ounce can (1⅓ cups) Eagle Brand sweetened condensed milk
Powdered sugar

In 2-quart saucepan combine ground peanuts and condensed milk. Cook and stir over medium heat about 5 minutes or till mixture forms a ball around the spoon and pulls away from sides of pan. Turn mixture out onto buttered plate to cool. When cool enough to handle, butter hands and form mixture into balls 1-inch in diameter; roll in powdered sugar. Cover and chill to store. Makes 6 dozen.

Brigadeiros

Brazil

1 14½-ounce can (1⅓ cups) Eagle Brand sweetened condensed milk
2 tablespoons unsweetened cocoa powder
1 tablespoon butter
⅓ cup chocolate-flavored sprinkles

In 2-quart saucepan combine condensed milk, cocoa powder, and butter. Cook and stir over medium heat about 5 minutes or till mixture forms a ball around the spoon and pulls away from sides of pan. Turn mixture out onto buttered plate to cool. When cool enough to handle, butter hands and form mixture into 1-inch balls; roll in chocolate sprinkles. Cover and chill to store. Makes 2 dozen.

SOUTH AMERICA

Brazilians are very fond of "churrasco," meat grilled on skewers over hot coals. Many restaurants are called "churrascarias" and feature a "churrasco" menu. The service is quick since the food is already prepared.

Waiters circle the tables, each brandishing a swordlike skewer that holds one kind of meat — lamb, beef, pork, hot and mild sausage, meatballs, or goat. At the gesture of a diner, the waiter carves off slice after slice of meat until he is stopped.

The overwhelmed guest scarcely touches one bite before the next waiter appears at his table with a different cut of meat.

Pictured from front to back
Fish with Salsa Fria (see recipe, page 156), Beef Heart Anticuchos, and Batida Paulista

Beef Heart Anticuchos   Peru

In Peru, *Beef Heart Anticuchos* are eaten as often as hamburgers are in the United States. The natives use feathers or cornhusks to brush the marinade onto these South American Indian kabobs as they cook.

1   2- to 2½-pound beef heart
1   cup vinegar
½   cup cooking oil
3   fresh green chili peppers, finely chopped (¼ cup)
2   cloves garlic, minced
1   teaspoon salt
½   teaspoon crushed annatto seed *or* paprika
½   teaspoon ground cumin
¼   teaspoon pepper
    Canned green chili peppers (optional)
    Cherry tomatoes (optional)

Rinse heart; remove outer membrane. Slit heart open; remove hard parts from center. Trim fat from heart; discard. Rinse and drain. Cut heart into 1-inch pieces; place in bowl. For marinade, combine vinegar, cooking oil, chili peppers, garlic, salt, annatto or paprika, cumin, and pepper; pour over meat. Cover; chill at least 4 hours.

Drain, reserving marinade. Thread meat on short skewers, using two cubes per skewer; brush with marinade. Grill over *hot* coals for 10 to 15 minutes, turning and brushing with marinade occasionally. (Or, broil 3 to 4 inches from heat for 15 minutes.) Serve with chili peppers and cherry tomatoes, if desired. Makes about 32 appetizers.

Batida Paulista   Brazil

Authentic *Batida* drinks contain "cachaça," a potent Brazilian rum distilled from sugar cane. This *Batida* sour takes its name from a nickname given to residents of San Paulo.

    Sugar
1   cup rum
2   egg whites
¼   cup lemon juice
2   tablespoons sugar
1   cup ice cubes (6 large cubes)
8   lemon peel curls (optional)

Moisten rims of chilled cocktail glasses with water; invert glass into a dish of sugar to make a sugared rim. In blender container combine rum, egg whites, lemon juice, and the 2 tablespoons sugar. With blender running, add ice cubes, one or two at a time, through hole in lid, blending till frothy. Serve at once in sugar-rimmed glasses. Trim with a lemon curl, if desired. Makes 8 (2¾-ounce) servings.

Cheese Pastries   Bolivia

2   cups all-purpose flour
1½   teaspoons baking powder
¼   teaspoon salt
½   cup butter *or* shortening
⅓   cup milk
2   slightly beaten egg yolks
2   slightly beaten egg whites
2   cups shredded Monterey Jack *or* Muenster cheese (8 ounces)
½   teaspoon finely shredded lime peel (optional)

For pastry, in mixing bowl stir together flour, baking powder, and salt. Cut in butter or shortening till pieces are size of small peas. Stir in milk and egg yolks. Form dough into a ball; cover and chill 1 hour. Divide dough in half. On a lightly floured surface roll *each* half to a 14x7-inch rectangle.

Combine egg whites, cheese, and lime peel, if desired. Spread *half* of the filling lengthwise down center of *each* rectangle. Fold two opposite edges to center, moisten to seal. Place rolls, seam side down, on ungreased baking sheet. Bake in a 400° oven for 20 minutes or till brown. Cool. Cut into 1-inch-thick slices. Makes 24 to 26 appetizers.

Corn Pancakes   Venezuela

1   cup frozen whole kernel corn, thawed, *or* canned whole kernel corn, drained
4   eggs
1   tablespoon all-purpose flour
¼   teaspoon salt
1   tablespoon snipped parsley
4   ounces Muenster cheese, thinly sliced

In a blender or food processor container combine corn, eggs, flour, and salt. Cover; blend or process till nearly smooth. Stir in parsley. For *each* pancake, pour a scant *1 tablespoon* of the mixture onto a lightly greased 10-inch skillet. Cook over medium heat, 4 pancakes at a time about 1 minute on each side. Remove; set aside and keep warm.

Serve pancakes with slices of Muenster cheese. Makes about 24 appetizer servings.

SOUTHEAST ASIA

During the Middle Ages, Southeast Asia was the center of the world's spice trade, and it is this region's spices that produce the unique flavors of dishes from India to Indonesia.

India's curry is not just one spice but a blend of many, freshly ground for each dish. Each cook prepares curry differently, choosing from anise seed, cloves, cardamom, cinnamon, coriander, fenugreek, cumin, ginger, saffron, and turmeric. In Indonesia and Malaysia, lemon grass, galingale and tamarind flavor local specialties.

From India to Vietnam, hot chili peppers are a favorite of all nationalities, but Thailand and Sri Lanka (Ceylon) are especially known for their love of extremely hot dishes.

The favorite flavoring ingredient of Thailand, Vietnam, and Kampuchea (formerly known as Cambodia) is "nuoc cham," a fish sauce without which no meal is complete. It is as essential to food preparation in that region as soy sauce is to China and Japan. The Vietnamese sometimes add fresh chili peppers, garlic, sugar, lime, lemon, and vinegar to "nuoc cham" to make it even more pungent.

A mainstay at all meals is rice, the dietary staple of Southeast Asia and a bland accompaniment to the region's highly seasoned dishes. Whether in Bangladesh or Kampuchea, all the dishes for a meal are served at once and diners help themselves. As in other Oriental cuisines, dessert is seldom served since sweets are considered snacktime treats. A more fitting conclusion to an exotic Asian meal is fresh fruit — a cool, refreshing finale.

Pictured clockwise from top right
Nasi Goreng (see recipe, page 171), Beef Satay (see recipe, page 164), Rice Cakes (see recipe, page 164), Chicken in Coconut Sauce (see recipe, page 168), Chapati (see recipe, page 175), Crispy Fried Fish (see recipe, page 171), and, center, Sweet Tomato Chutney (see recipe, page 174).

SOUTHEAST ASIA

Beef Satay   *pictured on page 162*   Malaysia

In Malaysia and Thailand a kabob is known as "satay" (also spelled "saté"). Small pieces of meat, poultry, or seafood are threaded on skewers, then they are charcoal-grilled. A marvelous spicy-hot peanut sauce and hot cooked rice are traditionally served with the "satay."

Traders and immigrants from China, India, Sri Lanka, the Arab countries, and Holland all influenced the culinary characteristics of Southeast Asian cooking. Kabobs and charcoal grilling are a legacy of Arab Moslems who settled in Southeast Asia. From India came the preference for using tantalizing hot curry spices such as red pepper, cumin, coriander, and turmeric. Cooking with soy sauce and serving rice are a carry-over from China.

Southeast Asian cooks took all these exciting culinary influences and combined them with some native foods — coconut milk, "nuoc cham" (fish sauce), peanuts, and hot chili peppers — resulting in this delectable and inviting specialty cuisine.

- **1 medium onion, finely chopped**
- **2 cloves garlic, minced**
- **½ teaspoon ground coriander**
- **½ teaspoon ground cumin**
- **½ teaspoon ground turmeric**
- **½ teaspoon chili powder**
- **2 tablespoons cooking oil**
- **½ cup Coconut Milk (see recipe, page 170) or milk**
- **¼ cup peanut butter**
- **1 teaspoon finely shredded lemon peel**
- **2 tablespoons lemon juice**
- **1 tablespoon soy sauce**
- **1 teaspoon brown sugar**
- **1½ pounds boneless beef, cut into 1-inch pieces**
- **Rice Cakes or hot cooked rice**

For sauce, in a small saucepan cook onion, garlic, coriander, cumin, turmeric, and chili powder in hot cooking oil till onion is tender but not brown. Stir together Coconut Milk or milk, peanut butter, lemon peel and juice, soy sauce, and brown sugar. Add peanut butter mixture to onion mixture; cook and stir till sauce is heated through, but *do not boil.*

Thread beef on 6 long skewers or 12 short skewers; brush with sauce. Grill beef over *hot* coals for 10 to 12 minutes, turning once; brush often with sauce. (Or, place beef on rack of unheated broiler pan. Broil 3 to 4 inches from heat about 20 minutes or to desired doneness, turning once; brush often with sauce.) Brush again and serve with Rice Cakes or hot cooked rice. Makes 6 servings.

Rice Cakes: In a saucepan combine 2 cups *water,* 1 cup medium *or* short grain *rice,* and ½ teaspoon *salt;* cover with tight-fitting lid. Bring to a rolling boil; reduce heat. Continue cooking 15 minutes *(do not lift cover).* Remove from heat; let stand, covered, 10 minutes or till all water is absorbed.

Line an 8x8x2-inch pan with waxed paper. Spread the hot rice in bottom of pan. Cover with waxed paper. Place a second 8x8x2-inch pan atop and press *very firmly* to compact mixture. Repeat pressing very firmly 3 more times. Remove top pan; invert rice mixture onto serving plate. (If rice falls apart, repeat the pressing procedure.) Remove remaining waxed paper. Cut into 6 pieces. Makes 6 servings.

Pork Satay   Thailand

- **1 tablespoon cooking oil**
- **1 teaspoon ground coriander**
- **1 teaspoon ground cumin**
- **1 teaspoon ground turmeric**
- **1 teaspoon paprika**
- **1 teaspoon shredded lemon peel**
- **½ teaspoon chili powder**
- **½ teaspoon ground ginger**
- **¼ teaspoon pepper**
- **¼ teaspoon garlic powder**
- **1½ pounds lean boneless pork, cut into 1-inch pieces**
- **1 cup Coconut Milk (see recipe, page 170) or milk**
- **¼ cup peanut butter**
- **1 tablespoon chopped canned green chili peppers**
- **½ teaspoon lemon peel**
- **½ teaspoon nuoc cham (fish sauce) or soy sauce**
- **¼ teaspoon dried basil, crushed Coconut Milk (see recipe, page 170) or milk**
- **Hot cooked rice**

For marinade, in a mixing bowl combine oil, coriander, cumin, turmeric, paprika, lemon peel, chili powder, ginger, pepper, and garlic powder. Stir in pork and thoroughly rub pork pieces with the marinade mixture. Cover and let stand 2 hours at room temperature or 4 to 6 hours in refrigerator. Thread pork on 6 long skewers or 12 short skewers.

For the sauce, in a small saucepan combine the 1 cup Coconut Milk or milk, peanut butter, chili peppers, lemon peel, nuoc cham (fish sauce) or soy sauce, and basil. Cook and stir over medium heat till mixture is bubbly; reduce heat. Simmer, uncovered, 5 to 10 minutes. Keep warm.

Grill pork over *hot* coals for 10 to 12 minutes, turning once; brush often with Coconut Milk or milk. (Or, place on rack of unheated broiler pan. Broil 3 to 4 inches from heat 20 minutes or till well done, turning once; brush often with Coconut Milk or milk.)

Pass the warm sauce. Serve the kabobs with Cucumber Salad (see recipe, page 175) and hot cooked rice, if desired. Makes 6 servings.

Barbecued Spareribs

Like the Chinese and Japanese, Vietnamese enjoy making their food beautiful by using techniques such as cutting vegetables into artful shapes.

For *Barbecued Spareribs,* Vietnamese cut carrots and daikon (Japanese white radish) into lovely floral shapes.

To make flower-shaped vegetables: Cut carrots into 3-inch pieces. Cook carrot pieces in boiling water for 4 minutes. Drain and cool. In each piece, cut 8 lengthwise triangular grooves (in the form of a V) about ¼ inch deep. Thinly slice the carrot pieces.

Cut the daikon into 3-inch pieces. Cut five thin lengthwise slices from each piece to form a five-sided radish piece. In the middle of each side, cut a lengthwise triangular groove (in the form of a V) about ⅛-inch deep. Thinly slice the 3-inch radish pieces.

Add the carrot and radish slices to the vinegar mixture (see recipe method).

- 2 **medium carrots**
- 1 **medium daikon (Japanese white radish)**
- 2 **cups ice water**
- 2 **tablespoons vinegar**
- 1 **tablespoon sugar**
- ½ **teaspoon salt**
- 3 **to 4 pounds pork spareribs**
- 5 **shallots *or* 1 medium onion, cut into wedges**
- 2 **cloves garlic**
- 3 **tablespoons lemon juice**
- 1 **tablespoon sugar**
- 1 **tablespoon nuoc cham (fish sauce) *or* soy sauce**
- ¼ **teaspoon pepper**
- 1 **cup coarsely chopped peanuts**
- 2 **tablespoons cooking oil**
  Hot cooked rice

Thinly bias-slice carrots and daikon. (Or, prepare as directed at left.) Combine ice water, vinegar, the 1 tablespoon sugar, and salt; stir to dissolve sugar. Add the carrot and radish slices. Refrigerate 2 to 3 hours or till crisp.

Cut ribs into 2-rib portions. In a large covered saucepan or Dutch oven cook ribs in enough boiling salted water to cover for 45 to 60 minutes or till ribs are just tender. Drain.

In a blender or food processor container combine shallots or onion wedges, garlic, lemon juice, the 1 tablespoon sugar, nuoc cham (fish sauce) or soy sauce, and pepper. Cover; blend or process mixture till smooth.

Place ribs in a pan. Brush shallot or onion mixture over ribs. Let stand 1 hour at room temperature. Place ribs over *slow* coals. (Hold hand, palm-side down, just above coals. Count "one thousand one, one thousand two," et cetera. If you need to withdraw your hand after five or six counts, the coals are slow.) Grill 45 minutes; turn occasionally.

In a small skillet cook and stir peanuts in hot oil for 2 minutes or till golden brown. To serve, place the hot cooked rice on a serving platter. Top with ribs; sprinkle with peanuts. Drain carrot and radish slices; arrange around the edge of the platter. Serves 4 or 5.

Lamb Koftas

- 1 **beaten egg**
- ¾ **cup soft bread crumbs**
- 2 **tablespoons plain yogurt**
- ¼ **teaspoon ground cinnamon**
- ¼ **teaspoon ground cardamom**
- ¼ **teaspoon ground cumin**
- ⅛ **teaspoon ground red pepper**
- ⅛ **teaspoon ground cloves**
- ⅛ **teaspoon ground mace**
- 1 **pound ground lamb *or* ground pork**
- 4 **hard-cooked eggs**
- 2 **tablespoons Usli Ghee (see recipe, page 166) *or* cooking oil**
- 1 **medium onion**
- 2 **cloves garlic, minced**
- 2 **teaspoons grated gingerroot**
- 1 **8-ounce can tomato sauce**
- 1 **4-ounce can green chili peppers, rinsed, seeded, and chopped**
- 1 **bay leaf**
- 1 **8-ounce carton plain yogurt**
- 1 **tablespoon snipped parsley**
  Hot cooked rice *or* Chapati (see recipe, page 175)

In a mixing bowl combine beaten egg, bread crumbs, the 2 tablespoons yogurt, and ½ teaspoon *salt.* Stir in cinnamon, cardamom, cumin, red pepper, cloves, and mace. (Or, use 1¼ teaspoons Garam Masala; see recipe, page 166.) Add ground lamb or ground pork; mix well. Shape *one-fourth* of the meat mixture around *each* hard-cooked egg, completely enclosing the egg.

In a large skillet brown meatballs in hot Usli Ghee or cooking oil, carefully turning to brown on all sides. Remove from skillet.

In the same skillet cook onion, garlic, and gingerroot in hot Usli Ghee or cooking oil till onion is tender but not brown. Drain off fat. Stir in tomato sauce, chili peppers, bay leaf, and ½ cup *water.* Bring to boiling; reduce heat. Simmer for 10 minutes. Add meatballs to tomato sauce mixture. Cover and simmer for 30 minutes, turning meatballs every 10 minutes and spooning sauce over. Remove meatballs. Skim fat from sauce.

Slowly add *1 cup* of the hot sauce to the yogurt. Return to skillet. Heat through, but *do not boil.* Remove bay leaf. Transfer sauce to a heated serving platter. Cut meatballs in half crosswise. Place meatballs, yolk side up, atop tomato sauce mixture. Sprinkle parsley atop. Serve with hot cooked rice or Chapati. Makes 4 servings.

SOUTHEAST ASIA

Lamb Korma   India

During the 16th century the Turkish Mongols settled in the northern plains of India, bringing with them their flavorful Moghul cuisine.

This cookery developed into the most popular and refined of all the regional cooking styles in northern India. It is famous for splendid yogurt and cream sauces, the delicate use of highly fragrant spices (cinnamon, cardamom, mace, nutmeg, and clove), and distinctive cooking techniques for meat dishes.

Several Moghul cooking techniques are similar to some that Westerners use. One of the techniques is braising ("korma").

2 cups chopped onion
2 cloves garlic, minced
1 teaspoon grated gingerroot
¼ cup Usli Ghee (see recipe below) or cooking oil
1 teaspoon Garam Masala (see recipe below)
1 teaspoon ground cumin
1 teaspoon ground mace
¾ teaspoon salt
¾ teaspoon ground cinnamon
¾ teaspoon ground turmeric
¾ teaspoon paprika
½ teaspoon ground red pepper
1½ pounds boneless lamb, cut into ¾-inch pieces
½ cup plain yogurt
½ cup dairy sour cream
1 tablespoon all-purpose flour
2 tablespoons snipped coriander or parsley
Hot cooked rice
Sweet Tomato Chutney (see recipe, page 174)

In a large skillet cook chopped onion, garlic, and gingerroot in hot Usli Ghee or cooking oil till onion is tender but not brown. Combine the 1 teaspoon Garam Masala, cumin, mace, salt, cinnamon, turmeric, paprika, and red pepper; stir into onion mixture. Remove from pan.

Brown meat, half at a time, in hot Usli Ghee or oil. (Add more Usli Ghee or oil to skillet, if necessary). Drain off excess fat. Return meat and onion mixture to pan. Add ¼ cup *water*. Cover and simmer about 1¼ hours or till meat is tender, stirring frequently to keep mixture from sticking. (If mixture becomes too thick during cooking, add 1 more tablespoon water.) Stir together yogurt, sour cream, and flour; stir mixture in skillet and heat through, but *do not boil*.

To serve, transfer meat mixture to a heated serving dish and sprinkle coriander or parsley atop. Serve with hot cooked rice and Sweet Tomato Chutney. Makes 6 servings.

Usli Ghee   India

1 pound butter

For clarified butter, in a heavy saucepan melt the butter over very low heat; do not stir. When butter is completely melted, increase heat just enough to bring to boiling. Stir once; reduce heat to low. Simmer butter, uncovered, for 30 minutes. Line a strainer with several layers of clean cheesecloth. Strain clear liquid through it, making sure none of the solids in bottom of pan goes through. Pour into a clean jar; cover, label, and store in refrigerator. Makes 1½ cups.

Garam Masala   India

Garam Masala is a mixture of several "hot" fragrant spices. Translated, "garam" means warm or hot, and "masala" means a blend of aromatic spices. Northern Indian cooking uses *Garam Masala* in so many of its classic dishes, this spicy ingredient is considered absolutely essential.

2 tablespoons whole black peppercorns
4 teaspoons cumin seed
1 tablespoon coriander seed
2 teaspoons whole cloves
1 teaspoon whole cardamom seed (without pods)
3 inches stick cinnamon, broken in half

Place all the spices in an 8x8x2-inch baking pan and heat in a 300° oven for 15 minutes. (This heats the oils, brings out the flavor, and dries the spices so they're easier to grind into a powder.)

In a blender container place heated spices; cover and blend till very fine. Store the spice mixture in a tightly covered container in a cool, dry place. Makes ⅓ cup.

Recipe note: Garam Masala may also be made by mixing pre-ground spices: 1 tablespoon ground *cumin*, 1 tablespoon ground *coriander*, 2 teaspoons *pepper*, 2 teaspoons ground *cardamom*, 1 teaspoon ground *cloves*, and 1 teaspoon ground *cinnamon*. Makes ¼ cup. (Or, purchase the spice mixture in a food specialty store.)

SOUTHEAST ASIA

Mee Krob

Thailand

Mee Krob is a classic Thai celebration dish. The crisp-fried rice sticks, along with pork, shrimp, and chicken, are flavored with "nuoc cham" (or "nuoc mam"), a pungent fish sauce. This sauce gives Thai food its characteristic salty flavor.

½ **pound fresh** *or* **frozen shrimp in shells**
¼ **pound boneless pork**
1 **whole large chicken breast, skinned, halved lengthwise, and boned**
2 **tablespoons soy sauce**
2 **tablespoons vinegar**
2 **teaspoons sugar**
1 **teaspoon nuoc cham (fish sauce)**
2 **tablespoons cooking oil**
⅓ **cup sliced green onion**
1 **clove garlic, minced**
  Deep-Fried Rice Sticks

Thaw shrimp, if frozen. Shell and devein shrimp. Halve shrimp lengthwise. Partially freeze pork; slice thinly into bite-size strips. Cut chicken into bite-size strips. Set aside.

In a small bowl stir together soy sauce, vinegar, sugar, and nuoc cham. Set aside.

Preheat a wok or large skillet over high heat; add 2 tablespoons cooking oil. Stir-fry green onion and garlic about 1 minute or till light brown. Add shrimp to onion mixture; stir-fry 2 to 3 minutes or till shrimp are done. Remove shrimp mixture. Add pork and chicken to hot wok or skillet; stir-fry 2 to 3 minutes or till brown. Return shrimp mixture to wok or skillet and add nuoc cham mixture. Cook and stir till bubbly. Cover and cook for 1 minute. Add Deep-Fried Rice Sticks. Toss to combine; heat through. Makes 4 or 5 servings.

Deep-Fried Rice Sticks: In a large saucepan fry 2 ounces unsoaked *rice sticks,* a few at a time, in deep hot *cooking oil* (375°) for 3 to 5 seconds or just till sticks puff and rise to the top. Remove; drain on paper toweling.

Chicken in Coconut Sauce *pictured on page 162*

India

For this recipe, known as "malai murgh" in India, chicken simmers in a spicy, thick coconut sauce. This rich sauce makes the dish ideal for eating with *Chapati,* thin flat bread.

Use the Chapati to scoop up the rich sauce — the flavor is so good you will want every drop.

1 **cup boiling water**
½ **cup flaked coconut**
1 **2½- to 3-pound broiler-fryer chicken, cut up**
2 **tablespoons Usli Ghee (see recipe, page 166) or cooking oil**
1 **medium onion, chopped**
2 **cloves garlic, minced**
2 **teaspoons grated gingerroot**
1 **teaspoon ground coriander**
½ **teaspoon ground turmeric**
¼ **teaspoon ground red pepper**
⅛ **teaspoon ground cloves**
⅛ **teaspoon ground cardamom**
1 **teaspoon salt**
1 **cup cashews** *or* **blanched whole almonds**
1 **tablespoon Usli Ghee (see recipe, page 166) or cooking oil**
1 **8-ounce carton plain yogurt**
½ **cup dairy sour cream**
2 **tablespoons all-purpose flour**
  Lime slices (optional)
  Mint sprigs (optional)
  Hot cooked rice
  Sweet Tomato Chutney (see recipe, page 174)

Pour boiling water over coconut; set aside.

In a large skillet brown chicken pieces on both sides in the 2 tablespoons hot Usli Ghee or cooking oil for 15 minutes; remove from skillet. Set chicken aside, reserving drippings.

Add the onion, garlic, and gingerroot to the drippings; cook till onion is tender but not brown. Stir in coriander, turmeric, red pepper, cloves, and cardamom. (Or, use 2 teaspoons Garam Masala, see recipe, page 166.) Cook and stir for 2 minutes. Stir in the coconut mixture and salt. Return chicken to skillet. Cover and simmer 35 to 45 minutes or till chicken is tender.

Transfer chicken to heated serving platter; keep warm. Skim fat from juices in skillet. In a small skillet heat cashews or almonds in the 1 tablespoon hot Usli Ghee or cooking oil for 1 to 2 minutes or till golden, stirring constantly.

For sauce, combine yogurt, sour cream, and flour. Stir into onion and juices in skillet. Cook and stir just till thickened, but *do not boil*. Stir in cashews or almonds. Pour sauce over chicken; garnish with lime slices and fresh mint sprigs, if desired. Serve with hot cooked rice and Sweet Tomato Chutney. Makes 6 servings.

In Pakistan and India, chicken isn't everyday fare — it's reserved for special, joyous events or religious occasions.

This is not only because chicken is very expensive but also because Hindus favor and relish it more than any other meat. Because of this high regard, Hindu chicken dishes are delightful creations with exquisite presentations.

Royal Chicken Pilaf is famous for its delicate flavor and lavish appearance.

¼ **cup Usli Ghee (see recipe, page 166) *or* cooking oil**
2 **cups chopped onion**
2 **teaspoons grated gingerroot**
2 **cloves garlic, minced**
½ **teaspooon ground cinnamon**
½ **teaspoon ground cardamom**
½ **teaspoon ground cumin**
¼ **teaspoon ground red pepper**
¼ **teaspoon ground cloves**
¼ **teaspoon ground mace**
1 **4-ounce can green chili peppers, rinsed, seeded, and chopped**
1 **8-ounce carton plain yogurt**
1 **teaspoon salt**
3 **whole large chicken breasts, skinned, halved lengthwise, and boned**
½ **cup boiling water**
½ **cup whipping cream**
½ **teaspoon thread saffron, crushed**
3 **cups chicken broth**
1 **cup long grain rice**
2 **tablespoons Usli Ghee (see recipe, page 166) *or* butter**
½ **teaspoon salt**
 Fried Onion Rings
 Cashews, toasted, *or* slivered almonds, toasted
 Seedless green grapes
 Sprigs of coriander *or* parsley

Preheat a wok or large skillet over high heat; add the ¼ cup Usli Ghee or cooking oil. Stir-fry chopped onion, gingerroot, and garlic for 2 minutes or till onion is tender but not brown. Stir in cinnamon, cardamom, cumin, red pepper, cloves, and mace. (*Or,* use 2 teaspoons Garam Masala, see recipe, page 166.) Reduce heat to medium. Stir in the chopped green chili peppers, 2 *tablespoons* of the yogurt, and the 1 teaspoon salt. Cook and stir till liquid is almost evaporated. Add remaining yogurt, 2 tablespoons at a time, stirring till nearly dry after each addition.

Cut *each* chicken breast half into 3 pieces. Place chicken in the wok or skillet; cook 8 minutes, spooning sauce over occasionally and turning chicken once. Stir in ¼ *cup* of the boiling water. Reduce heat; simmer, covered, for 20 minutes or till chicken is tender. Stir in whipping cream. Remove from heat. Meanwhile, combine remaining boiling water and saffron; let stand 20 minutes.

In a medium saucepan combine chicken broth, long grain rice, the 2 tablespoons Usli Ghee or butter, and the ½ teaspoon salt. Bring to boiling; reduce heat to low. Simmer, covered, for 15 minutes. *(Do not lift cover.)* Remove saucepan from heat. Let stand, covered, for 5 to 8 minutes. Rice should be tender but still slightly firm and the mixture should be creamy.

In a well-greased 2-quart casserole place *half* of the rice mixture. Drizzle with *1 tablespoon* of the saffron mixture, poking holes in rice mixture so saffron penetrates. Arrange *half* the chicken over rice and spoon *half* the yogurt mixture over. Drizzle with another *1 tablespoon* of the saffron mixture. Repeat layers. Place casserole on a baking sheet. Bake, uncovered, in a 325° oven for 30 minutes or till heated through. Let stand 10 minutes.

Invert casserole onto a heated serving platter. Garnish with Fried Onion Rings and cashews or almonds. Arrange small bunches of green grapes and sprigs of coriander or parsley around the edge of the platter. Makes 6 to 8 servings.

Fried Onion Rings: Melt 2 tablespoons *Usli Ghee* (see recipe, page 166) *or cooking oil* in skillet. Add 2 medium *Bermuda or mild white onions,* sliced ¼ inch thick and separated into rings. Cook and stir over medium heat for 5 to 10 minutes or till tender and golden. Drain on paper toweling.

SOUTHEAST ASIA

Chicken with Fried Noodles
Burma

This popular Burmese one-course meal, called "un-no kuakswe," is a favorite dish to serve at special family occasions.

A Burmese custom at these special celebrations is to invite a Buddhist monk to the house. The monk recites prayers and blessings for the family. He is then served *Chicken with Fried Noodles.*

In Burma, it is an honor to feed Buddhist monks. The Burmese believe it helps them earn merit — which will ensure them a better status in their next life.

1 2½- to 3-pound broiler-fryer chicken, cut up
3 cups water
1 teaspoon salt
½ teaspoon ground turmeric
6 ounces fine noodles
2 tablespoons peanut oil *or* cooking oil
1 cup Thick Coconut Milk (see recipe below)
3 tablespoons split pea flour, chick-pea (garbanzo) flour, *or* cornstarch
2 tablespoons peanut oil *or* cooking oil
1 cup finely chopped onion
1 clove garlic, minced
¾ teaspoon grated gingerroot
½ to 1 teaspoon chili powder
¼ teaspoon blachan (shrimp paste) *or* anchovy paste (optional)
3 green onions, thinly sliced
2 hard-cooked eggs, cut into quarters
1 lemon, cut into wedges

Place chicken in a large kettle; add water, salt, and turmeric. Bring to boiling; reduce heat. Cover and simmer about 1 hour or till chicken is tender.

Remove chicken, reserving the broth; strain broth and skim off fat. When chicken is cool enough to handle, remove meat from bones; discard skin and bones. Cut large pieces of chicken into bite-size pieces. Set chicken aside.

Meanwhile, cook fine noodles according to package directions; drain well. Rinse in cold water. Drain well. Preheat a wok or large skillet over high heat; add 2 tablespoons peanut oil or cooking oil. Add drained noodles and stir-fry 5 to 7 minutes or till just beginning to brown. Transfer noodles to serving dish. Keep warm.

Stir the Thick Coconut Milk into the split pea flour, chick-pea (garbanzo) flour, or cornstarch. Set the mixture aside.

To same wok or large skillet add 2 tablespoons peanut oil or cooking oil. Stir-fry onion, garlic, and gingerroot for 1 minute. Stir in chili powder and the blachan (shrimp paste) or anchovy paste, if desired. Add chicken; heat through.

Stir the coconut milk mixture; stir into chicken mixture along with the reserved broth. Cook and stir till thickened and bubbly. Reduce heat; simmer, uncovered, 10 minutes.

For each serving, place some of the noodles in an individual soup bowl, then ladle some of the chicken mixture atop. Top with some green onions and egg wedges. Squeeze lemon juice over to taste. Makes 4 to 6 servings.

Coconut Milk
Regional

1 fresh coconut
   Milk

Pierce coconut eyes; drain and reserve liquid. Remove shell; peel off brown skin. Rinse the coconut. Coarsely chop coconut. Add milk to reserved liquid to measure 2 cups; heat through but *do not boil.* Place chopped coconut and hot liquid in blender or food processor container. Cover; blend or process 1 minute. Makes about 3 cups.

• **Thick Coconut Milk:** Prepare Coconut Milk as above *except* add milk to the reserved liquid to measure 1 cup. Continue as directed. Makes about 2 cups.

Recipe note: Coconut Milk also may be made by using grated coconut. Stir together ¾ cup grated *coconut* and 1½ cups *boiling water.* (Or, to make Thick Coconut Milk use 1 cup grated *coconut* and stir in 1 cup *boiling water.*) Let stand 5 minutes. Place mixture in blender or food processor container. Cover; blend or process 1 minute.

Nasi Goreng *pictured on page 162* Indonesia

Indonesian cooks make rice the basis of every meal. Whether white or brown, long or short grain, highly polished or unpolished, the rice must always be perfectly cooked.

One of the most famous Indonesian rice dishes is *Nasi Goreng.* The rice is boiled ("nasi"), cooled completely, then fried ("goreng"). Shrimp, meat, and stir-fried vegetables make *Nasi Goreng* substantial enough to be served as a main dish.

½ **pound fresh *or* frozen shelled shrimp**
½ **pound boneless pork *or* beef top round steak**
2 **beaten eggs**
1 **tablespoon cooking oil**
1 **medium onion, finely chopped (½ cup)**
2 **cloves garlic, minced**
1 **teaspoon blachan (shrimp paste) *or* anchovy paste (optional)**
½ **teaspoon crushed red pepper *or* ¼ teaspoon ground red pepper**
2 **tablespoons cooking oil**
1 **cup coarsely chopped cabbage**
1 **cup fresh bean sprouts *or* ½ of a 16-ounce can bean sprouts, drained**
3 **green onions, bias sliced into 1-inch pieces**
4 **cups cooked rice, chilled**
¼ **cup soy sauce**
1 **medium cucumber, peeled and sliced**
2 **medium tomatoes, thinly sliced**

Thaw shrimp, if frozen; halve lengthwise. Partially freeze pork or beef; thinly slice across the grain into bite-size strips.

In a 12-inch skillet cook beaten eggs in the 1 tablespoon cooking oil, without stirring, till set. Invert skillet over a baking sheet to remove cooked eggs; cut into short, narrow strips.

Stir together the finely chopped onion; garlic; blachan (shrimp paste) or anchovy paste, if desired; and red pepper. In the same skillet cook onion mixture in the 2 tablespoons hot oil till onion is tender but not brown. Add shrimp and pork or beef strips; stir-fry 5 to 6 minutes. Add cabbage, bean sprouts, and green onions; stir-fry 2 minutes. Stir in cooked rice, soy sauce, and *half* of the egg strips; cover and heat through.

To serve, spoon the rice mixture onto a heated serving platter. Arrange the remaining egg strips atop the rice mixture. Garnish edge of platter with cucumber slices, if desired. Serve with sliced tomatoes. Makes 4 servings.

Crispy Fried Fish *pictured on page 162* Kampuchea

1 **pound fresh *or* frozen fish fillets**
2 **slightly beaten egg whites**
2 **tablespoons cornstarch**
Cooking oil *or* shortening for deep-fat frying
¼ **cup soy sauce**
2 **teaspoons cornstarch**
1 **tablespoon nuoc cham (fish sauce) *or* oyster sauce (optional)**
½ **teaspoon crushed red pepper *or* ¼ teaspoon ground red pepper**
2 **tablespoons cooking oil**
1 **teaspoon grated gingerroot**
1 **clove garlic, minced**
2 **cups chopped Chinese cabbage**
6 **green onions, bias sliced into 1-inch lengths**
1 **8-ounce can bamboo shoots, drained**
⅓ **cup coarsely chopped peanuts**

Thaw fish, if frozen; remove skin, if present. Cut fillets diagonally into 1-inch pieces. Press fish between layers of paper toweling to dry thoroughly. Sprinkle lightly with salt.

Dip each piece of fish into egg whites; drain off excess. Toss fish with the 2 tablespoons cornstarch in a plastic bag, a few pieces at a time.

Fry fish pieces, a few at a time, in deep hot fat (375°) about 5 minutes or till golden. Remove fish with slotted spoon or wire strainer; drain on paper toweling. Keep fish warm in 325° oven.

To make vegetable sauce, in a small bowl stir soy sauce into the 2 teaspoons cornstarch. Stir in nuoc cham (fish sauce) or oyster sauce, if desired; crushed or ground red pepper; and ⅓ cup *water.*

Preheat a wok or large skillet over high heat; add the 2 tablespoons cooking oil. Stir-fry gingerroot and garlic in hot oil for 30 seconds. Add Chinese cabbage; stir-fry 1 minute. Add green onions, bamboo shoots, and peanuts. Stir-fry 1 minute.

Stir soy mixture; stir into vegetables. Cook and stir till thickened and bubbly. Cover and cook 2 minutes more. Transfer vegetable sauce to a platter; arrange fish pieces on top. Serve with hot cooked rice, if desired. Serves 4.

SOUTHEAST ASIA

Thai Shrimp Larnar *pictured on front cover*   Thailand

Thai Shrimp Larnar contains a flavorful seasoned sauce Thais call "nam prik." This pungent, hot sauce is so popular that Thai people use it in almost everything they eat.

"Nam prik" probably has as many versions as the number of Thai cooks, but most include chili peppers or red pepper, garlic, and nuoc cham (fish sauce). Other seasonings can be added to please the palate of the cook.

Be very careful when you handle any kind of chili pepper. They contain oils that can burn your skin and eyes. Avoid direct contact as much as possible. Many cooks wear rubber gloves while handling chili peppers. In any case, after you have worked with chili peppers be sure to wash your hands and nails thoroughly with soap and water.

1 **pound fresh or frozen shrimp in shells**
2 **to 4 dried red chili peppers or ½ to 1 teaspoon crushed red pepper**
¼ **cup water**
2 **to 4 cloves garlic**
2 **tablespoons cooking oil**
2 **tablespoons lemon juice**
2 **tablespoons soy sauce**
1 **to 1½ teaspoons nuoc cham (fish sauce)**
4 **cups broccoli cut into 1-inch pieces**
2 **tablespoons cooking oil Deep-Fried Wonton Strips or hot cooked rice**

Thaw shrimp, if frozen. Shell shrimp. Leave shrimp tails on, if desired. Cut down back of each shrimp, using a knife point to remove and scrape out the vein. To butterfly, cut almost but not all the way through the shrimp. Cover and set aside in the refrigerator.

See tip at left for handling chili peppers. Cut the dried chili peppers open. Discard stems and seeds. Cut the peppers into pieces with scissors or knife. Place in bowl; cover with some boiling water. Let stand 45 to 60 minutes. Drain.

For the sauce, in a blender or food processor container combine the drained chili peppers or crushed red pepper, water, garlic, 2 tablespoons cooking oil, lemon juice, soy sauce, and nuoc cham (fish sauce). Cover; blend or process till smooth. Set aside.

In a large mixing bowl place the broccoli pieces; cover with cold water. Let stand about 15 minutes. Drain well. (Soaking the broccoli helps to retain its crispness.)

Preheat a wok or large skillet over high heat; add 2 tablespoons cooking oil. Stir-fry well-drained broccoli in oil for 3 minutes or till crisp-tender. Remove from wok. Add more oil, if necessary.

Add the shrimp to hot wok or skillet; stir-fry 5 to 7 minutes or till shrimp are done. Return broccoli to wok or skillet. Stir in the sauce, tossing shrimp and broccoli to coat evenly. Cover and cook 1 minute. Serve at once with Deep-Fried Wonton Strips or hot cooked rice. Makes 4 servings.

• **Thai Beef Larnar:** Prepare Thai Shrimp Larnar as above, *except* substitute 1 pound *beef top round steak* for the shrimp.

Partially freeze beef. Slice beef very thinly across the grain into bite-size strips. Add *half* of the beef to hot wok or skillet; stir-fry 2 to 3 minutes or till brown. Remove beef. Stir-fry remaining beef for 2 to 3 minutes. Return all meat to wok or skillet. Stir in 1 tablespoon toasted *sesame seed.* Continue as directed. Makes 4 servings.

Deep-Fried Wonton Strips: Cut ½ pound *egg roll skins or wonton skins* into 2x1-inch strips. Fry strips, a few at a time, in deep hot *cooking oil* (375°) about 10 seconds or just till strips are golden. Remove; drain on paper toweling. Keep the wonton strips warm in oven.

Pictured
Fried Fish with Ginger Sauce

Fried Fish with Ginger Sauce Thailand

Thai cooks add lemon grass to many of their dishes. Its distinctive flavor typifies Thai food.

Fresh lemon grass is available from Oriental stores. The lower third of the stalk, the bulb-like portion, is the part to use when a recipe specifies "chopped lemon grass."

Ground (or powdered) lemon grass is a good substitute. Or, 2 strips of very thinly sliced lemon peel can be used instead of the lemon grass called for in this recipe.

1 2- to 2½-pound fresh *or* frozen dressed red snapper, pike, *or* perch (with head and tail)
2 tablespoons grated gingerroot
1 clove garlic, minced
2 tablespoons cooking oil
¼ cup packed brown sugar
1 tablespoon cornstarch
⅓ cup vinegar
4 fresh green chili peppers *or* one 4-ounce can green chili peppers
¼ cup chopped lemon grass *or* 1 teaspoon ground lemon grass
½ to 1 teaspoon nuoc cham (fish sauce) *or* soy sauce
⅓ cup all-purpose flour
Cooking oil

Thaw fish, if frozen. For sauce, cook gingerroot and garlic in the 2 tablespoons hot oil. Combine brown sugar and cornstarch; stir into gingerroot mixture along with vinegar and ⅔ cup *water*. Cook and stir till thickened and bubbly.

Rinse fresh or canned green chili peppers; seed and chop. Stir chili peppers, lemon grass, and the nuoc cham (fish sauce) or soy sauce into gingerroot mixture; heat through. Keep warm.

Rinse fish; pat dry with paper toweling. Score fish with 6 diagonal cuts on each side, slicing almost through to the bone. Sprinkle fish with salt; coat both sides with flour. Place coated fish in a well-greased, shallow baking pan. Brush with oil. Bake in a 500° oven till golden and fish flakes easily when tested with a fork. (Allow 5 to 6 minutes for each ½ inch of thickness.)

Transfer to a platter; pour sauce over fish. Top with green onions, chopped parsley, and sliced green chili peppers, if desired. Serves 6.

SOUTHEAST ASIA

Sweet Tomato Chutney   *pictured on page 162*   India

In an Indian meal, chutneys or relishes are as important as the main dish. Traditional chutney ("chatni") literally means a touch-the-tongue flavoring.

This sweet-and-sour spicy chutney makes an excellent flavor contrast with *Lamb Korma* (see recipe, page 166) or *Chicken in Coconut Sauce* (see recipe, page 168).

- 1 **16-ounce can tomatoes, cut up**
- 1 **medium onion, finely chopped (½ cup)**
- 2 **cloves garlic, minced**
- 1 **teaspoon grated gingerroot**
- ¾ **cup sugar**
- ¾ **cup red wine vinegar**
- ½ **teaspoon salt**
- ½ **teaspoon paprika**
- ¼ **teaspoon ground red pepper**
- ¼ **teaspoon ground cloves**
- ½ **cup raisins *or* currants**
- ¼ **cup slivered almonds**

In a saucepan combine *undrained* tomatoes, onion, garlic, and gingerroot. Stir in sugar, vinegar, salt, paprika, red pepper, and cloves. Bring to boiling; reduce heat. Simmer, uncovered, for 30 minutes or till mixture is thickened (the consistency of catsup); stir frequently. Stir in raisins or currants and the almonds; heat through. Remove from heat. Cool. Pour into a container; cover and label. Store in refrigerator for up to 3 weeks. Makes 2 cups.

Gado-Gado   Indonesia

Wherever you go in Indonesia, you can find *Gado-Gado,* an imaginative vegetable salad. It's also popular in Malaysia and Singapore.

Indonesians traditionally serve a variety of cooked and fresh vegetables, attractively arranged on a platter, with a spicy peanut sauce.

Serve this salad for dinner with *Beef Satay* or *Pork Satay* (see recipes, page 164) and hot cooked rice.

Peanut Sauce
- 1 **8-ounce package fresh tofu (bean curd)**
- 2 **tablespoons cooking oil**
- 2 **large potatoes**
- 1 **9-ounce package frozen cut green beans**
- 3 **carrots, cut into julienne strips**
- 3 **cups torn fresh spinach**
- 3 **cups shredded cabbage**
  Lettuce leaves *or* watercress leaves
- 2 **cups fresh bean sprouts**
- 1 **medium cucumber**
- 3 **hard-cooked eggs, chilled and cut into wedges**
- 2 **medium tomatoes, cut into wedges**

Prepare the Peanut Sauce. Set aside.

Place tofu in double thickness of cheesecloth or paper toweling. Press gently to extract as much moisture as possible. Cube tofu. Preheat a wok or large skillet over high heat; add cooking oil. Stir-fry tofu in hot oil for 3 minutes, turning several times. Remove tofu; drain on paper toweling.

In covered saucepan cook potatoes in a small amount of boiling salted water for 20 to 25 minutes or till tender; drain. Peel and slice. In a covered saucepan cook green beans and carrots in boiling salted water for 4 to 5 minutes or till crisp-tender; drain. In saucepan cook spinach in boiling salted water for 30 seconds; drain. Place the shredded cabbage in a colander and pour boiling water over; drain well.

Line a large serving platter with lettuce leaves or watercress leaves. Arrange all of the vegetables atop the lettuce leaves. To score unpeeled cucumber, run tines of fork down sides; thinly slice cucumber. Garnish with cucumber slices, hard-cooked egg wedges, and tomatoes. Pass Peanut Sauce. Makes 10 servings.

Peanut Sauce: In a saucepan cook ½ cup finely chopped *onion* and 1 clove *garlic,* minced, in 1 tablespoon hot *butter or margarine* till tender but not brown. Stir in one 4-ounce can green *chili peppers,* rinsed, seeded, and chopped; 2 tablespoons *lemon juice;* 1 teaspoon *brown sugar;* ½ teaspoon *blachan* (shrimp paste) *or anchovy paste,* if desired; mix well. Stir together 1 cup *peanut butter* and 1½ cups *Coconut Milk* (see recipe, page 170) or *water.* Add peanut butter mixture to onion mixture, cooking and stirring till sauce is smooth and heated through, but *do not boil.* Cover surface with plastic wrap to prevent skin from forming. Makes 3 cups.

Chapati *pictured on page 162*   India

The most popular and widely eaten of all the northern Indian breads is *Chapati,* an unleavened bread. Similar in shape to the Mexican tortilla, *Chapati* is quite different in texture and flavor. *Chapati* is smooth, soft, and very pliable.

   Chapati is rolled out to thin rounds, then baked quickly on a griddle, and served while still warm. The bread complements just about any main dish.

   If you have made *Chapati* ahead, reheat before serving. Wrap a stack of *Chapati* in foil, then heat in a 325° oven for 10 to 15 minutes. If the *Chapati* seem dry, sprinkle them with a little water before reheating.

2 **cups whole wheat flour**
1 **cup all-purpose flour**
½ **teaspoon salt**
1 **cup warm water (110° to 115°)**
  Usli Ghee (see recipe, page 166) *or* **shortening**

In a large mixing bowl stir together whole wheat flour, all-purpose flour, and the salt. Add ¾ cup of the warm water while mixing constantly with hands till dough is moist. Add the remaining water, 1 tablespoon at a time, mixing constantly with hands. Keep working the dough with hands till dough forms a ball and holds its shape (dough will be stiff).

   Dampen hands. (Keep dough in mixing bowl to knead.) Knead in an additional 2 tablespoons all-purpose flour, if necessary, to make a moderately stiff dough. Knead dough till smooth and elastic (8 to 10 minutes). Continue dampening hands, as needed, during kneading. (The dough is ready for shaping when you can lightly and quickly press two fingertips ¼ inch into the dough and the dough springs back.)

   Shape dough into a ball. Cover bowl with a damp towel. Let the dough stand in a warm place for 30 to 60 minutes.

   Turn dough out onto a lightly floured surface. Knead dough 1 to 2 minutes more. Divide dough in half. Form *each* half into a 12-inch-long roll. Cut *each* roll into 12 one-inch pieces. Flatten each piece of dough with the palm of the hand.

   Sprinkle flour over the flattened balls. Cover with plastic wrap. Let rest 30 minutes.

   On a well-floured surface roll the flattened ball into a circle 7 to 8 inches in diameter, turning dough over once and firmly pressing and stretching dough with the rolling pin.

   Roll around rolling pin; transfer to a hot, greased griddle or heavy skillet. Cook over medium heat about ½ to 1 minute or till tiny brown spots appear. Using tongs, turn and cook 30 seconds more. Remove from heat; brush with Usli Ghee or shortening. Repeat with the remaining balls. Stack hot Chapati in a napkin-lined breadbasket to keep warm. Serve immediately. Makes 24.

Cucumber Salad   Thailand

2 **medium cucumbers**
1 **small onion, thinly sliced and separated into rings**
2 **tablespoons vinegar** *or* **lemon juice**
1 **tablespoon water**
1 **tablespoon sugar**
½ **to 1 teaspoon nuoc cham (fish sauce)** *or* **soy sauce**
⅛ **teaspoon crushed red pepper**
1 **fresh green chili pepper, rinsed, seeded, and chopped (optional)**

Peel the cucumbers. Halve the cucumbers lengthwise; seed. Thinly slice or coarsely shred the cucumbers. Combine cucumbers and onion.

   Combine vinegar or lemon juice, water, sugar, nuoc cham (fish sauce) or soy sauce, and crushed red pepper, stirring till sugar is dissolved. Pour over cucumber mixture and toss to coat. If desired, sprinkle with chopped chili pepper. Chill. Serve with slotted spoon. Makes 6 servings.

Spiced Rich Layer Cake
Indonesia

Because most Indonesians are Moslems (also spelled Muslims), the festival celebrating the end of the Islamic fasting month, "Ramadhan," is an occasion of great happiness and excitement.

"Id al-Fitr," the last day of the fast, is a very singular day in the year for Moslems. It is a time when quarrels are settled, grudges forgotten, and plans for a fresh start made.

An exciting part of this great celebration is holding an open house. Friends arrive, dressed in their best clothes, to sample an impressive array of sweet, fancy dishes.

Fancy cakes such as Spiced Rich Layer Cake ("spekkoek lapis legit") and delicious milk puddings such as Almond Pudding ("kheer") are offered to the open house visitors.

10 egg yolks
¾ cup butter or margarine, softened
¾ cup sugar
1 teaspoon vanilla
1 cup all-purpose flour
½ cup cornstarch
¼ teaspoon salt
10 egg whites
¼ cup sugar
1½ teaspoons ground cinnamon
½ teaspoon ground nutmeg
¼ teaspoon ground cloves
¼ teaspoon ground ginger
¼ teaspoon ground cardamom
Powdered sugar

In a small mixer bowl beat egg yolks at high speed of electric mixer about 10 minutes or till thick and light colored. In a large mixer bowl beat butter about 30 seconds; gradually add the ¾ cup sugar and vanilla. Add egg yolks; beat well.

In a large mixing bowl stir together flour, cornstarch, and salt; stir in butter mixture. Wash beaters and the large mixer bowl thoroughly. In a large mixer bowl beat egg whites till soft peaks form. Gradually add the ¼ cup sugar, beating till stiff peaks form. Fold into flour mixture.

Divide batter in half. Combine cinnamon, nutmeg, cloves, ginger, and cardamom. Gently fold spices into *half* of the batter till well combined.

Grease an 8- or 9-inch springform pan; spread ½ cup of the spiced batter evenly in the bottom. Place on oven broiler rack. Broil cake 5 inches from heat for 1 to 2 minutes or till brown. (Give pan a half-turn for even browning, if needed.) *Do not overbrown.* Remove from broiler. Spread ½ cup of the white batter atop first layer. Broil as before, turning as necessary. Repeat, alternating spice and white batter, making 10 to 15 layers in all.

Cool 10 minutes. Loosen cake and remove sides of pan; cool completely. Sprinkle powdered sugar atop. To serve, cut into thin wedges. Serves 20.

Almond Pudding
India

4 cups milk or light cream
2 tablespoons long grain rice
¼ teaspoon ground cardamom
¼ cup sugar
¼ cup chopped toasted almonds or chopped pistachio nuts
2 teaspoons rose water (optional)
Ground nutmeg
12 fresh whole strawberries

In a heavy 3-quart saucepan combine milk or light cream, rice, and cardamom. Bring to boiling. Reduce heat. Cook, uncovered, over low heat, stirring occasionally, about 1 hour or till milk mixture is reduced to about 2 cups. Remove from heat.

Stir in sugar and chopped almonds or pistachio nuts, continue stirring till sugar has dissolved. Cool 30 minutes; stir pudding. Stir in rose water, if desired.

Spoon mixture into 4 to 6 sherbet or dessert dishes. Chill in refrigerator. To serve, sprinkle with ground nutmeg and garnish each serving with 2 whole strawberries. Makes 4 to 6 servings.

Recipe note: To keep a "skin" from forming on the top of the pudding while cooling, carefully place a piece of clear plastic wrap or waxed paper directly on the surface of the hot pudding. After pudding has cooled, remove paper and spoon pudding into dessert dishes.

Coconut Candy

India

In India, candies and confections are called sweetmeats — and Indians adore them. A classic sweetmeat is "barfi," *Coconut Candy.*

If you have a sweet tooth, you will enjoy the interesting flavor of this candy. It's reminiscent of penuche in flavor and texture.

2 **cups sugar**
1 **cup milk**
1 **tablespoon butter** *or* **margarine**
¼ **teaspoon ground cardamom**
1 **cup grated coconut**
½ **cup chopped cashews**
½ **cup chopped almonds**

Butter sides of a heavy 2-quart saucepan. In it combine sugar and milk. Cook over medium heat, stirring constantly, till sugar dissolves and mixture comes to boiling. Continue cooking to 234° (soft-ball stage), for 20 to 25 minutes, stirring only as necessary to prevent sticking (mixture should boil gently over entire surface). Stir in butter or margarine and cardamom.

Immediately remove from heat; cool, without stirring, to lukewarm (110°). Beat vigorously about 3 minutes or till mixture is slightly thickened. Quickly stir in coconut and nuts. Immediately turn into a buttered 10x6x2-inch dish; pat down evenly. Score candy while warm into about 1-inch squares. Cool; cut through score marks. Makes 48 pieces.

Recipe note: Or, substitute 1 cup sugar and 1 cup packed brown sugar for the 2 cups sugar.

Spring Rolls

Thailand

"Poh pia" or *Spring Rolls* resemble a Chinese eggroll in that both have a tasty vegetable filling encased in a wrapper. The difference is that Thai people do not fry *Spring Rolls.*

Thais enjoy serving Spring Rolls as a snack. If you want, use them as a delightful first course to start off an international dinner.

⅔ **cup all-purpose flour**
2 **tablespoons cornstarch**
1 **cup water**
2 **eggs**
⅛ **teaspoon salt**
1 **beaten egg**
¼ **teaspoon nuoc cham (fish sauce)** *or* **soy sauce**
1½ **teaspoons cooking oil**
1½ **cups fresh bean sprouts**
½ **cup peeled and chopped cucumber**
¼ **cup thinly sliced Chinese sausage** *or* **salami**
2 **tablespoons chopped green onion**
Sweet-Sour Sauce
2 **tablespoons chopped green onion**

For the wrappers, in a bowl combine flour, cornstarch, water, the 2 eggs, and salt; beat with rotary beater till combined. Heat a lightly greased 6-inch skillet; remove from heat. Spoon in a scant *2 tablespoons* of the batter; lift and tilt skillet to spread batter evenly. Return to heat; cook but *do not brown.* Invert pan over paper toweling; remove. Repeat with remaining batter to make 16 wrappers, greasing skillet if necessary.

Combine the 1 egg and nuoc cham (fish sauce) or soy sauce. In a small skillet cook egg mixture in the hot oil, without stirring, till set. Invert skillet over a baking sheet to remove cooked eggs. Cut eggs into short, narrow strips.

In bowl combine bean sprouts, cucumber, Chinese sausage or salami, 2 tablespoons green onion, and the egg strips; toss lightly to mix together. Place about *2 tablespoons* of the bean sprout mixture in center of a wrapper. Fold about ⅓ of wrapper over filling; fold in the 2 sides atop filling, forming an envelope shape. Roll packet up toward remaining edge. Repeat with remaining wrappers and filling.

Set a bowl of Sweet-Sour Sauce in the center of a large round platter and arrange Spring Rolls around the sauce. Sprinkle the rolls with 2 tablespoons chopped green onion. Serve as a snack or as a first-course appetizer. Makes 16.

Sweet and Sour Sauce: Combine ¼ cup packed *brown sugar* and 1 tablespoon *cornstarch.* Stir in ⅓ cup *vinegar,* ⅓ cup *pineapple juice,* ⅓ cup *tomato juice,* and ¼ teaspoon *garlic powder.* Cook and stir till thickened and bubbly. Cook and stir 2 minutes more. Serve warm. Makes 1 cup.

Recipe note: Substitute store-purchased egg roll skins for the homemade wrappers.

SOUTH PACIFIC

Because miles of ocean separate the Pacific Islands, Australia and New Zealand, and the Philippines, each area has developed a distinctive cuisine rich in traditions.

The most indigenous cuisine of the three is that of the Pacific Islands, where the culinary style is authentic Polynesian. Taro, coconuts, and pork are the staples of the Pacific Islanders' diets. Coconut is indeed a versatile food: From it come its meat, milk, cream, and oil. Coconut oil is especially useful for frying the abundant fish and shellfish. But the special treat of the Pacific Islands is roast pig — cooked luau style in the smoke and steam of an earth oven.

Although the cuisine of Polynesia reflects its original inhabitants, the opposite is true of Australia and New Zealand. Years ago Australians occasionally ate kangaroo-tail soup (similar to ox-tail soup), but most dishes now are strictly English — almost as if eating back in the British Isles.

The English who settled these two countries brought their tea-drinking tradition and a love of simple foods. Australians are particularly fond of their traditional Sunday roast beef. New Zealanders have replaced this weekly favorite with an equally popular British meat — rack of lamb.

Both Australia and New Zealand are blessed with superb fruits. In Australia, exotic passion fruits, mangoes, papayas, and loquats are only samples of the many varieties available. And in New Zealand, the unusual, fuzzy green kiwi is plentiful.

Far away in the Philippines, Spain controlled the islands for more than 300 years and greatly influenced the local cuisine. But the Chinese and Malayans who settled there also added some of their cooking heritage. As a result, tastes vary throughout the islands. Filipinos enjoy foods flavored with everything from fish or shrimp paste, to garlic, pepper, and vinegar or tamarind.

Pictured clockwise from center right
Ensaimada Rolls (see recipe, page 183), Skewered Scallops (see recipe, page 181), Pancit Guisado (see recipe, page 180), and Luau Pork Roast (see recipe, page 181)

Carpetbag Steak
Australia

When Australians want beef, they often prepare *Carpetbag Steak,* a cut of meat stuffed with succulent oysters.

½ **pint shucked oysters, drained and cut in half**
2 **teaspoons lemon juice**
½ **teaspoon salt**
⅛ **teaspoon pepper**
1 **1¼- to 1½-pound beef sirloin steak, cut 1½ inches thick**
3 **tablespoons butter *or* margarine, melted**
  Rissole Potatoes

Pat oysters dry with paper toweling. In a small bowl combine oysters, lemon juice, salt, and pepper. Toss to coat oysters.

Slash fat edges of steak at 1-inch intervals (do not cut into meat). Cut a horizontal slit in one side of meat almost to bone, forming a pocket. Stuff pocket with oysters; skewer closed.

Place meat on an unheated rack in a broiler pan. Brush meat with *some* of the melted butter or margarine. Place under broiler; broil 4 inches from the heat for 14 to 16 minutes, turning once. Brush often with remaining melted butter. To serve, slice steak across grain. Serve with Rissole Potatoes. Makes 6 servings.

Rissole Potatoes: Thoroughly scrub 2 pounds *tiny new potatoes* or peel and quarter 6 medium *potatoes.* In a covered saucepan cook unpeeled new potatoes or peeled and quartered potatoes for 8 to 10 minutes or till tender. Drain potatoes. Peel the new potatoes. In a saucepan combine potatoes and ¼ cup *cooking oil;* toss potatoes in oil to coat evenly. Transfer the potatoes to an 11x7x1½-inch baking pan. Bake in a 425° oven for 20 minutes or till light brown. Makes 6 servings.

Pancit Guisado   *pictured on page 178*
Philippines

A dish similar to chow mein, *Pancit Guisado* reflects China's culinary influence in the Philippines.

"Pancit" refers to the fine Oriental noodles so prevalent in the Filipino cuisine.

"Patis," another ingredient in *Pancit Guisado,* is a salty, amber-colored fish sauce. It is a condiment as common in the Philippines as catsup is in the United States.

½ **pound boneless pork**
½ **pound fresh *or* frozen shelled shrimp**
6 **ounces fine noodles**
½ **cup chicken broth**
3 **tablespoons soy sauce**
2 **tablespoons patis (fish sauce) (optional)**
⅛ **teaspoon pepper**
¼ **cup cooking oil**
1 **tablespoon cooking oil**
2 **medium onions, chopped**
2 **cloves garlic, minced**
3 **cups shredded cabbage *or* chopped Chinese cabbage**
1 **whole large chicken breast, skinned, halved lengthwise, boned, and cut into 1-inch pieces**
2 **hard-cooked eggs, chilled and quartered**
2 **tablespoons sliced green onion**
1 **lemon, cut into wedges**

Partially freeze pork. Slice pork thinly into bite-size strips. Thaw shrimp, if frozen.

Meanwhile, in a saucepan cook the noodles in a large amount of boiling water just till tender; drain. Rinse in cold water; drain well. In a small mixing bowl combine chicken broth; soy sauce; patis (fish sauce), if desired; and pepper. Set aside.

Preheat a wok or large skillet over high heat; add the ¼ cup cooking oil. Fry noodles, a handful at a time, in hot oil for 5 to 7 minutes or till golden brown; drain noodles on paper toweling.

Add the 1 tablespoon cooking oil to wok or skillet. Stir-fry onions and garlic in hot oil for 1 minute. Remove onions and garlic. Add shredded cabbage or chopped Chinese cabbage; stir-fry for 2 minutes. Remove cabbage.

Add chicken pieces to hot wok or skillet; stir-fry for 2 minutes. Remove chicken. (Add more oil, if necessary.) Add pork strips; stir-fry for 2 minutes. Remove pork. Add shrimp; stir-fry for 4 to 5 minutes. Return the chicken and pork to wok or skillet. Stir chicken broth mixture into meat. Bring to boiling. Stir in the noodles, onion, garlic, and cabbage; cover and cook for 1 minute.

To serve, arrange mixture on a serving platter. Garnish with the egg quarters, green onions, and lemon wedges. Serve immediately. Serves 6.

Luau Pork Roast *pictured on page 178* Polynesia and Fiji

In the South Seas, important occasions are feted with a luau. When friends and relatives gather in honor of a baptism, birthday, or wedding, the order of the day is a traditional pig roast.

Long ago, the luau was a religious ceremony. Pigs and other animals were sacrificed to the gods. The men roasted and ate the meat the deities refused. Pigs were in such demand for these rituals that poor tenant farmers would give them to the wealthy landowners in lieu of rent.

For a luau, the pig is traditionally smoked in an "imu," an underground oven. Wood, coconut husks, and red-hot lava stones line the pit. Often, hot stones are stuffed into the pig's abdominal and neck cavities. The carcass is then lowered into the pit. It is covered by ti leaves, banana leaves, bread fruit, sweet potatoes, yams, shellfish, plantains, and sometimes sand to seal in the heat. The cooked meat and vegetables are presented on banana and ti leaves and are unabashedly eaten with the fingers. Until the 1800s, a religious taboo forbade women to prepare the feast or to eat alongside the men.

Luau Pork Roast with *Luau Sweet Potatoes* allows you to stage your own luau. Use bold floral prints, lush greenery, and colorful flowers to create a tropical atmosphere.

1   3- to 5-pound pork center loin roast
4 or 5   cloves garlic, halved
½   cup dry white wine
½   cup soy sauce
½   cup finely chopped onion
¼   cup vinegar *or* lemon juice
2   tablespoons brown sugar
1   tablespoon dry mustard
1   tablespoon grated gingerroot *or* 1 teaspoon ground ginger
¼   cup water
    Luau Sweet Potatoes
    Hot cooked rice

Have butcher loosen back bone of meat. Stud meat with garlic halves by inserting tip of knife into meat at even intervals and pushing garlic into meat as you remove knife.

For marinade, in a bowl combine white wine, soy sauce, onion, vinegar or lemon juice, brown sugar, dry mustard, and gingerroot or ground ginger. Place meat in a plastic bag set in a baking dish. Pour marinade over meat; close bag. Marinate in refrigerator 10 hours or overnight; turn often.

Remove roast, reserving marinade. Pat excess moisture from roast with paper toweling.

Arrange hot coals around edge of grill.* Place roast, rib side down, on heavy-duty foil drip pan on grill. Insert meat thermometer. Close hood; grill over *slow* coals for 2½ to 3 hours or till thermometer registers 170°. Brush frequently with marinade the last 30 minutes. Reserve ½ cup of the marinade; combine with the water. Bring to boiling; reduce heat. Keep warm. Transfer roast to a heated serving platter. Remove garlic from meat, if possible. Serve with Luau Sweet Potatoes, hot cooked rice, and pass the heated marinade. Serves 6 to 8.

*Note: For the oven method, place roast, rib side down, in shallow roasting pan. Insert meat thermometer. Roast, uncovered, in a 325° oven for 2½ to 3 hours or till thermometer registers 170°; brush frequently with marinade the last 30 minutes. Serve as above.

Luau Sweet Potatoes: Combine ½ cup packed *brown sugar,* ⅓ cup coarsely chopped *macadamia nuts or peanuts,* ½ teaspoon *salt,* and ¼ teaspoon *ground nutmeg or ground ginger.* In a 12x7½x2-inch baking dish arrange 5 or 6 medium *sweet potatoes* (2 pounds), cooked, peeled, and cut crosswise into thick pieces *or* two 18-ounce cans *sweet potatoes,* drained, and one 8¼-ounce can *pineapple chunks,* well-drained. Sprinkle brown sugar mixture atop. Dot with ¼ cup *butter or margarine.* Bake in a 325° oven for 30 to 40 minutes or till heated through. Makes 6 to 8 servings.

Skewered Scallops *pictured on page 178* Australia

1   pound fresh *or* frozen scallops
¼   cup dry white wine
3   tablespoons lemon juice
3   tablespoons butter *or* margarine, melted
1   clove garlic, minced
½   teaspoon salt
    Dash pepper
    Paprika
2   kiwi fruit, quartered (optional)

Thaw scallops, if frozen. Rinse in cold water; pat dry with paper toweling. Halve any large scallops. For marinade, in bowl combine dry white wine, lemon juice, butter or margarine, garlic, salt, and pepper. Add scallops; cover and marinate at room temperature for 1 hour. Drain; reserve marinade.

On 8 skewers thread scallops, allowing some space between scallops. Sprinkle lightly with paprika. Grill over *medium* coals for 8 to 10 minutes or till scallops are tender. Turn often and brush with reserved marinade. (Or, broil 4 inches from the heat about 10 minutes, turning once.) Serve with kiwi fruit, if desired. Serves 4.

SOUTH PACIFIC

In the Philippines, the Spanish influenced not only many dishes but also actual meal times. Because many Filipinos follow the Spanish practice of late dining, the time between meals is lengthy. To compensate for this time span, Filipinos have inserted two snack-meals or "meriendas" into their day.

The morning "merienda" takes the form of a coffee break. Sweet rolls, fruit, hot chocolate, and coffee provide a little nourishment before the luncheon hour arrives.

For their late-afternoon snack, Filipinos changed the Spanish tradition of cakes and tarts to a potpourri of sweet and savory dishes. Anything goes except plain cooked rice. As long as their staple rice is omitted from the menu, Filipinos do not consider themselves to be eating a meal.

The number and kind of dishes in a snack vary. *Beef and Pork Sour Soup* or "sinigang" might be accompanied by "puto" (sweet fluffy rice cakes). Tamarind water or lemon juice adds a tartness to this pungent soup. Another merienda classic is *Lumpia* (see recipe, page 185), a cousin of the Chinese egg roll. These often contain green beans and bean sprouts rolled inside a romaine leaf. A noodle dish such as *Pancit Guisado* (see recipe, page 180) might also appear on the table.

Ensaimada Rolls   *pictured on page 178*

Ensaimada Rolls are made from a dough rich in butter, sugar, and eggs. Their texture and flavor are reminiscent of brioche.

These cheese-filled sweet rolls may be topped with additional grated Edam cheese. Serve the rolls at a brunch or as a snack with mugs of hot chocolate or coffee.

 1 **package active dry yeast**
 ¼ **cup warm water (110° to 115°)**
 ½ **cup butter *or* margarine**
 ⅓ **cup sugar**
 ½ **teaspoon salt**
 4 **cups all-purpose flour**
 ½ **cup milk**
 4 **eggs**
 ½ **cup butter *or* margarine, melted**
 1 **cup grated Edam cheese Sugar**

Soften yeast in ¼ cup warm water. In a mixer bowl beat the ½ cup butter or margarine for 30 seconds. Add the ⅓ cup sugar and salt; beat well. Stir *1 cup* of the flour, the milk, and eggs into butter mixture. Add softened yeast; beat well. Stir in the remaining flour till mixture is smooth. Turn into a greased bowl. Cover and chill overnight; stir down.

Turn out onto a lightly floured surface. Divide dough in half. Cover; let rest 10 minutes. Roll *each* half into an 18x15-inch rectangle. Brush some of the melted butter over *each* rectangle of dough. Sprinkle *half* of the cheese over *each* rectangle. With a sharp knife cut *each* rectangle lengthwise into 3 strips, each 5 inches wide. Roll *each* strip up jelly-roll style, beginning from longest side. Cut *each* rolled strip into 3 pieces, each 6 inches long.

On a lightly floured surface, roll *each* piece of dough into a pencil-like strand about 10 inches long. Beginning at center, make a loose swirl with *each* strand forming a spiral-shaped roll; tuck ends under securely. Place 2 to 3 inches apart on lightly greased baking sheets. Cover; let rise in warm place till double (40 to 45 minutes). Bake in a 375° oven for 12 minutes. Remove from oven; brush *each* roll with some of the remaining melted butter or margarine. Sprinkle lightly with sugar. Serve warm. Makes 18 rolls.

Beef and Pork Sour Soup

 1 **pound boneless pork**
 2 **tablespoons olive oil *or* cooking oil**
 1 **pound beef stew meat, cut into ¾-inch pieces**
 1 **medium onion, chopped**
 7 **cups beef broth**
 2 **medium tomatoes, peeled and chopped**
 2 **medium sweet potatoes, peeled and cut into ½-inch cubes (2 cups)**
 1 **medium daikon (Japanese white radish), cut into ¼-inch slices**
 ¼ **cup tamarind water *or* lemon juice**
 1 **teaspoon salt**
 ¼ **teaspoon pepper**
 2 **cups torn fresh spinach**
 1 **tablespoon patis (fish sauce) (optional)**

Partially freeze pork; slice pork thinly into bite-size strips. In a Dutch oven or kettle brown pork in hot oil; remove from pan. Add beef and onion; cook till meat is brown and onion is tender. Return all meat to pan. Add beef broth. Bring to boiling; reduce heat. Cover and simmer about 1 hour.

Stir in the tomatoes, sweet potatoes, daikon (Japanese white radish), tamarind water or lemon juice, salt, and pepper. Cover; simmer for 15 to 20 minutes more or till meat and vegetables are tender. Stir in spinach and the patis (fish sauce), if desired; simmer for 3 to 5 minutes more. Season to taste with salt and pepper. Serve immediately. Makes 8 servings.

SOUTH PACIFIC

Mango Ice Cream

Long before calendars came to the Philippine Islands, mango seasons marked the passage of time. The tangy, juicy fruit was first cultivated over 4,000 years ago. Today, it appears in cobblers, pies, sherbets, and many other fruit dishes.

3 **fresh medium mangoes, peeled, seeded, and cut up, or two 15-ounce jars mango slices, drained***
1 **envelope unflavored gelatin**
¼ **cup cold water**
2 **egg yolks**
2 **cups whipping cream**
¾ **cup sugar***
1½ **teaspoons vanilla**
¼ **teaspoon salt**
2 **egg whites**
¼ **cup sugar**

In a blender or food processor container place mangoes. Cover; blend or process about 1 minute or till smooth (should have 2 cups mango mixture). In a small bowl soften gelatin in cold water; place over hot water and stir to dissolve. In a small mixer bowl beat egg yolks for 4 minutes or till thick and lemon-colored. In a mixing bowl combine mango mixture, egg yolks, whipping cream, the ¾ cup sugar, the vanilla, and salt. Add gelatin; mix well. Turn into a 13x9x2-inch baking pan. Cover and freeze till partially frozen.

Beat egg whites till soft peaks form; gradually add the ¼ cup sugar, beating till stiff peaks form. Break frozen mixture into chunks. Turn into a chilled mixer bowl. Beat with electric mixer till fluffy. Fold in beaten whites. Return to cold pan. Cover; freeze till firm. Makes about 2 quarts (16 servings).

*Note: If using canned mangoes, omit the ¾ cup sugar.

• Pineapple Ice Cream: Prepare Mango Ice Cream as above, except substitute 1 small fresh *pineapple* or three 8-ounce cans *crushed pineapple* (juice pack), drained, for the mangoes. Remove crown from fresh pineapple; remove eyes and core. Cut pineapple into chunks. Continue as directed above.

Pavlova

This chewy meringue dessert was named after a Russian ballerina who performed in Australia and New Zealand in the 1900s. The exterior rim should be firm, but the meringue shell under the fresh fruit should have a soft, marshmallow-like texture.

4 **egg whites**
2 **teaspoons vinegar**
¼ **teaspoon salt**
1 **cup sugar**
5 **cups sliced strawberries, kiwi fruit, bananas, peaches, papaya, or pineapple chunks**
1 **cup whipping cream**
¼ **cup sugar**
1 **teaspoon vanilla**

Bring egg whites to room temperature. Line a baking sheet or a 15x10x1-inch shallow baking pan with foil. Using an 8x1½-inch round cake pan as a guide, draw a circle on the foil. In a mixer bowl combine egg whites, vinegar, and salt; beat at medium speed of electric mixer till soft peaks form. Gradually add the 1 cup sugar, one tablespoon at a time, beating about 4 minutes more or till mixture forms stiff, glossy peaks and sugar is dissolved.

Spread some of the egg white mixture over the circle to ½-inch thickness. Spoon remaining mixture into a decorating bag fitted with a star tip. Pipe mixture around edge of circle, making sides 2 inches high. (Or, spread egg white mixture over circle. Shape into a shell with back of spoon, making the bottom ½ inch thick and sides 2 inches high.) Bake in a 275° oven for 1 hour. Turn off heat and let dry in oven with door closed for 2 to 3 hours more. *Do not open oven door while drying.*

Reserve about ¼ *cup* of the sliced fruit for garnish. Drain fruit slices well. Pat dry with paper toweling, if necessary.

Combine whipping cream, the ¼ cup sugar, and vanilla. Beat till soft peaks form. Carefully remove meringue shell from foil and place on a serving plate. Spoon fruit into meringue shell. Cover with the whipped cream. To serve, cut into wedges. Serve immediately. Makes 8 servings.

Anzac Biscuits

Australia and New Zealand

These biscuits are baked for Anzac Day (April 25), a memorial tribute to the soldiers killed in World War I. Anzac is an acronym for the combined Australia and New Zealand Army Corps.

Though called a biscuit in the two countries; Anzac biscuits are actually what Americans would term cookies.

1½ **cups self-rising flour***
½ **teaspoon ground cinnamon**
¼ **teaspoon ground nutmeg**
¼ **teaspoon ground allspice**
½ **cup butter** *or* **margarine**
½ **cup sugar**
1 **egg**
3 **tablespoons milk**
1 **cup light raisins**
½ **cup chopped almonds** *or* **walnuts**
¼ **cup chopped red candied cherries**

Stir together self-rising flour, cinnamon, nutmeg, and allspice. In a mixer bowl beat butter or margarine on medium speed of electric mixer for 30 seconds. Add sugar and beat till fluffy. Add egg and milk; beat well. Add dry ingredients to beaten mixture and beat till well combined. Stir in light raisins, nuts, and candied cherries.

Drop dough from a rounded teaspoon 2 inches apart onto a greased cookie sheet. Bake in a 375° oven for 8 to 10 minutes or till done. Cool on wire rack. Makes about 4 dozen cookies.

*Note: If desired, 1½ cups all-purpose *flour*, ¾ teaspoon *baking powder*, ¾ teaspoon *baking soda*, and ¼ teaspoon *salt* can be substituted for the self-rising flour.

Mai Tai *pictured on front cover*

Regional

The *Mai Tai* is a popular summer cooler on many of the balmy South Sea Islands.

In Australia and New Zealand, a favorite libation is "shandy," an equal-part mixture of carbonated lemon soda and strong Aussie beer. Men and women alike welcome the citrus-ale combination in December, January, and February, during the heat of the southern hemisphere's summer.

1½ **ounces orange juice**
1½ **ounces unsweetened pineapple juice**
1 **ounce light rum**
1 **ounce dark rum**
1 **ounce bottled sweetened lime juice**
½ **ounce orange liqueur**
Cracked ice
Lime slice (optional)
Fresh mint (optional)

In a tall glass stir together orange juice, pineapple juice, light rum, dark rum, lime juice, and orange liqueur. Add enough cracked ice to fill glass; stir. If desired, garnish the glass with a thin slice of lime and fresh mint. Makes 1 (6½-ounce) serving.

Lumpia

Philippines

2 **tablespoons cooking oil**
½ **cup finely chopped onion**
1 **clove garlic, minced**
¾ **cup finely chopped cooked pork** *or* **chicken**
¼ **cup finely chopped cooked shrimp**
1½ **cups finely shredded cabbage**
½ **of a 9-ounce package frozen French-style green beans, thawed and finely chopped**
1 **cup bean sprouts**
½ **cup shredded carrot**
2 **tablespoons soy sauce**
10 **egg roll skins**
10 **romaine leaves, ribs removed**
Dipping Sauce

For filling, preheat a wok or large skillet over high heat; add oil. Stir-fry onion and garlic in hot oil till tender. Add meat and shrimp; stir-fry for 2 minutes. Add the cabbage, green beans, bean sprouts, carrot, and soy; stir-fry 2 to 3 minutes or till vegetables are crisp-tender. Remove from wok or skillet; cool to room temperature. Brush a little cooking oil in a large shallow skillet; cook *one* egg roll skin, on *one* side only, about 1 minute or till light brown. Turn out onto paper toweling. Repeat with remaining skins. (Add more oil, if necessary.)

To assemble, place an egg roll skin, unbrowned side up, with one corner facing you; top with a romaine leaf. Spoon about ⅓ cup of the filling onto romaine. Roll up, folding in one side of egg roll skin and leaving other end open. Serve immediately with Dipping Sauce. Makes 10 rolls.

Dipping Sauce: In saucepan combine 3 tablespoons *brown sugar* and 2 tablespoons *cornstarch;* stir in 1 cup *chicken broth*, ½ cup *water*, and 2 tablespoons *soy sauce*. Cook and stir till thickened and bubbly. Cook and stir 2 minutes more. Cover surface with clear plastic wrap. Cool.

INDEX

Photographer Credits

Edgar Cheatum:
  Pages 53, 147
George de Gennaro:
  Pages 124, 127, 160
Bill Helms:
  Pages 12, 73, 81, 84, 107, 114
Jerome Klein:
  Page 35
Vincent Maselli
  Page 136
Carl Purcell:
  Left and bottom right on
  page 5; pages 93, 167, 182
William Sladcik:
  Pages 8, 15, 18, 23, 30, 38, 45,
  48, 56, 65, 70, 77, 88, 96, 102,
  111, 117, 120, 130, 150, 152, 162,
  173, 178, cover
Steven Stroud:
  Pages 4, 157
Jessie Walker:
  Background on pages 4, 5;
  upper right on pages 5, 61

A-B

Afghanistan
  Orange-Chicken Pilaf — 133
Africa
  Beef Pilau — 10
  Bobotie — 11
  Chicken Tajin — 13
  Couscous — 12
  Egyptian Eggplant Omelet — 10
  Ethiopian Flat Bread — 16
  Ethiopian Spicy Braised Chicken — 11
  Fish and Eggplant Stew — 14
  Fried Bread — 16
  Gazelle Horns — 17
  Groundnut Stew — 14
  Homemade Harissa Sauce — 12
  Jollof Rice — 10
  Lamb Bredie — 13
  Lamb Sosaties — 13
  Lamb Tajin — 13
  Melktert — 17
  Palaver Sauce — 14
  Pepper Chicken — 11
  Plantain Fritters — 16
Albondigas Tikal Soup — 51
Almond
  Almond-Baked Apples — 74
  Almond Braid — 146
  Almond Pudding — 176
Anzac Biscuits — 185
Appetizers
  Beef Heart Anticuchos — 161
  Bitterballen — 87
  Ceviche — 129
  Cheese-Filled Pastries — 140
  Cheese Pastries — 161
  Chicken and Crab Pot Stickers — 97
  Corn Pancakes — 161
  Fried Zucchini Appetizers — 99
  Guacamole con Tomatillos — 129
  Herring Salad — 151
  Kujol Pan — 100
  Liptói Cheese — 69
  Liver Pâté — 151
  Lumpia — 185
  Marinated Salmon — 29
  Mititei Sausages — 69
  Omelet-Wrapped Sushi — 101
  Pâté Maison — 87
  Piradzini — 69
  Pork and Shrimp Wontons — 98
  Pork Empanaditas — 55
  Salsa de Tomatillos — 129
  Savory Filled Triangles — 141
  Solomon Gundy — 37
  Spring Rolls — 177
  Steamed Buns with Sweet Filling — 99
  Steamed Pork Dumplings — 98
  Sweet Rice Eggs — 101
  Vitello Tonnato — 119
Apples
  Almond-Baked Apples — 74
  Apple Cake — 150
  Applesauce — 137

Apples (continued)
  Apple-Stuffed Salmon — 33
  Goose with Apple Stuffing — 75
  Rhubarb-Apple Pie — 36
Armenian SSR
  Lavash Bread — 63
Artichoke-Shallot Soufflé — 78
Asparagus Cream Soup — 78
Australia
  Anzac Biscuits — 185
  Carpetbag Steak — 180
  Pavlova — 184
  Rissole Potatoes — 180
  Skewered Scallops — 181
Austria
  Beef and Vegetable Platter — 73
  Beef Broth with Strudel Dumplings — 76
  Chocolate Butter Frosting — 82
  Coffee-Butter Cream Filling — 82
  Creamed Dilled Spinach — 81
  Creamed Spinach — 81
  Dill Sauce — 73
  Hazelnut Torte — 82
  Parslied Carrots — 80
Backwoods Pie — 36
Bahamas
  Papaya Salad — 44
Baked Kibbeh — 132
Balkans, The
  Ghivetci Vegetables — 59
Banana Daiquiri — 47
Banana Soufflé — 46
Bara Brith Bread — 26
Barbados
  Coo-Coo — 44
  Mango Mousse — 45
  Tomato Sauce — 44
Barbecued Spareribs — 165
Barley and Potato Soup — 62
Barley Kugel — 137
Basic Rich Pastry — 83
Batida Paulista — 161
Beans
  Caldo Gallego — 108
  Feijoada Bean Stew — 154
  Garbanzo Bean Soup — 108
  Lamb and Garbanzo Soup — 134
  Red Beans and Rice — 41
  Red Bean Soup — 52
  Refried Beans — 125
  Shredded Beef Tostadas — 122
Beef
  Beef and Pork Sour Soup — 183
  Beef and Vegetable Platter — 73
  Beef Broth with Strudel Dumplings — 76
  Beef Heart Anticuchos — 161
  Beef Pilau — 10
  Beef Satay — 164
  Beef with Mustard Greens — 50
  Carne en Adobo — 50
  Carpetbag Steak — 180
  Grilled Marinated Short Ribs — 91
  Hussar Roast — 58
  Kujol Pan — 100
  Minced Collops — 20

Beef (continued)
Nasi Goreng ___ 171
Palaver Sauce ___ 14
Pot-au-Feu ___ 32
Ranch Steak ___ 32
Sancocho Beef Stew ___ 51
Shredded Beef Tostadas ___ 122
Shredded Flank Steak ___ 40
Szechwan Dry-Fried Beef ___ 90
Teppanyaki ___ 91
Thai Beef Larnar ___ 172
Vegetable-Beef Stir-Fry ___ 90
Wine-Braised Beef ___ 72

Beef, Ground
Albondigas Tikal Soup ___ 51
Beef Dumpling Soup ___ 94
Bitterballen ___ 87
Cheese-Filled Manicotti ___ 106
Dolmas ___ 132
Frikadeller Meatballs ___ 144
Mititei Sausages ___ 69
Plantain Circles ___ 40
Potatoes Rellenos ___ 157
Stuffed Peppers with Walnut Sauce 122

Belgium
Brussels Sprouts Puree ___ 80
Flemish Eel Waterzooi ___ 79
Flemish Fish Waterzooi ___ 79
Berry Soup ___ 151

Beverages, Alcoholic
Banana Daiquiri ___ 47
Batida Paulista ___ 161
Bisschop ___ 86
Daiquiri ___ 47
Frozen Daiquiri ___ 47
Irish Coffee ___ 29
Limonada ___ 119
Mai Tai ___ 185
Margarita ___ 128
Piña Colada ___ 47
Pineapple Daiquiri ___ 47
Planter's Punch ___ 47
Spiced Wassail ___ 29
Syllabub ___ 29
Tequila Sunrise ___ 128

Beverages, Nonalcoholic
Chocolate Mexicano ___ 128
Peach Chicha ___ 55
Walnut Tea ___ 101
Bisschop ___ 86
Bitterballen ___ 87
Black Bun ___ 27
Bobotie ___ 11
Bolillo ___ 116

Bolivia
Cheese Pastries ___ 161
Potatoes with Hot Sauce ___ 158
Boxty ___ 25

Brazil
Batida Paulista ___ 161
Brigadeiros ___ 159
Chicken Empadao ___ 155
Coconut Quindins ___ 159
Feijoada Bean Stew ___ 154
Peanut Balls ___ 159

Brazil (continued)
Pumpkin Custard ___ 158
Soufflé-Topped Shrimp ___ 155
Tomato Rice ___ 156
Bread and Wine Dessert ___ 54
Bread Pudding, Cherry ___ 86

Breads, Quick
Brown Irish Soda Bread ___ 27
Chapati ___ 175
Churros ___ 126
Corn Soupbread ___ 158
Ethiopian Flat Bread ___ 16
Fried Bread ___ 16
Fried Butter Biscuits ___ 44
Gingerbread ___ 46
Lavash Bread ___ 63
Lefse ___ 149
Oatcakes ___ 34
Sopaipillas ___ 126
Sourdough Biscuits ___ 35
Treacle Tea Scones ___ 26

Breads, Yeast
Almond Braid ___ 146
Bara Brith Bread ___ 26
Bolillo Rolls ___ 116
Christmas Braid ___ 64
Christopsomo Bread ___ 115
Doughnut Spheres ___ 138
Egg Bread Rosettes ___ 54
Ensaimada Rolls ___ 183
Homemade Bread Dough ___ 141
King's Cake ___ 116
Love Feast Buns ___ 66
Lucia Buns ___ 148
Massa Sovada Bread ___ 115
Pita Bread ___ 138
Poppy Seed Kolache ___ 64
Steamed Buns with Sweet Filling ___ 99
Sweet Raisin Bread ___ 148
Brigadeiros ___ 159

British Isles
Michaelmas Goose ___ 21
Syllabub ___ 29
Treacle Tea Scones ___ 26
Brown Irish Soda Bread ___ 27
Brussels Sprouts Puree ___ 80

Bulgaria
Tarator Yogurt Soup ___ 62

Burma
Chicken with Fried Noodles ___ 170
Burnt Cream ___ 29

C-E

Cabbage
Lamb with Cabbage ___ 144
Seasoned Sauerkraut ___ 63
Stuffed Cabbage Rolls ___ 59
Sweet and Sour Red Cabbage ___ 146
Swiss Cheese-Cabbage Soup ___ 76
Cabbie Claw ___ 22

Cakes
Cake of Juices ___ 54
Hazelnut Torte ___ 82
Heavenly Cake ___ 126

Cakes (continued)
Honey Cake ___ 66
Kirsch Torte ___ 84
Malakoff Torte ___ 85
Spiced Rich Layer Cake ___ 176
Zagreb Cake ___ 67
Caldeirada Fish Stew ___ 108
Caldo Gallego ___ 108
Caldo Verde ___ 109
Callaloo ___ 42

Canada
Apple-Stuffed Salmon ___ 33
Backwoods Pie ___ 36
Cherry-Nut Roly-Poly ___ 37
Hodgepodge ___ 34
Hugger-in-Buff ___ 33
Maple Divinity ___ 37
Oatcakes ___ 34
Pot-au-Feu ___ 32
Ranch Steak ___ 32
Rhubarb-Apple Pie ___ 36
Seafood Chowder ___ 33
Solomon Gundy ___ 37
Sourdough Biscuits ___ 35
Sourdough Starter ___ 35
Split Pea Soup ___ 34
Tourtière ___ 32
Tourtière Pastry ___ 32
Wild Rice Bake ___ 34

Candies
Brigadeiros ___ 159
Coconut Candy ___ 177
Coconut Quindins ___ 159
Loukomi Candy ___ 140
Maple Divinity ___ 37
Peanut Balls ___ 159

Caribbean
Banana Daiquiri ___ 47
Daiquiri ___ 47
Frozen Daiquiri ___ 47
Piña Colada ___ 47
Pineapple Daiquiri ___ 47
Planter's Punch ___ 47
Carne en Adobo ___ 50
Carpetbag Steak ___ 180

Carrots
Carrot Custard ___ 146
Carrot Tzimmes ___ 135
Lemon-Basil Carrots ___ 112
Parslied Carrots ___ 80

Central America
Pork Empanaditas ___ 55
Rice with Peas ___ 52
Sweet Potato Buñeulos ___ 52
Ceviche ___ 129
Chapati ___ 175

Cheese
Cheese and Onion Tart ___ 78
Cheese-Filled Manicotti ___ 106
Cheese-Filled Pastries ___ 140
Cheese Pastries ___ 161
Ensaimada Rolls ___ 183
Potatoes with Hot Sauce ___ 158
Cherry Bread Pudding ___ 86
Cherry-Nut Roly-Poly ___ 37

Chicken
Chicken and Crab Pot Stickers —— 97
Chicken Asopao —— 43
Chicken Empadao —— 155
Chicken Enchiladas —— 123
Chicken in Coconut Sauce —— 168
Chicken in Pepitoria —— 104
Chicken in Phyllo —— 105
Chicken in Wine Sauce —— 50
Chicken Mole —— 123
Chicken Tajin —— 13
Chicken with Cider and Cream —— 74
Chicken with Fried Noodles —— 170
Cock-a-Leekie Soup —— 24
Ethiopian Spicy Braised Chicken —— 11
Fuji Chicken in Miso —— 92
Groundnut Stew —— 14
Howtowdie with Drappit Eggs —— 22
Jollof Rice —— 10
Lime Soup —— 124
Mulligatawny —— 23
Pancit Guisado —— 180
Pepper Chicken —— 11
Orange-Chicken Pilaf —— 133
Royal Chicken Pilaf —— 169
Chile
Potatoes Rellenos —— 157
Puffed Corn Pies —— 154
China
Chicken and Crab Pot Stickers —— 97
Chinese Mustard Sauce —— 97
Kowloon Duckling —— 92
Lobster Cantonese —— 94
Plum-Orange Sauce —— 92
Pork and Shrimp Wontons —— 99
Pork-Vegetable Soup —— 94
Soy-Ginger Sauce —— 97
Steamed Buns with Sweet Filling —— 99
Steamed Pork Dumplings —— 98
Szechwan Dry-Fried Beef —— 90
Vegetarian Fried Rice —— 95
Walnut Tea —— 101
Chocolate
Brigadeiros —— 159
Chicken Mole —— 123
Chocolate Butter Frosting —— 82
Chocolate Mexicano —— 128
Zagreb Cake —— 67
Christmas Braid —— 64
Christopsomo Bread —— 115
Churros —— 126
Cock-a-Leekie Soup —— 24
Coconut
Chicken in Coconut Sauce —— 168
Coconut Candy —— 177
Coconut Empanadas —— 55
Coconut Milk —— 170
Coconut Quindins —— 159
Coconut Tarts —— 119
Thick Coconut Milk —— 170
Cod and Potato Casserole —— 105
Coffee-Butter Cream Filling —— 82
Colcannon —— 25
Colombia
Fish with Salsa Fria —— 156

Condiments
Guacamole con Tomatillos —— 129
Homemade Harissa Sauce —— 12
Homemade Tahini —— 134
Kimchi —— 95
Salsa de Tomatillos —— 129
Salsa Fria —— 156
Sweet Tomato Chutney —— 174
Coo-Coo —— 44
Cookies
Anzac Biscuits —— 185
Coconut Tarts —— 119
Gazelle Horns —— 17
Jan Hagels —— 86
Koulourakia Cookies —— 117
Mamool Cookies —— 139
Melamakárona Cookies —— 118
Napoleon's Hats —— 149
Piparkukas —— 66
Richmond Maids of Honor —— 27
Sandbakkelse —— 149
Corn
Corn Pancakes —— 161
Corn Soupbread —— 158
Puffed Corn Pies —— 154
Costa Rica
Beef with Mustard Greens —— 50
Cottage Cheese Patties —— 59
Couscous —— 12
Cream Crowdie —— 28
Creamed Dilled Spinach —— 81
Creamed Spinach —— 81
Crème Fraîche —— 74
Crispy Fried Fish —— 171
Cuba
Shredded Flank Steak —— 40
Cucumber Salad —— 175
Custard and Fruit Dessert —— 128
Czechoslovakia
Christmas Braid —— 64
Love Feast Buns —— 66
Poppy Seed Kolache —— 64
Daiquiri —— 47
Daiquiri, Banana —— 47
Daiquiri, Frozen —— 47
Daiquiri, Pineapple —— 47
Deep-Fried Rice Sticks —— 168
Deep-Fried Wonton Strips —— 172
Denmark
Apple Cake —— 150
Frikadeller Meatballs —— 144
Liver Pâté —— 151
Napoleon's Hats —— 149
Desserts (see also Cakes, Candies, Cookies, Pies, and Puddings)
Apple Cake —— 150
Berry Soup —— 151
Bread and Wine Dessert —— 54
Burnt Cream —— 29
Cherry-Nut Roly-Poly —— 37
Cream Crowdie —— 28
Custard and Fruit Dessert —— 128
Fresh Fruit Compote —— 67
Fruit Trifle —— 28
Galaktoboúreko Pastry —— 118

Desserts (continued)
Little Devils —— 67
Mango Ice Cream —— 184
Mango Mousse —— 45
Pavlova —— 184
Pineapple Ice Cream —— 184
Plantain Fritters —— 16
Pumpkin Custard —— 158
Vargabéles Rétes —— 68
Dipping Sauce —— 185
Dolmas —— 132
Doughnut Spheres —— 138
Dublin Coddle —— 21
Duck with Apple Stuffing —— 75
Eastern Europe
Fish with Sour Cream Sauce —— 60
Potato Salad —— 63
Seasoned Sauerkraut —— 63
Stuffed Cabbage Rolls —— 59
Egg Bread Rosettes —— 54
Eggplant
Egyptian Eggplant Omelet —— 10
Fish and Eggplant Stew —— 14
Lamb-Eggplant Avgolemono —— 104
Eggs
Artichoke-Shallot Soufflé —— 78
Banana Soufflé —— 46
Egyptian Eggplant Omelet —— 10
Howtowdie with Drappit Eggs —— 22
Huevos a la Flamenca —— 106
Japanese Omelet —— 101
Lamb Koftas —— 165
Omelet-Wrapped Sushi —— 101
Scotch Eggs —— 21
Soufflé-Topped Shrimp —— 155
El Salvador
Chicken in Wine Sauce —— 50
Red Bean Soup —— 52
England
Fruit Trifle —— 28
Lemon Steamed Pudding —— 28
Marinated Salmon —— 29
Melton Mowbray Pie —— 20
Mulligatawny —— 23
Richmond Maids of Honor —— 27
Salmon Kedgeree —— 24
Spiced Wassail —— 29
Ensaimado Rolls —— 183
Ensalada de Esparragos —— 111
Ensalada Mixta —— 156
Ethiopian Flat Bread —— 16
Ethiopian Spicy Braised Chicken —— 11

F-K

Feijoada Bean Stew —— 154
Figs in Syrup —— 139
Finland
Carrot Custard —— 146
Liver and Raisin Bake —— 144
Summer Vegetable Soup —— 145
Fish
Apple-Stuffed Salmon —— 33
Cabbie Claw —— 22
Caldeirada Fish Stew —— 108

Fish *(continued)*
Callaloo — 42
Ceviche — 129
Cod and Potato Casserole — 105
Crispy Fried Fish — 171
Fish and Eggplant Stew — 14
Fish Vinaigrette — 41
Fish with Salsa Fria — 156
Fish with Sour Cream Sauce — 60
Fish with Tahini Sauce — 134
Fish with Walnut Sauce — 60
Fish with White Butter Sauce — 79
Fiskeboller — 145
Flemish Fish Waterzooi — 79
Fried Fish with Ginger Sauce — 173
Herring Salad — 151
Hugger-in-Buff — 33
Kulebiaka — 61
Marinated Salmon — 29
Salmon Kedgeree — 24
Solomon Gundy — 37
Stuffed Salmon — 60
Vitello Tonnato — 1
Flemish Eel Waterzooi — 79
France
Almond-Baked Apples — 74
Artichoke-Shallot Soufflé — 78
Basic Rich Pastry — 83
Chicken with Cider and Cream — 74
Crème Fraîche — 74
Fish with White Butter Sauce — 79
Fruit Tarte — 83
Pâté Maison — 87
Wine-Braised Beef — 72
Fresh Fruit Compote — 67
Fresh Vegetable Marinade — 110
Fried Bread — 16
Fried Butter Biscuits — 44
Fried Fish with Ginger Sauce — 173
Fried Onion Rings — 169
Fried Potato Cake — 80
Fried Zucchini Appetizers — 99
Frikadeller Meatballs — 144
Frozen Daiquiri — 47
Fruit *(see also* Apple, Banana, Pineapple, *and* Plantain)
Figs in Syrup — 139
Fresh Fruit Compote — 67
Fruit Tarte — 83
Fruit Trifle — 28
Mango Ice Cream — 184
Orange-Chicken Pilaf — 133
Papaya Salad — 44
Pavlova — 184
Peach Chicha — 55
Plum-Orange Sauce — 92
Rhubarb-Apple Pie — 36
Fuji Chicken in Miso — 92
Gado-Gado — 174
Galaktoboúreko Pastry — 118
Garam Masala — 166
Garbanzo Bean Soup — 108
Garbanzo Soup, Lamb and — 134
Gazelle Horns — 17
Gazpacho — 109

Georgian SSR
Fish with Walnut Sauce — 60
Germany
Asparagus Cream Soup — 78
Goose with Apple Stuffing — 75
Kirsch Torte — 84
Malakoff Torte — 85
Ghivetci Vegetables — 59
Giblets, Risotto with — 113
Gingerbread — 46
Goose with Apple Stuffing — 75
Greece
Chicken in Phyllo — 105
Christopsomo Bread — 115
Galaktoboúreko Pastry — 118
Greek Dressing — 109
Koulourakia Cookies — 117
Lamb-Eggplant Avgolemono — 104
Lemon-Basil Carrots — 112
Melamakárona Cookies — 118
Peasant Salad — 109
Green Beans with Miso Dressing — 95
Grilled Marinated Short Ribs — 91
Groundnut Stew — 14
Guacamole con Tomatillos — 129
Guadeloupe
Pineapple-Rum Duckling — 41
Guatemala
Albondigas Tikal Soup — 51
Haiti
Banana Soufflé — 46
Hangover Soup — 62
Hazelnut Torte — 82
Heavenly Cake — 126
Herring Salad — 151
Hodgepodge — 34
Holland
Bisschop — 86
Bitterballen — 87
Jan Hagels — 86
Stamppot — 74
Homemade Bread Dough — 141
Homemade Harissa Sauce — 12
Honduras
Bread and Wine Dessert — 54
Honey Cake — 66
Hot Mustard Sauce — 100
Howtowdie with Drappit Eggs — 22
Huevos a la Flamenca — 106
Hugger-in-Buff — 33
Hungary
Hangover Soup — 62
Liptói Cheese — 69
Little Devils — 67
Pork Pörkölt — 58
Strudel Dough — 68
Vargabéles Rétes — 68
Hussar Roast — 58
India
Almond Pudding — 176
Chapati — 175
Chicken in Coconut Sauce — 168
Coconut Candy — 177
Garam Masala — 166
Lamb Koftas — 165

India *(continued)*
Lamb Korma — 166
Sweet Tomato Chutney — 174
Usli Ghee — 166
Indonesia
Gado-Gado — 174
Nasi Goreng — 171
Peanut Sauce — 174
Spiced Rich Layer Cake — 176
Iran
Lamb and Garbanzo Soup — 134
Spinach-Yogurt Salad — 135
Ireland
Boxty — 25
Brown Irish Soda Bread — 27
Colcannon — 25
Dublin Coddle — 21
Irish Coffee — 29
Irish Stew — 24
Israel
Applesauce — 137
Barley Kugel — 137
Carrot Tzimmes — 135
Doughnut Spheres — 138
Knish — 141
Potato Latkes — 137
Sour Cream Latkes — 137
Italy
Cheese-Filled Manicotti — 106
Fresh Vegetable Marinade — 110
Garbanzo Bean Soup — 108
Linguine with White Clam Sauce — 105
Risotto with Giblets — 113
Spaghetti with Four Cheeses — 106
Spaghetti with Marinara Sauce — 112
Spinach-Stuffed Conchiglione — 112
Straw and Hay — 113
Stuffed Escarole — 110
Vitello Tonnato — 119
Jamaica
Fish Vinaigrette — 41
Gingerbread — 46
Jan Hagels — 86
Japan
Fuji Chicken in Miso — 92
Green Beans with Miso Dressing — 95
Japanese Omelets — 101
Omelet-Wrapped Sushi — 101
Sweet Rice Eggs — 101
Teppanyaki — 91
Jollof Rice — 10
Jordan
Mansaf — 132
Kampuchea
Crispy Fried Fish — 171
Kimchi — 95
King's Cake — 116
Kirsch Torte — 84
Knish — 141
Korea
Beef Dumpling Soup — 94
Fried Zucchini Appetizers — 99
Grilled Marinated Short Ribs — 91
Hot Mustard Sauce — 100
Kimchi — 95

189

Korea (continued)
Korean Pancakes _____ 100
Kujol Pan _____ 100
Soy Dipping Sauce _____ 100
Vegetable-Beef Stir-Fry _____ 90
Koulourakia Cookies _____ 117
Kowloon Duckling _____ 92
Kujol Pan _____ 100
Kulebiaka _____ 61

L-P

Lamb
Baked Kibbeh _____ 132
Bobotie _____ 11
Couscous _____ 12
Dolmas _____ 132
Irish Stew _____ 24
Lamb-Eggplant Avgolemono _____ 104
Lamb and Garbanzo Soup _____ 134
Lamb Bredie _____ 13
Lamb Koftas _____ 165
Lamb Korma _____ 166
Lamb Sosaties _____ 13
Lamb Tajin _____ 13
Lamb with Cabbage _____ 144
Mansaf _____ 132
Savory Filled Triangles _____ 141
Shish Kabob _____ 133
Latvian SSR
Fresh Fruit Compote _____ 67
Piparkukas _____ 66
Piradzini _____ 69
Stuffed Salmon _____ 60
Veal Ragout _____ 58
Lavash Bread _____ 63
Lebanon
Baked Kibbeh _____ 132
Fish with Tahini Sauce _____ 134
Mamool Cookies _____ 139
Savory Filled Triangles _____ 141
Tabouleh Salad _____ 134
Leek Salad _____ 25
Lefse _____ 149
Lemon-Basil Carrots _____ 112
Lemon Steamed Pudding _____ 28
Lime Soup _____ 124
Limonada _____ 119
Linguine with White Clam Sauce _____ 105
Liptói Cheese _____ 69
Little Devils _____ 67
Liver and Raisin Bake _____ 144
Liver Pâté _____ 151
Lobster Cantonese _____ 94
Loukomi Candy _____ 140
Love Feast Buns _____ 66
Luau Pork Roast _____ 181
Luau Sweet Potatoes _____ 181
Lucia Buns _____ 148
Lumpia _____ 185
Mai Tai _____ 185
Malakoff Torte _____ 84
Malaysia
Beef Satay _____ 164
Rice Cakes _____ 164

Mamool Cookies _____ 139
Mango Ice Cream _____ 184
Mango Mousse _____ 45
Mansaf _____ 132
Maple Divinity _____ 37
Margarita _____ 128
Marinated Salmon _____ 29
Massa Sovada Bread _____ 115
Mee Krob _____ 168
Melamakárona Cookies _____ 118
Melktert _____ 17
Melton Mowbray Pie _____ 20
Mexico
Ceviche _____ 129
Chicken Enchiladas _____ 123
Chicken Mole _____ 123
Chocolate Mexicano _____ 128
Churros _____ 126
Custard and Fruit Dessert _____ 128
Guacamole con Tomatillos _____ 129
Heavenly Cake _____ 126
Lime Soup _____ 124
Margarita _____ 128
Refried Beans _____ 125
Salsa de Tomatillos _____ 129
Sausage-Stuffed Zucchini _____ 125
Shredded Beef Tostadas _____ 122
Sopaipillas _____ 126
Stuffed Peppers
with Walnut Sauce _____ 122
Tequila Sunrise _____ 128
Tortilla Casserole _____ 125
Michaelmas Goose _____ 21
Middle East
Dolmas _____ 132
Pita Bread _____ 138
Minced Collops _____ 20
Miso Dressing, Green Beans with _____ 95
Mititei Sausages _____ 69
Mixed Vegetable Salad _____ 52
Mulligatawny _____ 23
Napoleon's Hats _____ 149
Nasi Goreng _____ 171
New Zealand
Anzac Biscuits _____ 185
Nicaragua
Coconut Empanadas _____ 55
Mixed Vegetable Salad _____ 52
Noah's Pudding _____ 139
Noodles with Nuts _____ 68
Norway
Fiskeboller _____ 145
Herring Salad _____ 151
Lefse _____ 149
Mushroom Sauce _____ 145
Sandbakkelse _____ 149
Sweet Raisin Bread _____ 148
Oatcakes _____ 34
Okra in Oil _____ 135
Omelet-Wrapped Sushi _____ 101
Orange-Chicken Pilaf _____ 133
Pakistan
Fried Onion Rings _____ 169
Royal Chicken Pilaf _____ 169
Palaver Sauce _____ 14

Panama
Cake of Juices _____ 54
Carne en Adobo _____ 50
Egg Bread Rosettes _____ 54
Peach Chicha _____ 55
Sancocho Beef Stew _____ 51
Pancit Guisado _____ 180
Papaya Salad _____ 44
Paraguay
Corn Soupbread _____ 158
Parslied Carrots _____ 80
Pasta
Cheese-Filled Manicotti _____ 106
Linguine with White Clam Sauce _____ 105
Noodles with Nuts _____ 68
Pancit Guisado _____ 180
Spaghetti with Four Cheeses _____ 106
Spaghetti with Marinara Sauce _____ 112
Spinach-Stuffed Conchiglione _____ 112
Straw and Hay _____ 113
Pastry
Basic Rich Pastry _____ 83
Kulebiaka Pastry _____ 61
Pastry for Double-Crust Pie _____ 27, 141
Pastry for Single-Crust Pie _____ 36
Strudel Dough _____ 68
Tourtière Pastry _____ 32
Pâté Maison _____ 87
Pavlova _____ 184
Peach Chicha _____ 55
Peanut Balls _____ 159
Peanut Sauce _____ 174
Peasant Salad _____ 109
Pepper Chicken _____ 11
Peru
Beef Heart Anticuchos _____ 161
Philippines
Beef and Pork Sour Soup _____ 183
Dipping Sauce _____ 185
Ensaimada Rolls _____ 183
Lumpia _____ 185
Mango Ice Cream _____ 184
Pancit Guisado _____ 180
Pineapple Ice Cream _____ 184
Pies
Backwoods Pie _____ 36
Chicken Empadao _____ 155
Melktert _____ 17
Melton Mowbray Pie _____ 20
Rhubarb-Apple Pie _____ 36
Tourtière _____ 32
Piña Colada _____ 47
Pineapple
Pineapple Daiquiri _____ 47
Pineapple Ice Cream _____ 184
Pineapple-Rum Duckling _____ 41
Piparkukas _____ 66
Piradzini _____ 69
Pisto _____ 110
Pita Bread _____ 138
Plantain
Plantain Circles _____ 40
Plantain Fritters _____ 16
Plantain Tostones _____ 43
Planter's Punch _____ 47

Plum-Orange Sauce _____ 92
Poland
   Barley and Potato Soup_____ 62
   Hussar Roast _____ 58
Polynesia and Fiji
   Luau Pork Roast _____ 181
   Luau Sweet Potatoes _____ 181
Poppy Seed Kolache _____ 64
Pork
   Albondigas Tikal Soup _____ 51
   Barbecued Spareribs _____ 165
   Beef and Pork Sour Soup_____ 183
   Dublin Coddle _____ 21
   Frikadeller Meatballs _____ 144
   Ghivetci Vegetables _____ 59
   Kujol Pan _____ 100
   Liver Pâté _____ 151
   Luau Pork Roast_____ 181
   Melton Mowbray Pie _____ 20
   Nasi Goreng _____ 171
   Pancit Guisado _____ 180
   Pâté Maison _____ 87
   Pork Alentejana _____ 104
   Pork and Shrimp Wontons _____ 98
   Pork Empanaditas_____ 55
   Pork Pörkölt _____ 58
   Pork Satay _____ 164
   Pork-Vegetable Soup _____ 94
   Steamed Pork Dumplings _____ 98
   Stuffed Cabbage Rolls _____ 59
   Tourtière _____ 32
Portugal
   Caldeirada Fish Stew_____ 108
   Caldo Verde _____ 109
   Coconut Tarts _____ 119
   Cod and Potato Casserole ____ 105
   King's Cake _____ 116
   Massa Sovada Bread _____ 115
   Pork Alentejana_____ 104
Potatoes
   Barley and Potato Soup_____ 62
   Boxty _____ 25
   Cod and Potato Casserole ____ 105
   Colcannon _____ 25
   Fried Potato Cake_____ 80
   Knish_____ 141
   Potatoes Rellenos _____ 157
   Potatoes with Hot Sauce _____ 158
   Potato Latkes _____ 137
   Potato Salad _____ 63
   Rissole Potatoes _____ 180
   Stamppot _____ 74
Pot-au-Feu _____ 32
Poultry (see also Chicken)
   Duck with Apple Stuffing _____ 75
   Goose with Apple Stuffing _____ 75
   Kowloon Duckling _____ 92
   Michaelmas Goose _____ 21
   Pineapple-Rum Duckling _____ 41
Puddings
   Almond Pudding _____ 176
   Cherry Bread Pudding _____ 86
   Lemon Steamed Pudding _____ 28
   Noah's Pudding _____ 139
   Pumpkin Pudding _____ 46

Puerto Rico
   Adobo_____ 43
   Chicken Asopao _____ 43
   Plantain Circles _____ 40
   Plantain Tostones _____ 43
   Pumpkin Pudding _____ 46
   Red Beans and Rice _____ 41
   Sofrito _____ 41
Puffed Corn Pies _____ 154
Pumpkin Custard _____ 158
Pumpkin Pudding _____ 46

R-S

Ranch Steak _____ 32
Red Beans and Rice _____ 41
Red Bean Soup _____ 52
Refried Beans_____ 125
Rhubarb-Apple Pie _____ 36
Rice
   Almond Pudding_____ 176
   Beef Pilau _____ 10
   Deep-Fried Rice Sticks_____ 168
   Jollof Rice _____ 10
   Liver and Raisin Bake _____ 144
   Mansaf _____ 132
   Nasi Goreng _____ 171
   Noah's Pudding_____ 139
   Omelet-Wrapped Sushi _____ 101
   Orange-Chicken Pilaf _____ 133
   Red Beans and Rice _____ 41
   Rice Cakes _____ 164
   Rice with Peas _____ 52
   Risotto with Giblets _____ 113
   Royal Chicken Pilaf _____ 169
   Salmon Kedgeree _____ 24
   Sweet Rice Eggs _____ 101
   Tomato Rice _____ 156
   Vegetarian Fried Rice _____ 95
   Wild Rice Bake _____ 34
Richmond Maids of Honor _____ 27
Risotto with Giblets _____ 113
Rissole Potatoes _____ 180
Romania
   Mititei Sausages _____ 69
   Noodles with Nuts _____ 68
Royal Chicken Pilaf _____ 169
Salad Dressings
   Greek Dressing _____ 109
   Hot Pepper Dressing_____ 156
   Miso Dressing _____ 95
   Peanut Sauce _____ 174
Salads
   Cucumber Salad _____ 175
   Ensalada de Esparragos_____ 111
   Ensalada Mixta _____ 156
   Fresh Vegetable Marinade_____ 110
   Herring Salad _____ 151
   Leek Salad _____ 25
   Mixed Vegetable Salad _____ 52
   Papaya Salad _____ 44
   Peasant Salad _____ 109
   Spinach-Yogurt Salad _____ 135
   Tabouleh Salad _____ 134
Salmon Kedgeree_____ 24

Salsa de Tomatillos _____ 129
Sancocho Beef Stew _____ 51
Sandbakkelse _____ 149
Sauces
   Adobo_____ 43
   Chinese Mustard Sauce_____ 97
   Dill Sauce _____ 73
   Dipping Sauce _____ 185
   Hot Mustard Sauce _____ 100
   Mushroom Sauce _____ 145
   Plum-Orange Sauce_____ 92
   Sofrito_____ 41
   Soy Dipping Sauce_____ 100
   Soy-Ginger Sauce _____ 97
   Sweet and Sour Sauce _____ 177
   Tomato Sauce _____ 44
   Walnut Sauce_____ 122
Saudi Arabia
   Figs in Syrup _____ 139
   Okra in Oil_____ 135
Sausage
   Caldo Gallego _____ 108
   Feijoada Bean Stew_____ 154
   Hangover Soup _____ 62
   Huevos a la Flamenca_____ 106
   Red Beans and Rice _____ 41
   Sancocho Beef Stew _____ 51
   Sausage-Stuffed Zucchini _____ 125
   Scotch Eggs _____ 21
   Spring Rolls _____ 177
   Stamppot _____ 74
Savory Filled Triangles _____ 141
Scandinavia
   Berry Soup _____ 151
   Lamb with Cabbage _____ 144
   Sweet and Sour Red Cabbage_____ 146
Scotland
   Black Bun _____ 27
   Burnt Cream _____ 29
   Cabbie Claw _____ 22
   Cock-a-Leekie Soup _____ 24
   Cream Crowdie_____ 28
   Howtowdie with Drappit Eggs _____ 22
   Minced Collops _____ 20
   Scotch Eggs _____ 21
Seafood (see also Fish and Shrimp)
   Caldeirada Fish Stew_____ 108
   Callaloo _____ 42
   Carpetbag Steak _____ 180
   Chicken and Crab Pot Stickers _____ 97
   Flemish Eel Waterzooi _____ 79
   Linguine with White Clam Sauce_____ 105
   Lobster Cantonese _____ 94
   Pork Alentejana _____ 104
   Seafood Chowder _____ 33
   Skewered Scallops _____ 181
Seasoned Sauerkraut _____ 63
Shallot Soufflé, Artichoke- _____ 78
Shish Kabob _____ 133
Shredded Beef Tostadas _____ 122
Shredded Flank Steak _____ 40
Shrimp
   Mee Krob _____ 168
   Pork and Shrimp Wontons _____ 98
   Soufflé-Topped Shrimp_____ 155

Shrimp *(continued)*
Teppanyaki — 91
Thai Shrimp Larnar — 172
Skewered Scallops — 181
Solomon Gundy — 37
Sopaipillas — 126
Soufflé, Artichoke-Shallot — 78
Soufflé, Banana — 46
Soufflé-Topped Shrimp — 155
Soups
Albondigas Tikal Soup — 51
Asparagus Cream Soup — 78
Barley and Potato Soup — 62
Beef and Pork Sour Soup — 183
Beef Dumpling Soup — 94
Berry Soup — 151
Caldo Gallego — 108
Caldo Verde — 109
Callaloo — 42
Cock-a-Leekie Soup — 24
Garbanzo Bean Soup — 108
Gazpacho — 109
Hangover Soup — 62
Lamb and Garbanzo Soup — 134
Lime Soup — 124
Mulligatawny — 23
Pork-Vegetable Soup — 94
Seafood Chowder — 33
Split Pea Soup — 34
Summer Vegetable Soup — 145
Swiss Cheese-Cabbage Soup — 76
Swiss Cheese Soup — 76
Tarator Yogurt Soup — 62
Sour Cream Latkes — 137
Sour Cream Sauce, Fish with — 60
Sourdough Biscuits — 35
Sourdough Starter — 35
Southeast Asia
Coconut Milk — 170
Thick Coconut Milk — 170
South Pacific
Mai Tai — 185
Soy Dipping Sauce — 100
Soy-Ginger Sauce — 97
Spaghetti with Four Cheeses — 106
Spaghetti with Marinara Sauce — 112
Spain
Bolillo — 116
Caldo Gallego — 108
Chicken in Pepitoria — 104
Ensalada de Esparragos — 111
Gazpacho — 109
Huevos a la Flamenca — 106
Limonada — 119
Pisto — 110
Spiced Rich Layer Cake — 176
Spicy Stewed Liver — 133
Spinach
Creamed Dilled Spinach — 81
Creamed Spinach — 81
Spinach-Stuffed Conchiglione — 112
Spinach-Yogurt Salad — 135
Split Pea Soup — 34
Spring Rolls — 177
Stamppot — 74

Steamed Buns with Sweet Filling — 99
Steamed Pork Dumplings — 98
Stews
Caldeirada Fish Stew — 108
Feijoada Bean Stew — 154
Fish and Eggplant Stew — 14
Groundnut Stew — 14
Irish Stew — 24
Pork Pörkölt — 58
Pot-au-Feu — 33
Sancocho Beef Stew — 51
Wine-Braised Beef — 72
Straw and Hay — 113
Stuffed Cabbage Rolls — 59
Stuffed Escarole — 110
Stuffed Peppers with Walnut Sauce — 122
Stuffed Salmon — 60
Summer Vegetable Soup — 145
Sweden
Almond Braid — 146
Lucia Buns — 148
Sweet and Sour Red Cabbage — 146
Sweet Potato Buñeulos — 52
Sweet Raisin Bread — 148
Sweet Rice Eggs — 101
Sweet Tomato Chutney — 174
Switzerland
Cheese and Onion Tart — 78
Cherry Bread Pudding — 86
Fried Potato Cake — 80
Swiss Cheese-Cabbage Soup — 76
Swiss Cheese Soup — 76
Veal with Cream Sauce — 72
Syllabub — 29
Syria
Baked Kibbeh — 132
Fish with Tahini Sauce — 134
Mamool Cookies — 139
Savory Filled Triangles — 141
Tabouleh Salad — 134
Szechwan Dry-Fried Beef — 90

T-Z

Tabouleh Salad — 134
Tarator Yogurt Soup — 62
Teppanyaki — 91
Tequila Sunrise — 128
Thailand
Cucumber Salad — 175
Deep-Fried Rice Sticks — 168
Deep-Fried Wonton Strips — 172
Fried Fish with Ginger Sauce — 173
Mee Krob — 168
Pork Satay — 164
Spring Rolls — 177
Sweet and Sour Sauce — 177
Thai Beef Larnar — 172
Thai Shrimp Larnar — 172
Tomatoes
Dolmas — 132
Gazpacho — 109
Salsa Fria — 156
Spaghetti with Marinara Sauce — 112
Sweet Tomato Chutney — 174

Tomatoes *(continued)*
Tomato Rice — 156
Tomato Sauce — 44
Tortilla Casserole — 125
Tourtière — 32
Treacle Tea Scones — 26
Trinidad
Callaloo — 42
Fried Butter Biscuits — 44
Turkey
Cheese-Filled Pastries — 140
Loukomi Candy — 140
Noah's Pudding — 139
Shish Kabob — 133
Ukrainian SSR
Cottage Cheese Patties — 59
Honey Cake — 66
Usli Ghee — 166
USSR
Kulebiaka — 61
Kulebiaka Pastry — 61
Vargabéles Retés — 68
Variety Meats
Beef Heart Anticuchos — 161
Liver and Raisin Bake — 144
Liver Pâté — 151
Risotto with Giblets — 113
Spicy Stewed Liver — 133
Veal
Veal Ragout — 58
Veal with Cream Sauce — 72
Vitello Tonnato — 119
Vegetables *(see also* Beans, Cabbage, Carrots, Corn, Eggplant, Potatoes, Spinach, *and* Tomatoes)
Asparagus Cream Soup — 78
Brussels Sprouts Puree — 80
Fresh Vegetable Marinade — 110
Fried Onion Rings — 169
Gado-Gado — 174
Ghivetci Vegetables — 59
Hodgepodge — 34
Okra in Oil — 135
Pisto — 110
Pork-Vegetable Soup — 94
Summer Vegetable Soup — 145
Vegetable-Beef Stir-Fry — 90
Vegetarian Fried Rice — 95
Venezuela
Corn Pancakes — 161
Ensalada Mixta — 156
Hot Pepper Dressing — 156
Vietnam
Barbecued Spareribs — 165
Vitello Tonnato — 119
Wales
Bara Brith Bread — 26
Leek Salad — 25
Walnut Tea — 101
Wild Rice Bake — 34
Wine-Braised Beef — 72
Yemen
Spicy Stewed Liver — 133
Yugoslavia
Zagreb Cake — 67